Isaiah 1–39

Isaiah 1–39

A Commentary

MICHAEL E. W. THOMPSON

CASCADE Books • Eugene, Oregon

ISAIAH 1–39
A Commentary

Copyright © 2022 Michael E. W. Thompson. All rights reserved. Except for brief quotations in critical publications or reviews, no part of this book may be reproduced in any manner without prior written permission from the publisher. Write: Permissions, Wipf and Stock Publishers, 199 W. 8th Ave., Suite 3, Eugene, OR 97401.

Cascade Books
An imprint of Wipf and Stock Publishers
199 W. 8th Ave., Suite 3
Eugene, OR 97401

www.wipfandstock.com

PAPERBACK ISBN: 978-1-6667-3638-0
HARDCOVER ISBN: 978-1-6667-9459-5
EBOOK ISBN: 978-1-6667-9460-1

Cataloguing-in-Publication data:

Names: Thompson, Michael E. W. [author].

Title: Isaiah 1–39 : a commentary / Michael E. W. Thompson.

Description: Eugene, OR: Cascade Books, 2022 | Includes bibliographical references.

Identifiers: ISBN 978-1-6667-3638-0 (paperback) | ISBN 978-1-6667-9459-5 (hardcover) | ISBN 978-1-6667-9460-1 (ebook)

Subjects: LCSH: Bible.—Isaiah I–XXXIX—Commentaries | Bible.—Isaiah—Commentaries

Classification: BS1515.53 T46 2022 (print) | BS1515.53 (ebook)

11/30/22

Contents

Preface | ix
Abbreviations | xi
Introduction | xiii
    The Book of Isaiah | xiii
    Historical Background | xv
    The Prophetical Ministries | xvi
    The Book Called Isaiah | xviii
    Dominant Theological Themes of Isaiah 1–39 | xix
    The Development of the Book of Isaiah | xxi
    The Arrangement of Isaiah 1–39 | xxiii
    Isaiah 1–39 in the Book of Isaiah | xxvi

I. Isaiah 1–12: The Lord and His People | 3
    The Divine Judgement and Mercy upon Israel 1:1–31 | 3
    Jerusalem and the Nations 2:1–5 | 11
    The Day of the Lord 2:6–22 | 13
    Judah's Anarchy 3:1–9 | 14
    The Lord and His People 3:10–15 | 16
    The Pride of the Daughters of Zion 3:16—4:1 | 17
    Zion's Final Glory 4:2–6 | 18

The Song of the Vineyard 5:1–7 | 20
A Series of Woe-Oracles 5:8–24 | 21
Judgement Is Coming 5:25–30 | 24
The Prophet Isaiah's Call 6:1–13 | 25
The Syro-Ephraimite War 7:1—8:22 | 31
    Isaiah and His Son 7:1–9 | 31
    Isaiah and His Sign of Immanuel 7:10–17 | 33
    Coming Devastation 7:18–25 | 35
    The Sign of Maher-shalal-hash-baz 8:1–4 | 37
    Another Word about Immanuel 8:5–10 | 38
    Trusting and Obeying the LORD 8:11–22 | 39
A Great Light 9:1–7 [Hebrew 8:23—9:6] | 41
The Judgement of the LORD 9:8–21 [Hebrew 9:7–20] and 10:1–4 | 44
Assyria's Pride 10:5–15 | 46
Light and Fire 10:16–19 | 47
A Remnant Will Return 10:20–23 | 49
The Day of Midian 10:24–27a | 50
Invasion . . . and the Trees 10:27b–34 | 51
The Kingdom of Peace 11:1–9 | 52
Israel and the Nations 11:10–16 | 55
Song of Thanksgiving 12:1–6 | 57

II. Isaiah 13–23: Prophetic Words about Foreign Nations | 59

Prophecies about Babylon 13:1—14:23 | 60
    Isaiah's Vision of Babylon 13:1–22 | 60
    The End of Babylon 14:1–23 | 63
Doom for Assyria 14:24–27 | 65
Beware, Philistia 14:28–32 | 66
Concerning Moab 15:1—16:14 | 67
Concerning Damascus and Ephraim 17:1–14 | 69
Concerning Nubia 18:1–7 | 71
Egypt under Judgement 19:1–15 | 72
Egypt in the Future 19:16–25 | 74
Egypt and Ethiopia 20:1–6 | 76
The Fall of Babylon 21:1–10 | 77
Prophecies about Arabia 21:11–17 | 79

Complacency in Jerusalem 22:1–14 | 80
Shebna and Eliakim 22:15–25 | 82
Tyre of Phoenicia 23:1–18 | 84

III. **Isaiah 24–27: Visions of the Future** | 87
Judgement on the World 24:1–23 | 87
Banquet on Mount Zion 25:1–12 | 90
New Life 26:1–21 | 93
Past, Present, and Future 27:1–13 | 95

IV. **Isaiah 28–32: Isaiah and Judah** | 99
Ephraimite Drunkards 28:1–6 | 99
Failed Leadership 28:7–13 | 100
More Failed Leaders 28:14–22 | 102
The Good Farmer's Wisdom 28:23–29 | 104
The City Punished and Delivered 29:1–8 | 105
Not Wishing to See 29:9–14 | 106
Better Days in the Future 29:15–24 | 107
A Rebellious People 30:1–5 | 109
The Source of Real Help 30:6–7 | 110
Written Prophecy 30:8–17 | 110
Salvation Coming 30:18–26 | 113
Divine Judgement on Assyria 30:27–33 | 114
No Help in Egypt 31:1–9 | 116
Kingdom of Righteousness 32:1–8 | 119
A Warning and an Assurance 32:9–20 | 120

V. **Isaiah 33–39: The Center of the Isaiah Book** | 123
From Vision to Life and Worship 33:1–24 | 124
Judgement and Salvation Chapters 34 and 35 | 127
Judgement on Edom 34:1–17 | 128
Return to Zion 35:1–10 | 129
The Isaiah Narratives, chapters 36–39 | 131
Jerusalem in Danger 36:1—37:8 | 132
Sennacherib, Hezekiah, and Isaiah 37:9–38 | 135
Hezekiah's Sickness and Recovery 38:1–22 | 138
Hezekiah, and Merodach-Baladan's Delegation 39:1–8 | 142

Table of Dates | 145
Select Bibliography | 147

Preface

I HAD LONG WISHED to write about the first thirty-nine chapters of the book of Isaiah, having many years earlier been invited by the erstwhile Epworth Press to write their commentary on Isaiah 40–66, as sadly the scholar, minister, and author David Stacey had died having completed the work on chapters 1–39 but not being able to go on and expound chs 40–66. I am therefore most grateful now to Wipf and Stock—who have taken over the Epworth series of biblical commentaries—for agreeing now to publish my own contribution in this present modest volume on chs 1–39, and thereafter to reissue my earlier work on chs 40–66, taking into account various movements and changes in the views of scholars over the authorship and composition of those latter chapters. Thus, in these matters I am particularly grateful to the editor Robin Parry and the staff of the publishers Wipf and Stock. I trust that this modest-sized commentary will be of service and help in particular to those in church, college, and home settings who wish to have some guidance in their understanding of the meaning, the significance, and the relevance of these chapters of the book of Isaiah. Thus I do frequently at the close of my treatment of particular units of the Isaiah book add a quotation from one of the scholars who have worked on this biblical book, in particular regarding what it perhaps has to say to us about our pursuit of the biblical faith in our lives, works, and biblical expositions these days. Following the usual practice of Wipf and Stock as publishers I have used the American Version of the New Revised Standard Version of the Bible in this book, my biblical quotations being from that version.

Preface

Once more, I am so grateful to my wife Hazel who has been involved both in the beginnings and also in the development of this book project. As ever I am indebted to her for help in matters to do with computers and printers, for guiding me here and there in my texts to certain more felicitous wordings than I had earlier chosen, and above all for our sharing in commitments to matters of religious faith and church, never mind to reading books on a wide range of subjects.

Michael E. W. Thompson
On the Feast of the Epiphany
6th January 2022

Abbreviations

BCE	Before the Common Era
c.	circa, approximately
CE	The Common Era
Cf.	Compare
chs	chapters
ed.	Editor
Eng	English translation
ICC	International Critical Commentary
JSOT	*Journal for the Study of the Old Testament*
LXX	Septuagint (Greek translation of the Old Testament)
MT	Masoretic Text (Hebrew Text)
NEB	New English Bible
NIV	New International Version of the Bible,
NRSV	New Revised Standard Version of the Bible, American Edition, 1994
REB	Revised English Bible, 1989
RSV	Revised Standard Version, 1952
RV	Revised Version of the Bible, 1881–85
Tr.	Translator
V	Vulgate (Latin translation of the Bible)

Introduction

THE BOOK OF ISAIAH

THE BOOK OF ISAIAH begins with the words, "The vision of Isaiah son of Amoz, which he saw concerning Judah and Jerusalem in the days of Uzziah, Jotham, Ahaz, and Hezekiah, kings of Judah" (1:1). This statement covers the historical period that lies behind a good deal, but not all, of what we are hearing about in Isaiah 1–39.

What follows in this present work seeks to be a commentary on these chapters, material that is generally referred to as "the first part" of this biblical book. The remaining parts of the book of Isaiah appear to speak respectively about the times and opportunities of Judah's exiles returning from Babylonian captivity to their old homeland (chs 40–55) and then about leaders and peoples having to find new ways of living out their faith back in the promised land, but now in a new age (chs 56–66).[1]

The one who is doing this seeing, experiencing this vision, we are told, is the prophet named Isaiah, about whom unfortunately we can say very little, apart from what we are able to learn from chapters 1–39. Yet one thing we do read about him in this part of the Isaiah book is his call by the LORD to a prophetical ministry, and the essentials of the message he is to proclaim to his people (6:1–13). Clearly, as we shall see as we work through this biblical material, other writers—other prophetical individuals perhaps—appear to have been responsible for certain parts of the text that has come down to

---

1. For a study of these chapters, see Thompson, *Isaiah 40–66*.

us as the Isaiah book. Even in chs 1–39 passages frequently appear to come from later times than those of Isaiah of Jerusalem, being written in a different style of writing and expressing different theological thinking from texts generally assigned by scholars to Isaiah himself.

The ministry of Isaiah the son of Amoz (not to be confused with Amos, another of the Old Testament prophets) took place in a time of turbulent events for the people of Judah and Jerusalem. This was a historical period when the situation for Israel and Judah was considerably dictated by the affairs of the nations around them, by their needs and at times their ambitions, and in a particular way by the powerful Assyrian empire to the east, an empire that was to grow in might in the years during which there was in Judah and Jerusalem a prophet called Isaiah.

Below there is an attempt to represent in outline by means of a chronological chart the comparative happenings in Judah, Israel (the northern kingdom of Israel), and Assyria.[2] It should be understood that we are constrained by having to be somewhat vague regarding dates, for as yet in Old Testament scholarly circles there are no agreed dating schemes, so that different scholars inevitably come up with various different dates for sundry happenings in the ancient world.[3] Further, we should be aware of the fact that as far as "all Israel" is concerned, it ceased to be such in c. 722 BCE, when the northern kingdom of Israel was besieged by Assyria, and as a result of that many of their people were deported to Assyria (see 2 Kgs 18:9–12), and we hear no more about them. The Old Testament becomes silent about those people, and largely also about details concerning their erstwhile lands in the north of Israel, though we do read of some events in those lands.[4]

Thus it is that after that date any references to Israel generally inevitably indicate in fact Judah alone, the southern kingdom with its capital city, Jerusalem. Hence, in the Chronological Table below for the period of the ministry of the prophet Isaiah, after 722 BCE there is only Judah with the city of Jerusalem remaining. Moreover, we need to note that this is not a complete list of, for example, all the kings of Judah and Israel, but only certain of them.

---

2. See the Table of Dates below, 145–46.

3. Essentially, the dating scheme I have used in this work is that of W. F. Albright, an understanding that is also adopted by Joseph Blenkinsopp in his recent detailed work of three volumes on the book of Isaiah. On this subject of dating in the Old Testament, see Hayes and Miller, *Israelite and Judaean History*, 678–83.

4. For example, see the references in Isa 9:8–12; 17:4–11; 28:1–6 and the note thereon in this present work, 41, 66, 99.

HISTORICAL BACKGROUND

The long period during which Isaiah ministered—comprising parts of the eighth and seventh centuries BCE—was a time of very considerable change for the peoples of Israel and Judah, and their principal cities of Samaria and Jerusalem, all too soon to become just Judah and Jerusalem. In the hands and powers of Assyria, the people of the northern kingdom of Israel are hardly heard of any more after 722 BCE, in which year Samaria was under siege to the Assyrians, and thus lost its separate identity as an independent nation. In fact, after this happening there is precious little concerning them to be read in the Old Testament. Henceforth Israelite history will somewhat inevitably be written from the points of view and understanding of various people and leaders of the Judean capital city, Jerusalem.

Yet so much in that ongoing life of the remaining southern kingdom of Judah and Jerusalem was to be under the worldly lordship of the kingdom of Assyria, and in particular under a succession of Assyrian kings, namely, Tiglath Pileser III, Shalmaneser V, Sargon II, and Sennacherib who, collectively, reigned from around 744 BCE to about 681 BCE. This meant that the kings and peoples of Judah and Jerusalem were not "free people" in the world in the way and in the style that they had enjoyed in the days of the Judean kings David and Solomon. Now Israel (until her fall in c. 722 BCE) and Judah were not ultimately the self-governing and independent peoples they had been earlier, but rather they were under the rule, and also theoretically the "protection," of this major power.

A military matter that we are told occurred for Judah and Jerusalem during the kingship of Ahaz of Judah was the attack upon Judah and Jerusalem of a coalition of Israel and Aram, an attack that failed, although we read that Ahaz was in a considerable panic over it. We read about this incident in Isa 7:1—8:22, and also in other parts of the Old Testament.[5] The siege took place around 734 BCE, and somewhat later there was a rebellion in the northern kingdom of Israel which brought to an end the independent life of that nation and people. Now Judah and Jerusalem were on their own as the "Israelite" peoples, yet still, of course, subject to the overall rule of Assyria.

As ever there was a temptation on the part of certain rulers to rebel against their foreign overlord, and one incident of that nature took place under the rule of the King Hezekiah of Jerusalem in 705 BCE, but this, alas, was destined to result in Hezekiah's eventual surrender to the Assyrians. We read of this in 2 Kgs 18:13–16 and also in Isa 36–37, about which see below

---

5. For further on the matter of this war see Irvine, *Isaiah, Ahaz, and the Syro-Ephraimitic Crisis*; Thompson, *Situation and Theology*.

132–141. Around this time, moreover, it does seem that we come to the end of the historical ministry of the prophet Isaiah of Jerusalem.

Further, as far as the people of Jerusalem and the surroundings were concerned, the somewhat inevitable result of developing international events, with the rise of the Babylonian Empire to replace the Assyrian one, was that many of them were taken away to live as exiles in Babylon for some fifty years. Yet events after those fifty years of exile did truly constitute a new beginning, and it was in all probability another prophet of the LORD who proclaimed that exceedingly good news of post-exilic restoration, yet one whose prophecies would come to be made into a further part of the Old Testament's book of Isaiah (chs 40–55). That new prophet had a remarkable message of comfort, assurance, and indeed real hope for his people in exile, seeking to reassure them that their LORD God had fresh, indeed vital purposes for them back in their old land. Thus he began his prophecy with the confident words, "Comfort, O comfort my people, says your God" (40:1).

THE PROPHETICAL MINISTRIES

Yet back in the period of the ministry of the prophet Isaiah of Jerusalem, in the late eighth and early seventh centuries BCE, there were some remarkable Yahwistic interpretations being made of the historical events of the time. Isaiah was among those offering such a religious interpretation of events, and Ronald Clements is surely correct to speak of him as "one of the greatest figures of the religious and political story of ancient Israel."[6] It was not that the Israelite phenomenon of prophecy began in this historical moment, for earlier than this there had been prophets such as Amos and Hosea. Even before those prophets there had been the prophetical-style ministries of such persons as Elijah and Elisha. What however is different with the ministries of Amos and Hosea is the fact that we have *written records* of at least some of the matters about which they preached and prophesied. These writing prophets ministered in historical moments of large political change, change that in a special way demanded and drew forth the prophetical ministries of various individuals such as Isaiah of Jerusalem.[7] Indeed, the purpose of these prophetical ministries it seems was to enable the LORD's people to have some understanding of what was happening in the world, that world of which they found themselves to be a part, and this particularly in a religious sense.

---

6. See, Clements, *Isaiah 1–39*, 11.

7. For a recent introductory study of these prophets, see Lundblom, *Hebrew Prophets*.

Further, this was indeed a much expanded and wider political world than the one the Israelite and Judean peoples had known before. How then were these peoples to continue to be the people of the LORD God in this changing situation? For now there was the whole issue of their having a powerful overlord in a neighboring and very much larger country than their own. Thus it was that Assyrians and later Babylonians, and then others who followed them, exerted a large and at times dominating presence that had to be taken seriously. Moreover, now there were taxes to pay to the overlord. Yet on the positive side there could at times be help available for the subject peoples from their overlords should their military and/or political situation demand such. Thus inevitably the nature of the kingships in both Israel and Judah were changed from what they had been in earlier times in the reigns of David and then of Solomon. These changes affected fundamental matters about the government and the direction the kings were to take for their countries, and about the degree of control they had of their own political destiny.

Yet more, the fact was that from a geographical point of view Israel and Judah (and later Judah and Jerusalem on their own) were very much boundary states of the Assyrian empire. This meant that if there was to be an attack upon that empire from their direction then they, the Judeans, would be some of the first to be attacked, and thus to suffer. Such was the negative aspect of their geographic setting, being very much in the midst of various countries and nations. (Even so, at the same time, and this from a more positive point of view, this location would one day be seen as being of considerable importance and opportunity by at least some of their people, who would come to appreciate that they had a religious message to proclaim to other peoples in the world. Nevertheless, that would be a concern coming to these peoples later, albeit one that could certainly be seen in the Old Testament in Isa 40–55 and 56–66, and I would suggest also in such works as the book of Jonah.)

Despite such significant challenges, the peoples of Israel and Judah—and later of Judah with its capital city of Jerusalem alone—were still called to be the people of God in the world of their day, which, as their prophets reminded them, involved a very great deal more than just living out their lives for their own sakes.

It was out of the international situation described above that from the states of Judah and Israel there came three great Hebrew prophetical books, those named after the prophets whose ministries in particular ways featured in various periods of the times from the eighth to the sixth centuries BCE, the ministries respectively of Isaiah, Jeremiah, and Ezekiel. It is just the first of these that is our present concern, and then only a part of the book, chs

1–39, which concern the message of the prophet Isaiah himself, parts of which may even have been written by him.

THE BOOK CALLED ISAIAH

The complete book Isaiah is a remarkably wide-ranging work making up in total no less than sixty-six chapters. These are not-infrequently regarded, and treated, as three distinct parts, each one of which, generally speaking, addresses matters occurring in one of three historical periods for the people of Judah and Jerusalem: namely, first the years before the exile (ch. 1–39), then second the period of the Babylonian exile (chs 40–55), and third the years of opportunity to return to their own homeland (chs 56–66). Nevertheless, all of these parts are engaged in a deep and ongoing concern about the relationship between the religious faith, life, and actions of the people of Judah, on the one hand, and their political lives as a people subject to a powerful political overlord. What is of prime importance in all parts of the book is the people's ongoing faithfulness to the will and purposes of their Lord God.

The three historical settings in the book of Isaiah are first, what appears to be—that is, is portrayed as—pre-exilic (chs 1–39). The prophet here usually being called Isaiah (of Jerusalem). The second historical setting (chs 40–55) concerns the time of exile, and yet at a historical moment when for the Jewish people there was indeed a "new" time of opportunity to return to their old land and capital city, Judah and Jerusalem. For this was indeed a time of a fresh political rule with the anticipated fall of Babylon. The third historical setting, underlying chs 56–66, appears to be about life back in Judah and Jerusalem to which the Hebrew people have been allowed to return. These chapters are about a now inevitably somewhat changed situation, so that certain matters of faith and action back in the land of Judah may also have to be changed. The matter of the authorship of chs 40–55 and 56–66 is much discussed by scholars, and I deal with it in my commentary on those chapters, believing personally that the responsibility for the writing of these three main blocks did lie with three principal authors, generally referred to in the Old Testament scholarly world as Isaiah, the Second Isaiah, and the Third Isaiah.[8] There have recently been certain developments in our thinking about this period, and I shall be dealing with this below, in particular in the section concerned with the arrangement of chs 1–39 of the book of Isaiah, and also about the relationships between these three major blocks of biblical material.

8. See Thompson, *Isaiah 40–66*.

Returning to our present concern with Isa 1–39, and taking something of an overall view regarding their contents, we observe the wide and deep concerns that the prophet Isaiah seems clearly to have had concerning some of those happenings and issues about which he proclaimed his prophecies (words believed to have been given to him by the LORD God, which he and/ or others wrote down). Thus it is that when we examine the opening chapter of the work we note that it is concerned with *both* the divine judgement upon, *and also* the divine mercy for, the people of Israel and Judah. That is, there is talk here *both* of the judgement of the LORD upon his people, *and also* about his salvation of them when they are repentant. Then ch. 2 of the book of Isaiah is taken up with the twin themes of the LORD's relationship with Jerusalem and the nations, along with concerns and issues regarding the Day of the LORD.

DOMINANT THEOLOGICAL THEMES OF ISAIAH 1–39

It is surely not unreasonable to regard what is said in Isa 1–39 about the otherness, the greatness, and the glory of the LORD God as being one of the primary theological themes of the book, perhaps indeed *the* primary theme. This, of course, is spoken about above all in the account in Isa 6 of the remarkable and awesome vision of this deity that Isaiah the son of Amoz saw in what is surely portrayed as the Jerusalem temple (6:1). The writer struggles to express the greatness and the divine grandeur—which is humanly inexpressible—with mere human words. He writes of the divine one being *high and lofty,* while it was merely *the hem of his robe* that was sufficient to fill that great temple in Jerusalem (see 6:1)! Yet this holy, this totally other Being, so utterly other than anything or anyone on earth, is there working his works and seeking to speak his words in situation after situation through all the ages being addressed in the book. Further, in the chapters of the Isaiah book there is portrayed the ongoing presence of this Holy Being, who forgives sins, gives strength, along with new hopes and purposes for his people in the world, and who calls those people to live lives of holiness and purpose. He is indeed the King (6:5; 33:22), who will reign in righteousness (32:1), and who will one day be seen in "his beauty" (33:17). Further, he is indeed the "Holy One of Israel," this title being particularly common in this biblical book (1:4; 5:19, 24; 10:20; 12:6; 17:7; 29:19; 30:11–12, 15; 31:1; 37:23), a matter of descriptive theological wording to which we shall return (see under 1:4 below).

Then there is the issue of the worldly setting where these divine activities and deeds are to be enacted and lived out, and where certain of the lands are particularly chosen, namely, Israel and Judah. If the LORD does have to be portrayed as having an earthly dwelling, then it is to be Jerusalem, on Mount Zion (8:18), and he will indeed defend and save it (37:35). Yet increasingly in the biblical book of Isaiah the wider world is portrayed too as being the realm of the divine activity, in a particular way in those Mesopotamian lands to the east of the more traditional biblical lands. Further, we shall see the divine activity expanding into those lands where in no small ways certain of the worldly powers would be growing and developing in strength. Whether they realized it or not, these non-Israelite national leaders would be coming to be progressively more involved in the divine will and purposes of the LORD God of Israel. Thus it is necessary that in the study of the Old Testament book of Isaiah we deal with both geographical and historical matters, and consider the importance such matters had for the lives of the LORD's chosen people. Of some particular importance for us is the matter of grappling with issues of the political leadership over the years and centuries of the larger and more dominant nations round about, particularly those in the Mesopotamian lands.

Further, there are both small conflicts and also much larger international conflicts in which Israelite and Judean leaders and peoples are involved. Eventually Israel and Judah come to be in conflict with the great nations, in particular with the leaders and forces of Assyria and later of Babylon, while at an earlier time the people of Judah and Jerusalem would find themselves attacked by a coalition of Israelite and Syrian forces, the so-called Syro-Ephraimite war. For that particular crisis the prophet Isaiah would be around, and would be the one advising the Judean king that in fact things were not as bad as they looked (7:1–17). Yet also, in considering the matter of the relation of Judah and Jerusalem to the nations around them, we must take seriously a whole section of prophetic oracles directed *against* a series of those nations (chs 13–23), oracles similar to those found elsewhere among the books of a number of the Old Testament prophets.

Another subject that is presented in this Old Testament prophetical book is a full section of materials concerning a distant future, when things for the human lands, along with their peoples and leaders would change dramatically. This we read about in chs 24–27 and 34–35, where we find a type of writing that bears similarities to later apocalyptic texts, such as Daniel 7–12 or 1 Enoch, indicating the end of the current world order and the dawning and beginning of a new and divine world order. Thus is envisaged the divine bringing in of a new age. More will be said about this when we come to these chapters in the commentary that follows. Meanwhile, in what we may refer to as the more immediate future, the book of Isaiah portrays visions of better, wiser, more God-centered and God-guided kings, exercising their high calling. Such leaders are envisaged, for example, in passages such as Isa 9:2–7 and 11:1–9.

Then, there are the people of Israel to be considered, and there is a good deal about them in this part of the book of Isaiah, but sadly much of it is made up of words of the divine judgement upon them, their sins and failings being set forth in situation after situation. The prophet is critical of the people, as well as of their leaders, for their exploitation of those who are needy and poor (see for example 5:8–13), and for their failures in being faithful to what is required of them in regard to their established system of religious beliefs and rituals (1:10–17). Nor for much of the time do those concerned pay proper attention to the requirements of the judicial system, and we hear too often of bribes on the parts of those who have the money to pay them (1:23; 5:23; 10:1–2; 33:15). Further, there are people who have a tendency to panic in situations when they should have been quietly putting their trust in the Lord God (7:2). Moreover, the peoples' leaders so often did not lead and guide them as they should have done (1:21, 23, 26; 3:14; 5:13–14; 28:14).

Nevertheless, these people of God on earth were ever being called to a life of holiness, so that indeed one day there would indeed be peace on the earth, and no hurting or destroying on the Lord's holy mountain (11:9). Further, a life of inner peace for the people of Israel will only be found when they believe in the Lord, then they will be "established" (7:9), and moreover for them the promise is, "In returning and rest you shall be saved; in quietness and in trust shall be your strength" (30:15). What is more, great and good things are promised for that day: "On that day the branch of the Lord shall be beautiful and glorious, and the fruit of the land shall be the pride and glory of the survivors of Israel" (4:2).[9]

THE DEVELOPMENT OF THE BOOK OF ISAIAH

It is clear that the book of Isaiah is made up of a series of pieces of writing, the first being chs 1–39 concerning matters appertaining to the particular situations in the eighth century BCE. These culminate in the account of many people of Judah and Jerusalem being taken away to what would be something like half-a-century of the life of exile in Babylon and elsewhere. However, this large block of material can be seen to be made up of a number of distinctive parts. Thus ch. 1 reads like an introduction, while chs 2–12 comprise prophecies concerning Judah and Jerusalem. Then chs 13–23 are

---

9. On this subject of the main theological themes in the book of Isaiah, see Goldingay, "The Theology of Isaiah."

about foreign nations, while the block of material in chs 24–27 is made up of "apocalyptic" material. Chapters 28–33 go back to being prophecies concerning Judah and Jerusalem, while chs 34–35 are again about apocalyptic matters. Finally, chs 36–39 make up an extended narrative about the prophet Isaiah, about king Hezekiah, and also concerning the city of Jerusalem.

Who was responsible—whether one person or many—for compiling this material to pass on to generations then unborn, so that others at later dates would be able to read the prophetic words in their own settings and situations? We can understand that materials like the main contents of the introductory chapter (ch. 1) came from the prophet Isaiah himself, or at least from someone close to him and his spiritual and worldly concerns. One would expect that the prophet Isaiah was in one way or another involved in the presentation of the material concerning his own call to be a prophet (ch. 6), and also in the literature concerning the Syro-Ephraimite war which we find spoken about in Isa 7:1—8:22 (and maybe going even further than that, and also including Isa 8:23—9:6).

Yet what about the later materials in the book, not only such parts that have the "apocalyptic" materials, but also those parts that come in the material at the closing of this part of the book of Isaiah, the fall of Jerusalem and thus the beginning of the exile in Babylon (chs 33–39)? That fall of Jerusalem and the associated exile took place in the year 587 BCE, while we are told that the call of the man Isaiah to be a prophet of the LORD was in the year when King Uzziah died (6:1), which is most likely to have been 742 BCE—that is, nearly 150 years earlier. This clearly suggests that Isaiah could hardly have been the LORD's prophet acting through all of these times. Others must somehow have been involved, other prophetic figures perhaps. Yet who they were, and when and in what ways they acted and worked we are not told.

Who then, in particular, can have been responsible for the drawing together of all the material that makes up the biblical material before us in Isa 1–39? We have to say that we do not know who was responsible. Nor, in the cases of certain passages and selections of passages, is it surprising that various individuals or groups have over the years and decades been suggested as the writers, or the editors, or the gatherers of materials, all of which suggestions have thus far failed to convince many of us. And thus, in this situation and setting of ignorance, we have indeed to accept that we simply do not know.[10]

10. I suggest here two possible studies for those who are concerned with such matters that they might find useful. The first is R. E. Clements, who in his commentary on *Isaiah 1–39*, 3–8, sets out his view coming from German Old Testament scholarship propounding that there were those who drew together materials about these events,

THE ARRANGEMENT OF ISAIAH 1-39

The first chapter of the book of Isaiah seems to have been intended to serve as an introduction to all that will follow, in particular to chs 2-39, and perhaps even to the completed book, chs 2-66, though we cannot be sure as far as that last possibility is concerned, there being such great changes occurring in the styles and the messages of the materials we read in chs 40-55 and 56-66. Clearly, as suggested by the fact that there is a new introductory verse at 2:1, here in ch. 1 we are being introduced in a clear way to the issues facing the prophet, and also no doubt others, as they contemplated the general situation for Judah and Jerusalem in the days of the reign of King Uzziah. Thus Isa 1:1-31 concerns the divine judgement and mercy upon the leaders and people of Israel and Judah at that time.

With Isa 2:1 we move onto an extensive block of material that runs to the end of ch. 12 and that concerns the situations and lives of the peoples of both Judah and Jerusalem, and in certain parts of Israel as well. This is a large block of material that records difficulties experienced by the people of Judah not only concerning their apparent lack of faithfulness to the LORD, but also in regard to their being under the divine judgement. For an overview of this section of the book of Isaiah see the table of contents above (pp. v-viii).

Then, with chs 13-23, we read of a development of the material in Isa 1-39 into another aspect of the Isaianic message recorded in the book bearing his name, namely the prophetic words about foreign nations, and in particular about those nations, or their leaders, who in their different ways, ambitions, concerns, and actions affected and influenced the ongoing life of the people of Judah and Jerusalem. Thus, chapters 13-23 are usually designated "prophecies concerning foreign nations." Such blocks of material on the subject of foreign nations are also to be found in other books of the Old Testament prophets: Jeremiah 46-51, Ezekiel 25-32, Amos 1:3—2:16, and Zephaniah 2:4-15, and also in the books of Nahum and Obadiah. Thus it is not only here in the book of Isaiah 13-23 that we are given what we might call a sustained treatment of certain aspects of the life and activities of the nations among whom in succeeding years and ages the peoples of Israel and Judah found themselves to be in contact, sometimes in strife, at other times at peace.

---

and thus wrote about them. The second is the study of H. G. M. Williamson, *The Book Called Isaiah*, who suggests that it was the so-called Deutero-Isaiah, the Second Isaiah, the author behind Isa 40-55, who gathered this material together. For more details see below, xxviii, and also Clements, *Isaiah 1-39*, 5-8.

The relationship of the Israelite people with the people and country of Egypt changed and developed over the years. At times it was seen as a place of refuge and help, at other times a place of oppression, one that fed the desire, and even the need, for liberation from unfriendly rule. Then later there would be relationships for good or for ill with the near-neighboring peoples of Canaan, and Syria, and elsewhere. Even later there would arise the larger and more dominant powers of the ancient Near East, who not infrequently desired to have the surrounding nations within their grasp, even under their rule. In these ways did the peoples of Israel and Judah find themselves under a certain rulership, or even political supervision, by the great and growing nations of the ancient Near East, nations such as Assyria, then Babylonia, followed by Persia, later Greece, and eventually Rome. For this reason it is not surprising that in the books of the Hebrew prophets we should frequently find a part, or at least a section, devoted to what have come to be called prophetic oracles about the nations, that is, written materials in which we read about what particular prophets, and sometimes also their successors, had to say regarding the presence, either for good or for ill, of the neighboring nations. The oracles against the nations in this section of Isaiah begin with an extensive passage about Babylon and the Babylonians (13:1—14:32) before moving on to Assyria and then other nations.

With chs 24–27 the book of Isaiah begins a further new section, not a lengthy one, but rather one of just four chapters, that is concerned with visions of the future. These chapters are in a style of language and writing similar to those we find in other parts of the Bible that has been called apocalyptic, a word that comes from the Greek, meaning "unveiling, uncovering". The most extensive passages in the Bible in this apocalyptic style are in the books of Daniel (chs 7–12) and Revelation, both of these being concerned with future events about which certain aspects are revealed, that is, "uncovered." Yet apocalyptic writings occur also in comparatively smaller compositions in the Old Testament, as here in Isaiah 24–27, and in the New Testament in Mark's Gospel at ch 13. It is further encountered in some of the inter-testamental writings such as 2 Esdras (4 Ezra) and 1 Enoch.

The apocalyptic style of writing seems generally to have come from times of crisis and upheaval, and particularly those times that bear the suggestion of being "end times" in some sense, perhaps being called, "latter days." What has been written is not infrequently portrayed as having come from the spiritual experience of writers who have received "revelations," during times when things seem to be heading for end-times, and when there may be perceived to be a struggle between forces of good and evil. Often in apocalyptic writings matters are expressed in somewhat extreme language, not infrequently we find in them references to dreams and visions, in the talk using the symbolism of the Beast and the Harlot to speak of those who would use their powers for their own good, and if at all possible to gain power and influence for themselves. Here in the apocalyptic writings we read words about the desolate earth (see Isa 24:1), or parts of the earth that have darkened skies (24:4), and yet we also hear of great and new things for the peoples (see 25:6-9), as perhaps above all the beginnings of some assurance concerning life after death—see Isa 26:19.

There are some very hopeful aspects for people expressed in the Bible's apocalyptic literature, including Isa 24-27. Whereas for so much of the time in age after age there are people who have to confront sufferings and difficulties, here in this biblical material are various writings that are surely intended to give some meaning and sense to these experiences, and maybe also to give hope to those peoples who are suffering.[11]

Having considered a number of chapters in the book of Isaiah that range quite widely in matters of both history and also geography, we are now brought to a series of texts that concern in the main Judah and Jerusalem, and that amongst other things speak about the protest and rebellion of Judah in the years 705-1 BCE against the Assyrians. These issues are presented in chs 28-32. Also being spoken about here is condemnation of the leaders of the people of Israel in Samaria, those who at an earlier date rebelled against the lordship of the Assyrians over them.

We now come to chapters 33-39, which are called here the "center of the book," that is, the center of the *whole* book of Isaiah (all sixty-six chapters). We need to take note of the fact that there is a change in the style and language used here from the overall majority of the material in chs 1-32, which in the main is speaking about what was taking place for the peoples of Israel and Judah *before* the Babylonian conquest of Jerusalem and surrounding lands in 587 BCE, which resulted in the deportation of the leaders and many of their peoples to exile in Babylon. That situation was to last for some fifty years, by which time Babylon had fallen into Persian hands, and Cyrus, the Achaemenian, the Persian, became the ruler in Babylon. One of the great changes that Cyrus effected was to allow his Jewish and other subject peoples, under certain conditions, to return to their own lands. Thus indeed, chapters 33-39 have come to be called by some scholars "the center of the book," to indicate that there is material in the book of Isaiah about three settings, namely, (a) the time *before* the Babylonian exile (ch. 33-38 [parts]), (b) the time of Judah's fall to Babylon (ch. 39), and (c) the time after the Babylonian captivity (chs. 33 [parts], 34-35). Chapters 33-39 are thus the pivot of the book.

---

11. For the biblical apocalyptic writings, see Rowland, *The Open Heaven*.

Alongside, as it were, our Isaiah book's accounts of these two enormous, life-changing events—first, exile in Babylon, far away from the homeland in Judah and Jerusalem, and second, the courage to take to the desert ways and return home when, with a change of imperial government, there would be that possibility—are inserted these chapters, Isa 33–39, that we are now considering. These chapters fall into three main sections, namely ch 33, chs 34–35, and chs 36–39. The first of these (ch 33) is a much-discussed and written-about chapter, both regarding its authorship, and also its form, that is, what sort of literature is it? A number of us believe we can explain its purpose by seeing it as being expressed in the form of a liturgy, but first we need to study its contents, and then go on to consider the matters of its purpose and central message, its form and style, and further, if possible, the issue of its authorship.

The second section of these three parts at the center of the Isaiah book is Isa 34–35, and these two chapters have emphasis both on future divine judgement and also assurances of new life. There is a certain similarity of style here with chs 24–27 of Isaiah, chapters that have come down to us in what has been called the apocalyptic style. Further, these chapters appear to be particularly concerned with the divine punishment of Edom (ch. 34), and the contrasting glorification of Mount Zion in Judah. See pp. xxiv–xxv above for a summary of the characteristic features of the Old Testament's apocalyptic writings.

The third piece is what has been called The Isaiah Narrative, and takes up all of Isa 36–39. The highly distinctive feature of these chapters is that they are *very* similar to the material that we find in 2 Kings 18:17—20:19, with the addition of a psalm attributed to the Judean king Hezekiah in Isa 38:9–20. In fact, this material is presented in the style, and very largely in the words, of the above 2 Kings passage, and it does seem that the material, the writing, we have here in the book of Isaiah is based upon the Old Testament books of Kings. Yet there are a few differences here in the Isaiah account from that found in Kings, and we must consider how it is, and for what reasons and purposes, that we have this material, apparently from the books of Kings, here in the book of Isaiah.

ISAIAH 1–39 IN THE BOOK OF ISAIAH

Although this particular study of the book of Isaiah is only of chs 1–39, we should take notice of the fact that there has been in recent years a certain movement to see and understand the complete sixty-six chapters of the Isaiah book as having been—at least in its final form—intended to make one integrated whole. Undoubtedly there are individual parts to this whole prophetic book, parts that were composed in and speak of events in a series of historical settings, but they have been brought together, and now function as individual parts of a new whole that has evolved. These "parts" would seem to have been a series of writings that have come from a range of authors working in different times. Those times clearly range over a whole series of decades, indeed of centuries, but their literary and theological labors it would seem must have been fired and sustained by the desire to produce a completed literary and theological whole that tells of the events and happenings of the Lord's chosen people from c. 742 BCE, that is, from around the time Isaiah had his vision of the Lord in the Jerusalem temple, right up to around at least 539 BCE, when Cyrus the Persian came to power in Babylon, and allowed exiled people there to return to their own lands, and then beyond that into times of renewed life in their own land.

This is to suggest that the completed book of Isaiah covered a period of over perhaps 350 years, and thus for its writing and compilation there presumably must have been involved the labors of a number of generations of writers, compilers, authors, theological historians.

There has for a long time been a scholarly consensus that the three main parts of the text of the book of Isaiah, that is chs 1–39, 40–55, and 56–66, must have come from different authors. That said, especially in conservative communities, there have been those scholars and readers of the book who believe that the whole composition of sixty-six chapters is the work of a single author, Isaiah, who under divine inspiration speaks about his present, but also of what were, from his perspective, future happenings and events, seen in prophetic visions. Yet even if this traditional view of authorship is unlikely, for a number of reasons, it has the advantage of reading the book as an integrated whole. More recently there have been a number of scholarly contributions to the debate drawing attention to the fact that there are some common themes and uses of vocabulary that are to be observed traversing the various and varied parts of the completed book. These suggest that the parts were edited together to be read as a single work.

Thus, for example, though the title "The Holy One of Israel" is found throughout in chs 1–39 (see 1:4; 5:19, 24; 10:17, 20; 12:6; 17:7; 29:19, 23; 30:11, 12, 15; 31:1; 37:23), it is also there in a number of occurrences in chs 40–55 (see 40:25; 41:14, 16, 20; 43:3, 14, 15; 45:11; 47:4; 48:17; 49:7 [twice]; 54:5; 55:5), and further is also present in chs 56–66 (see 60:9, 14). Apart from these usages in the book of Isaiah, occurrences elsewhere in the Old Testament of this expression, "The Holy One of Israel," may be said to be occasional, but certainly not frequent.

Another consideration pointing to a later editor tying the parts together is the fact that the collection of prophecies against the nations in Isa 13:1—14:23 contains oracles about individual nations that appear to be coming from later times than those of the pre-exilic period.[12] This fact surely suggests that some editorial work on the pre-exilic part of the book (chs 1-39) was still in fact taking place at a *later* time than the pre-exilic period. In a not dissimilar way the material in ch 35 looks and reads very much as if it comes from either exilic, or more likely post-exilic, times. This, for example, speaks so hopefully about a highway on which "the ransomed of the LORD shall return, and come to Zion with singing; everlasting joy shall be upon their heads . . ." (35:10), again suggesting authorship in the post-exilic period, both because of where the material is placed and also the language used being that of, or at least being so similar to, the material—never mind the overall theme—we find in Isa 40-55. A further theme that we find coming from what are presented as very different times is that conveyed in the so-called Song of the Vineyard. This we find "first" in Isa 5:1-7—that is, in the pre-exilic part of the book—but yet being repeated among the apparently post-exilic materials in 37:30 and 65:21.

The whole issue of the development and growth of the Isaiah book into the composition of sixty-six chapters we know today has been much studied, but in spite of the presentation of various theories, in particular as regards authorship, no clear agreement has as yet been arrived at. One significant and detailed academic study was that of the scholar Hermann Barth in which he suggested a pattern and the progress of the history of the composition of the Isaiah book into the form we know, what has come to be known in scholarly circles as a "Josianic Redaction," but while some scholars have found this to be helpful, others remain unconvinced there was such a redaction (that is, editing, revising for further usage) at that particular time.[13]

All this is to say that whereas at one time many Old Testament scholars were convinced of the three distinct parts of the book of Isaiah, each apparently coming from very different historical times, and those times being so different as to suggest that we should be thinking about earlier and later authors, now we are less certain about such matters, and we await further developments in these matters by Old Testament scholars. It is clear that there are three distinct parts of the book of Isaiah, and that they each speaks about three distinctive historical eras. What, however, we lack is a sense of

---

12. See below, pp. 60–86 for further details.

13. See the contribution of H. G. M. Williamson, "The Theory of a Josianic Edition of the First Part of the Book of Isaiah."

sure knowledge about the historical development of what became the documents that make-up something by way of the records of those eras.[14]

It can surely be said that there is a certain commonality of themes we find in the various parts of the book of Isaiah. Yet also there is the consideration that the very considerable time-span between the days when Isaiah the son of Amoz was called to be a prophet (c. 742 BCE) and the days when the people of Judah and Jerusalem were being promised an end to their exile in Babylon (c. 539 BCE) does inevitably for some of us suggest the multiple authorship of certain parts of the Isaiah book that has come down to us. Further, when we consider also the addition of the materials in chs 56–66 in the book of Isaiah, most likely coming from an even later period, we would seem to be considering the matter of an even further change of authorship. Yet within these parts of the completed book of Isaiah, in spite of apparent different and varied authorships, there are undoubtedly similarities in styles, and an overall theological concern to witness to the work of the LORD through his people and their earthly leaders in a succession of historical eras. Moreover, it surely has to be said that in spite of what comes over to us as an essentially negative situation for the LORD's people portrayed in the closing verses of Isaiah ch. 39, there is indeed great hope yet to be spoken of, not least in the opening verses of Isaiah ch. 40 with their "Comfort, O comfort my people, says your God. Speak tenderly to Jerusalem . . ." (40:1–2a). Further, there is much else besides, not only of challenge, but also of both divine and human purpose, and for the latter of ongoing discoveries, in the materials that are presented to us in chs 40–55 and 56–66 of the continuing book of Isaiah.

---

14. In reference to these matters see the very stimulating article, to which I am particularly indebted, by Clements, "The Unity of the Book of Isaiah." See also the helpful chapter concerning the relationships between Isa 1–39; 40–55; 56–66, by Goldingay, "Isaiah 56–66: An Isaianic and a Postcolonial Reading."

Isaiah 1–39 Commentary

I

Isaiah 1–12
The Lord and His People

THE DIVINE JUDGEMENT AND MERCY UPON ISRAEL
1:1–31

In this first chapter of the book of Isaiah we are given an introduction to all that is to follow, in particular to that block of written materials in chapters 1 to 12 of the book. In this sense it is something in the nature of an explanation, an exposition of the grievous sins at one particular historical time period of those very peoples whose leaders believed that they, the peoples, had a special calling and role both in their individual and also in their national lives to be nothing less than the chosen people of God. That place and time is identified as being the time when four kings reigned successively in Jerusalem, all of them of the line of and descended from David, the first real king of Israel and Judah and Jerusalem, namely Uzziah, Jotham, Ahaz, and Hezekiah. Something will be said about each of these rulers as we come to those parts of the Isaiah book where they and their reigns are treated. In the meantime here, and this continues throughout the material in chapters 1–5, right at the beginning of this prophetical book is set forth the Lord's fundamental complaint about his people. In short, *they are unfaithful to their Lord and God*.

The opening verse, or indeed title, of the book of Isaiah (1:1) spells out the fact that what follows is the *vision* of the prophet Isaiah son of Amoz concerning Judah and Jerusalem in the days of those four kings mentioned above. The word *vision* is intended to indicate and give proper emphasis to the fact that this is some particular and divine word that has been given to Isaiah as the Lord's prophet. Further, it is given by no less than God directly to this man, who is thus divinely called to be the particular spokesperson for the Lord, that is to declare what it is that God has to say to his people in that particular age, and at that particular moment in history, and in their particular setting.

As we shall come to see, those were indeed to be stirring and event-filled days and times for which Isaiah the son of Amoz was called to be the Lord's prophet, that is the Lord's servant, his appointed spokesperson. Isaiah was thus called to utter words both of judgement and also of hope and assurance, and even further of guidance to his people for their present and future lives. This man was to proclaim these matters and words as being nothing less than the word of God himself for his people. See on Isa 6:1–13 below for the divine call to Isaiah and what was to be his role, his significance, and his prophetic ministry in the continuing life of his people. Meanwhile, this opening verse of the whole Isaiah book is maybe intended to be an introduction to the first chapter of the book, the first section of the book, and also to all the rest of the work that follows. Further, such titles will occur again in Isa 2:1 and 13:1. Moreover, it appears to have been the serious purpose of this prophet—or perhaps of his editors?—that before we are told about the man Isaiah's call (6:1–13), we need to read and hear about what is the situation on the earth, what is happening there; what is the will of the Lord for his people; what it is that the Lord's people are doing; what it is they are not thinking about and what in fact they should be thinking about.

In 1:1 we are given a title to what is to follow, and it is similar to those that we find in the books of Amos and Hosea (Amos 1:1; Hos 1:1). The present title speaks of the prophet Isaiah's vision only of the southern kingdom of Judah and Jerusalem, omitting any mention of the northern kingdom of Israel, which would admittedly come to an end long before the southern kingdom did, falling to the Assyrian army in 722 BCE, its people being deported to Assyria (2 Kgs 17:6). Meanwhile in the southern kingdom of Judah, with its capital city of Jerusalem, there was a succession of kings of the line of David, and Isaiah speaks here of some of them, namely, Uzziah, Jotham, Ahaz, and Hezekiah.[1]

In 1:2–9 the prophet begins to spell out the Lord God's complaint about his people: it concerns their sins and their failings in being the people of the Lord in the life of the world of their day. For Isaiah, the fundamental problem for God with his people is that the intended relationship between God and his people does not appear to be known by these people, and

---

1. See the time chart below on 145–46.

certainly is not understood (1:3). In verse 2 this basic complaint of the LORD is set forth—and it is necessary that all parts of the universe, both heaven and earth, should take notice of this—namely that *the heavens and the earth* should hear, and attend seriously to what the LORD is saying. The LORD has reared *children* and brought them up, and yet they have *rebelled* against him. And this is not the only place in the Isaiah book where this particular divine complaint will be expressed (see also 1:10; 28:23; 32:9; 42:23; 51:4; 64:3). Yet here is declared for the first time in this prophetical book the divine will that all creation shall both listen and also take notice of what the LORD wishes to say to his people.

Then in v. 3 is expressed the further divine complaint, namely, the truly shocking fact that the animals do better in these matters than do God's people; at least the animals know to whom they belong, what is the source of their rest, where their food and drink are to be found, and information and guidance about their own places and roles in the world of the day. Yet as far as these basic matters of food, rest, shelter are concerned God's people are apparently without understanding, and thus in their lives they have come to a situation in which they are in a state of nothing less than what the prophet calls *rebellion* (vv. 2–3). Alas, the matter of *rebellion* on the part of God's people against their Lord is still being expressed in the very last verse of the book of Isaiah (66:24).

The LORD's complaint about, and rebuke of, his people continues in v. 4, the LORD here being called the *Holy One of Israel*. This is a title for the LORD that occurs very largely in the book of Isaiah, mainly in chs. 1–39 and 40–55. The title, as we can see from the above, holds together twin aspects of the divinity, stressing both his greatness and otherness, his far distance from the life of earth, indeed his holiness, and yet at the same time his very particular relationship with his own people, Israel. That is, in the mystery of his divine being the LORD is both great and far beyond the people and things of earth, and yet at the same time, he has a particular and what appears to be a close and dedicated relationship with his chosen people of earth. In Isa 1–39 this expression is to be found in 1:4; 5:19, 24; 10:20; 12:6; 17:7; 29:19; 30:11–12, 15; 31:1; 37:23. This title for the LORD will continue to be used with some frequency in Isa 40–55, but then less so in chs. 56–66. The prophet's complaint about his people here in 1:4 is that they have despised their Lord, thus becoming utterly estranged from the very source of their being, the God of the whole earth, but in a special and particular way, the *Holy One of Israel*.[2]

---

2. For the expression "Holy One of Israel" see Oswalt, *The Holy One of Israel*, 21, 39–58.

In vv. 5 and 6 the prophet's word concerning the divine complaint about the attitudes and lives of the Israelite peoples is fleshed out, and the focus of the matter is individual lives. The question is posed as to why it is that the peoples seek further ills by their thoroughly sinful lives? The prophet maintains that in fact these people are sick throughout every part of their corporate, national life. So many parts of the body corporate are infected—and no doubt this must be intended to apply individually also—that this sickness, this illness they have, reaches from *head* to *heart* and *from the sole of the foot even to the head*.

With vv. 7–9 the prophetic complaint turns to the corporate aspect of the people's sinfulness, and speaks of the whole land as being in a parlous state. Who the envisaged peoples bringing about all this chaos and destruction are we are not told. Plenty have been the historical proposals made, but the fact is that we are not told who the enemy was, nor are we given an indication of a date.[3] In this short passage the city of Jerusalem is referred to as *daughter Zion*, an expression that is also to be found in the Isaiah book at 10:32; 16:1; 37:22; 52:2; 62:11. *Zion* appears to be an ancient name for the city of Jerusalem, with the term *daughter Zion* thus giving it a certain personification, as if it were a living being.

The crisis for the city is further expressed and detailed by the use of the expressions *booth in a vineyard* (a shelter for a night for a person who was on watch during the harvest season—see Lev 23:42–43), a *shelter in a cucumber field* (perhaps a provision for the same purpose), indeed the whole impression is of being a *besieged city*. In fact, if it had not been for there being a few survivors in Jerusalem the people of Israel would have been *like Sodom . . . like Gomorrah*, whose total destruction by fire we read about in Gen 19:24–29. The impression is surely intended to make abundantly clear that failure to follow in the ways of the LORD will bring grim results for his people. With v. 9 the talk of *Sodom* and *Gomorrah* continues, making the point that without a few survivors the land and the people of Israel would have experienced the same fate as those legendary evil places, which were portrayed as suffering dreadful fates because of their sins.

Verses 10–17 may be felt to be very much more positive material than what has been presented previously. Nevertheless, the preceding materials were needed to set the scene regarding the inadequacies and sins of the people of Israel and their leaders, both in the period of the ministry of Isaiah and also earlier. However, the sins and failures of the people having been presented, the time has surely come that the prophet can set forth a number

---

3. For references to other nations in the book of Isaiah, see Oswalt, "The Nations in Isaiah," 94–105, in Oswalt, *The Holy One of Israel*.

of present ways in which individual and national life could display more aspects of true faithfulness to God. Further, such would present both concerns and also appropriate responses on the part of the people of God.

The focus of the vv. 10-17 concerns the worship of the LORD, and what there is in present practices that is either inappropriate to be offered to God, or else lacks in usefulness regarding the approach to the holy God for his forgiveness of his people's sins. At the beginning of this prophetic word the people are again addressed as those having connections with the cities of *Sodom* and *Gomorrah*, and this—it seems to be suggested—is because they are stained with varieties of their failures and sins (v. 10). Yet why is it that what elsewhere the Old Testament presents as the valid means and aid in the approach to God, namely sacrifices and offerings, are here condemned as inappropriate and worthless? The answer would surely seem to be located both in the spirit in which such offerings are made, and also the nature and activities of the lives of those making the offerings come. In fact, the people have to make some fundamental changes in their lives, which must be put into effect *before* they can come and make their true religious offerings to the LORD. The reference to those who *trample my courts* (v. 12) is about those who are in attendance at happenings in the Jerusalem temple, but whose efforts are made void by the way they live outside the temple walls.

For the fact is clearly that the prophet has in mind here certain aspects of, and offerings made in, worship that have become unacceptable to God. Thus are mentioned *burnt offerings* and *sacrifices* (v. 11), the use of *incense* (v. 13), these being aspects and parts of the worship of God spoken about in the Old Testament and what were understood to be highly desirable to the LORD God. Also mentioned are the particular rites on days of *new moon*, and *sabbath* devotions (v. 13) involving the stretching out of hands in *prayer*, and various other religious rites and offerings. But if those hands of the worshippers are *full of blood* (v. 15), then will there be no worth, perhaps even no value before the LORD, in what are in fact in earthly terms the most valuable offerings! Rather, let there be a dramatic change in the lives and the attitudes of the worshippers—they must rid themselves of their unacceptable social and religious habits and tendencies. Yet there is clearly envisaged in the Old Testament a high level of importance attached to the place of blood in the sacrificial system. The Old Testament clearly regards blood (representing the life of the animal) as a great gift to the people of earth, and while blood is not to be consumed by humans, it is regarded as a most desirable offering to God, and for the continuing good of the life of humanity (see Lev 17:11).[4] So the issue here is not that sacrifice is rejected but that sacrifice from *brazen and unrepentant sinners* is.

The required life-changes are set out in vv. 16–17, in particular, matters to do with the people removing their evil ways from their lives. Changing from doing evil to doing good is required, each person turning round their priorities so that they might advance to rescuing the oppressed, to *defend the orphan*, and to *plead for the widow*. When these matters are attended to, and human lives are being changed accordingly, then *justice* (v. 17) will have been done—that is, the right and correct treatment of other people, not least those who are in need of help and acceptance in the society of the day, in particular those who lack the strength, the standing, or the acceptance into religious and corporate social life. Thus it is of great importance that the community ensures that all receive their fair shares of life's goods and gifts, and that thereby something more of *justice* will have been done.

Verses 18–20 present an invitation to the people of God to repent and to seek the forgiveness of the LORD for their present and past sins. The verb at the beginning of v. 18, which NRSV translates as *let us argue it out*, could be rendered "let us settle our differences," or "let us reach an agreement." These words certainly seem to be coming from a situation of dispute, one between the LORD God and his people. It is the peoples' sins that constitute the fundamental problem in the divine-human relationship, that is, those definitively *red* or *scarlet* sinful failings in the lives of God's people. Yet these human sinners are being offered by the LORD the possibility of turning to a different way of life. For the fact is that with the LORD there can indeed be for penitent people the reality of forgiveness, the opportunity, as it were, to begin again, each and all to be transformed from looking *scarlet* to being white like *snow*, being changed from *red* to white *wool* (v. 18). The deeply beneficial results of this turning from the one to the other way of life is that henceforward there will be the possibility for these human people of being able to *eat* the good things of life. Presumably there is the thought here of a transformation both in these people's earthly lives and also in their spiritual lives. Yet without the turning from sin, the LORD warns the people that the sword will play over them in their lives. This is indeed a divine possibility the prophet says, *for the mouth of the LORD has spoken* (v. 20). That is, we are being assured that this is truly something that the prophet is bringing to his people from their God.

Before we go on further, we need to return to v. 19 with its reference to the blessings on the Israelite people: they will be able to *eat the good of*

---

4. On this subject of the worship spoken about in the Old Testament, see Thompson, *Greatly to Be Praised*.

the land. This is not the first occurrence of the word *land* (Hebrew *'erez*) in the book Isaiah. It occurs earlier in v. 7, but there the NRSV translates it *country*. Yet the word, and the associated concept, is there in so many parts of the Old Testament. Indeed, it frequently occurs in the book of Isaiah (see a concordance for the many references). In the Old Testament the "land" is understood as being the gift of the LORD to his people, and the whole of the lengthy drama of the exodus from Egypt is that the Israelites may come eventually into their promised land. Land is home, provision, identity, security. However, that land was already occupied, and thus some aggressive activity took place so that Israel could take possession of what they understood to be their share. And thus it has been since then, for in no small way the whole theme of land possession and sharing remains a serious issue in our world of today, when so many peoples are seeking for their shares of, and places in, the lands where there is peace, being ready to brave many perilous ways through parts of the world to find a place to dwell.[5]

Williamson in his commentary on these chapters points out that here—in the presentation of divine judgement upon the people, followed by the possibility of forgiveness, and invitation by divine call to choose the right path thereafter—is reflected the basic shape of the book of Isaiah as a whole in its three main parts, by which he means chapters 1–39; 40–55; 56–66.[6]

Verses 21–26 continue the thought of the preceding verses, and express that thought in bold and outspoken language. They speak in some detail of the necessary renewal of the city of Jerusalem that must take place if it is to become once again *the faithful city*. The dreadful religious plight that now so seriously threatens all who are involved, is that the once *faithful city* has become like a *whore*, a prostitute; the community that had once been full of *justice* and *righteousness* is now dominated by *murderers* (v. 21). The city that was full of *justice* and *righteousness*—that is, of people who act fairly, who treat others in good and correct ways (*justice*), and who lead such lives that from them comes goodness and true morality (*righteousness*)—has sunk, gone downhill, become debased, apparently both in the practice of individuals, yet also in families, and further moreover in the people's corporate life. Thus there has come about inattention to the *orphan's* and the *widow's* causes; that now they do not come before the *princes* of the land, as they should have been able to do. In fact, those princes are *rebels*, and *companions of thieves*, people concerned alone for their own well-being

---

5. On this whole subject, see Brueggemann's study *The Land*; see also Habel, *The Land Is Mine*.

6. Williamson, *Isaiah 1–5*, 113.

(v. 23). Therefore the judgement of the LORD will fall upon such leaders, and also bring about transformation and renewal, so that afterwards the words for the city will be *righteousness* and *the faithful city* (v. 26). In this way will the city be purified.

Verses 27–31 tell in plain straightforward words the possible futures for the people of Israel, those called to be the people of the Lord. Are they to be ransomed or are they to be broken, crushed? These two possibilities are set out in the opening two verses of this section: v. 27 speaks of the possibility of being *redeemed* through living lives practising *justice* and *righteousness,* putting into good effect those issues and concerns spoken about above in v. 21. However, the expression here (justice and righteousness) seems to be using two words to speak of one thought (*hendiadys*). They are used in this way elsewhere in this part of the Isaiah book (see 1:17, 27; 5:7, 16; 9:7; 16:5; 28:17; 32:1, 16; 33:5). Sometimes, however, these two words seem intended to have slightly different meanings or significances. Be that as it may, what the words *justice* and *righteousness* are intended to signify is a society where there is social justice, where every member may be able to enjoy freedom and equality, and where there is mutual concern for one another.

In order to make this a real possibility there is the call here to turn away from those idolatrous things that in the past have been believed to be of religious value, for example, objects such as terebinths (*oaks*) and supposedly sacred *gardens* (vv. 29, 30), earthly objects (and also individuals) that are regarded as having strength, and possibly even delivering power, but which in reality are not *strong* at all, and are liable to *burn* up—with no one *to quench* their flames (v. 31). To be seeking help and strength in such idols is a sinful failure in not going to the LORD, the real source of help and strength for his people. Thus are the people being sinful and are liable to find that they and their works shall burn together, with no one to quench them (v. 31).

What we have here in the first chapter of the book of Isaiah is something of a series of fundamental concerns of the prophet that will continue to be found not only in the first section of the long book of Isaiah, but in fact throughout its various parts, and even as far as the very closing verse of the whole work (see Isa 66:24). This surely suggests an ongoing concern with such issues on the part of all those responsible for giving us this remarkable prophetic book. We repeatedly find the pattern that in seeking the salvation that has over the years been revealed and proclaimed to them, God's people have often in fact searched for help in places where no help could possibly have been found. Further, this search for help in such places, and from such sources, is not only an ongoing major mistake, but is also a major and ever-prevalent sin. Also to be noted is the warning—and reassurance—to the readers and hearers at the end of the dramatic and most important chapter detailing the call of the prophet Isaiah (6:1–13). It is as if those words about sinful and useless seeking that we read in Isa 1 are being spoken again. Even in the apparently most desperate of situations for the people of God there can be, there surely will be, divine possibilities of new growth that may, by the grace and help of the LORD, come out of the LORD's holy seed (6:13).

This opening chapter of the book of Isaiah seems to be presented to us as a summary of an important aspect of Old Testament faith. It has been pointed out by some scholars that the wording and the emphases here are reminding us of what we are told about the Yahwistic religious life in Deuteronomy 28 and 32.[7] Further, Wildberger,[8] in his very detailed commentaries on Isa 1–39, speaks of there being here certain catchwords that emphasize both Israel's failures in the past and the expected religious searches of future peoples. Thus may apostasy (vv. 2–3) followed by divine judgement and grace (vv. 4–9) provoke a turning to God (vv. 10–20), fidelity (vv. 21–28), and an end to false worship (vv. 29–31). Ronald Clements says of this first chapter of Isaiah, "The inner spiritual challenge and the repeated re-emergence of hope and renewal build on the ideals of peace and righteousness which are set out in [Isa] 1:26. Only when they are re-established can the message which the book sets out attain fulfilment: 'Afterwards you shall be called the city of righteousness, the faithful city' (Isa 1:26)."[9]

JERUSALEM AND THE NATIONS 2:1–5

This short passage begins with a new title, this time a shorter one than that found at the beginning of the first chapter. This one has briefly *The word that Isaiah son of Amoz saw concerning Judah and Jerusalem*, and the differences here are that what was the *vision* at the beginning of chapter 1 here becomes the *word*, that is the issue, the matter. There has been much scholarly discussion as to possibilities of which of these passages is the original, but in truth it hardly matters. As we work through the first part of the Isaiah book we shall come across further new beginnings, and simply accept that this prophet, and maybe others with him too, have many things to say, many different issues to speak about, an extensive range of historical happenings in which the workings of God are there to be spoken about and possibly interpreted. It is, therefore, hardly surprising that there should be divisions and breaks in this long written work.

7. Clements, "Isaiah 1:1–31: Israel Summoned to Repentance . . ." See esp. 228.
8. Wildberger, *Isaiah 1–12*, 79.
9. Clements, "Isaiah 1:1–31: Israel Summoned to Repentance . . ." See esp. 228.

The new heading is followed by four verses (2:2–5) in which a renewed future for the people of God is spoken about, one in which there are some dramatic changes for the people of God, and further, one in which others of earth could find new help and renewal of their lives, both individual and corporate. However, first there is another question to note—even if we cannot answer it in any definitive way. The content of Isa 2:2–4, with much the same wording and in much the same order, is to be found in Mic 4:1–3. It has to be said that we cannot be sure which of these versions came first, or whether in fact they both came out of an independent source. The very fact that we do find the wording and message in the two places suggests that in the minds of certain people there was real significance to be found in this wording and the emphasis of the promise being set forth. Perhaps we need to accept that we cannot be certain about their original authorship.[10]

Returning to the Isaiah passage as we find it in Isa 2:1–5, we have here an affirmation of the great importance and worth of the house of the LORD coming to be situated on the highest (literally, the head) of the mountains, and to it the nations will stream (v. 2). Presumably its place on the heights will give expression to the fact that here is something of the greatest importance for the people of God, and that it is hardly surprising that it became what must have been a rather obvious site for the temple building, which is here called *the house of the God of Jacob*. Moreover, there will, at least on the parts of some of the residents, have been the appreciation of the fact that from this holy building, on this supremely high place, there would naturally proceed the word of the LORD, and his divine instructions as to how all are to walk in obedience as God's faithful people (v. 3). Here, proceeding from *Zion* there will also be the necessary teachings (*instruction* [v. 3]) about the way of the LORD, and what he calls for from his earthly followers regarding the ending of their dependence on weapons of war to settle their differences—and even to the end of a need on their parts to learn the ways and arts of war. Thus come the memorable words about beating *their swords into plowshares, and their spears into pruning hooks*. Further, there follows the command about the fundamental national and individual action needed, *neither shall they learn war any more* (v. 4). This brief but remarkable vision of a totally peaceful future is concluded with the bold invitation to the nation, here referred to as the house of Jacob, to *come* and *walk in the light of the LORD* (v. 5). Nevertheless, how much strife and warfare is there yet to speak about in this first part (chs. 1–39) of the book of Isaiah. In particular we may note with at least some anguish that in Joel 3:10, which comes from

---

10. Duhm, *Jesaia*, 39.

a totally different historical situation, there can be the call to *Beat your plowshares into swords, and your pruning hooks into spears.*[11]

Surely, every re-reading of this short passage from Isaiah comes to us as a most urgent reminder that we should in our contemporary world be seeking to beat our swords into plowshares, and our spears into pruning hooks. For tragically the situation in this regard is indeed as yet hardly any better after so many centuries of our reading these words of the prophet Isaiah. Concerning the book of Isaiah, and in a particular way this verse (2:5), Blenkinsopp says, "In view of our own sad and guilty knowledge of the violence we continue to visit on each other, on other creatures, and on the environment in general, the eschatological horizon of the abolition of war, and even of violence in the animal world (11:6–9), is one of the most poignant motifs in the book."[12]

THE DAY OF THE LORD 2:6–22

This is not an easy passage to study; it seems to lack order and organization. In fact, many years ago the German Old Testament scholar Bernard Duhm wrote in his 1892 commentary on Isaiah that this passage was the worst preserved in the entire book of Isaiah.[13] It has to be said that a good number of scholars today still accept such a view of these verses. Nevertheless, there is an emphasis here on the theme of the "Day of the LORD" (see v. 12), and in this regard there is some similarity with the concerns and proclamations of others of the Hebrew prophets. See for example, Amos 5:18–20; Joel 1:15; Zeph 1:14. Further, there are complaints that the land is full of those who seek to bring to the peoples their own religious beliefs, their own chosen leaders, and their own artefacts. Thus, there is talk in v. 6 of *diviners* from the east and *soothsayers* like the Philistines; in v. 7 it is *silver, gold, horses,* and *chariots*; in v. 8 *idols* to which people bow down. There are warnings too about the judgement of the LORD upon those Israelites who may worship such false gods (v. 10), and that if they do, then Israelite peoples will be humbled and brought low (vv. 10, 11, 12). In fact, there are warnings here of the judgement of the LORD upon all sorts and conditions of things and beings—see v. 13 for the warning against *lofty* trees, and v. 14 against *high mountains*. Still the tirade continues: divine judgement against *high towers* (v. 15), against *ships of Tarshish* (v. 16), against haughty and proud peoples (v. 17). Yet also there is talk of a day that will dawn when there are much

11. Blenkinsopp, *Isa 1–39*, 191.
12. Blenkinsopp, *Isa 1–39*, 191.
13. Duhm, *Jesaia*, 39.

better things—when, for example, *idols* will pass away (v. 18), or indeed, have been thrown away (v. 20). Meanwhile, the people should be preparing themselves for what is to come, by going into *caverns/caves, holes* in the rocks (vv. 19, 21). Above all they should be turning away from that sort of apparent mortal assistance, help that, in fact, is of little use at all (vv. 20, 22).

There is surely a serious message here of both warning and also of hope for peoples in all ages who may be looking to this Lord for help and strength in their lives, and in particular in times of crisis. Certainly, in the arrangement of the stories and the prophecies in Isaiah there is a real sense at this stage of things in the architecture of the book that it seeks to assist us in preparing ourselves for the *glory* of the *majesty* of the Lord (v. 21). J. J. M. Roberts says about this passage, "Only in walking in Yahweh's light is there true security. When the scramble for security alienates one from God, when it takes precedence over God's commandments, one may be sure that an idol has been erected. Such idolatry may find expression in[, for instance,] a campaign to promote a Star Wars military defense . . ."[14] Are we not here being challenged over the matter of what emphases we adopt in our lives, especially in times of challenge or crisis. Where do we place our ultimate trust? In God . . . or an idol?

JUDAH'S ANARCHY 3:1–9

Those issues of prophetical concern that begin to be spoken about in Isa 2:6–22, are now continued in the present passage, and in fact will go on to the end of chapter 4. The serious matters that make up the contents of these chapters are issues that the prophet—or those who were responsible for these parts of the book—believed were an affront to the Lord, with such sinfulness being especially shocking because it comes from the chosen people of the Lord. There is surely being expressed here the prophetic view that as things stand at the moment in Judah and Jerusalem those who are called to be the people of God are in fact under the serious judgement of the Lord.

The section begins with the warning that the Lord is taking away so many of the necessities of life; spoken of in v. 1 is the impending loss even of those dietary basics of *bread* and *water*. Verses 2–3 speak of the forthcoming loss of certain national and local leaders, those who are called to sustain earthly, physical life (*warrior and soldier, judge and prophet, diviner and elder*). With the loss of the *judge* there would be no proper administration of justice; without the *prophet* there would be the lack of the personnel called to bring the word of the Lord to the people and their leaders—most likely

14. Roberts, *First Isaiah*, 48–49.

not those who became the biblical Isaiahs and Jeremiahs and other such "major prophets," but rather perhaps those individuals who had been given general mediatory ministries from the LORD to earthly individuals and groups, such as the ministry of cultic prophets. Also with messages from the LORD would be the *diviner*. The term *elder* was a somewhat general one to indicate those who were held in particular respect in Israelite society. *Captain* must refer to a military person, while the *counselor* filled a more political appointment, and the *magician* was one who was believed to speak and perform various duties, either of a military or other nature. There is also the warning that the nation's future and fate is in the hands of those who are totally inexperienced.

Yet there are more changes ahead even than all of these. The people are given warning that they are to be led by *boys* in place of their present *princes*, and that it will be as if they are having *babes* ruling over them (v. 4). Further, there is to be much internal national strife; people will *oppress* one another, *neighbors* will be embattled one against another. In fact, social life will be thrown into situations of general chaos and aggression (vv. 5–6). This is because of the sins of Judah and Jerusalem, both of them exhibiting ways of life that are contrary to the ways of the LORD, and that, as it were, deny any real sense of the LORD's *glorious presence*. Indeed, there is a general failure of neighbors seeking to help neighbors in their various needs (vv. 7–8). With v. 9 we have what looks like a summarizing statement of the happenings that have been detailed in the preceding verses, this giving particular mention of the city named *Sodom*, a place spoken of alongside *Gomorrah* in the Old Testament as a setting and locality of extreme sinfulness, that, as we read in Gen 18–19, were places scheduled to be destroyed by the LORD—and which events, we are told, did take place (Gen 19:24–29). Thus, in the Old Testament these cities come to be presented as legendary places where human sinfulness was followed by divine judgement.

Here, surely, is being presented some of the details of the state of Judah and Jerusalem, which it would seem the prophet (or prophets) and the editor (or editors) needed to present to readers and hearers before certain new and salvific events could be spoken about. Thus does the prophet present, both to his contemporaries and also to all the later generations of leaders, a serious challenge about walking in the ways of God, and sharing in his concerns for all peoples.

THE LORD AND HIS PEOPLE 3:10–15

At the beginning of this passage it is as if the prophet surveys the people of his day, their individual and corporate lives, and the state of Judah. There are some good individuals, there are righteous ones, these being spoken about in v. 10, and they are assured that they will be recipients of good things. This is expressed in the somewhat homely words about being able to eat well after doing their good deeds. In stark contrast are the wicked, those we read about in v. 11, who must expect things to go badly for them, for surely *what their hands have done shall be done to them*. This is a common expression found in Old Testament thought: harmful things being done to others were believed in some Israelite circles to rebound on those who do them. Yet the Old Testament itself joins in something of a challenge to this point of view, and in parts maintains that this is no adequate way to explain the problems of suffering that come to people who do not appear to have committed any particularly gross sins.[15]

Verse 12 may well cause us some further difficulties. NRSV translates a Hebrew word here *women*, but more likely is the translation that has come down to us in other Versions, in particular in the Greek and the Targums, "usurers, creditors." What is being condemned here is lenders of money gaining unreasonable profits for themselves, when in fact they had been called to give help to those in financial difficulties.

Nevertheless, above and beyond all these earthly issues and problems, so we are told in v. 13, there stands the LORD to *argue his case* and that it is he who will judge the people, that is, presumably in the place of those earthly appointees who rather than fulfilling their God-given duties are in fact concerned only with their own needs and desires. The imagined setting here would seem to be that of a law court, for indeed on the Israelite part of the earth there is a whole series of human appointments to national leadership and legal responsibilities, these being intended to ensure that as much as is humanly possible there are maintained justice and peace in the land. Thus, we are told in v. 14 that the LORD *enters into judgment* with the national leaders and elders, and also those who have *devoured the vineyard* and appropriated for themselves even the few possessions of the poor. Further, those leaders are guilty of *crushing* God's people, and *grinding the face of the poor* (v. 15) rather than exercising their intended ministry of caring for them.

The prophet has yet a good deal more to say about vineyards and the people of Israel's and their leaders' responsibilities regarding them, as we shall read in forthcoming chapters of book (see in particular Isa 5:1–7).

---

15. For a discussion of this and of other aspects of the problems of suffering, as spoken about in the Old Testament, see Thompson, *Where Is the God of Justice?*

What the LORD of all has presented to his people on earth needs earthly care and attention, and moreover attention to what the LORD requires from human leaders as they exercise their stewardship, and so care for all their peoples. And those divinely chosen leaders are always to practise this living and leading in justice and in righteousness. So may they thus ever lead their peoples in justice and righteousness.

THE PRIDE OF THE DAUGHTERS OF ZION 3:16—4:1

One commentator on the book of Isaiah has referred to this passage as a "tirade against the court ladies" of Jerusalem (*the daughters of Zion*, v. 16).[16] His description is certainly appropriate, and one might have expected the point to have been made within a few verses. Instead we have an extended description, and one that uses a considerable number of rare words as far as the Old Testament is concerned, no small number of them being Hebrew words that make their sole Hebrew Bible appearance here. We find not dissimilar outbursts against what we must presumably regard as the inappropriate privilege of station and possessions, especially monies, in Amos 4:1–3 and 6:4–5. See also on this subject Isa 32:9–12 and Jer 44:15–20.

This passage is about a religiously unacceptable attitude concerning human wealth. Here the focus is upon the women of wealth in Jerusalem, who we are told in v. 16 were walking in their haughty and even seductive ways. With v. 17 we find some variation in different translations: namely, what has been commonly translated "foreheads" in the fourth line, is in NRSV rendered *secret parts*, this being a not-unreasonable translation of a Hebrew word. Then in vv. 18–23 we have an extended list of women's clothes and ornaments, a good number of which make their only Old Testament/Hebrew Bible appearance here, and therefore raise serious questions for translators as to just what is intended to be understood. What however is more straightforwardly understandable is that a series of rare Hebrew words refer to a number of seriously expensive items of women's clothing and ornaments. Even so, this situation, the reader is warned, will not last.

Thus with v. 24 there is a change of emphasis, this being due to a whole change of fortunes for the city and people of Jerusalem—and in particular for those Jerusalem women we have considered, who appear to have been enjoying such privilege, not forgetting those finest of clothings. This would appear to be the result of some disasters in war, but which war we do not know, and indeed we cannot be at all sure about the historical date, even the period, from which this passage comes. The fact that there is a lack of men

---

16. Blenkinsopp, *Isaiah 1–39*, 201.

in the city available for the women is maybe due to the men having been called away to join the city's protecting forces. This is how many scholars understand the language of vv. 24–26. That would certainly seem to be the emphasis in the new subject being spoken about in v. 25, *Your men shall fall by the sword and your warriors in battle.* Thus shall there be the sad situation when even the city gates appear to be among those who *lament and mourn* (v. 26), all this leading to the drastically changed circumstances in which no less than seven women are having to ask one man to help them. Whether that is literally correct or whether it is prophetic use of hyperbole (4:1) is open to question.

This reminds us how swiftly such totally changed situations for the people of the world's communities can come about, in age after age. And surely not only for those once-fortunate ones who had so much and were able to enjoy such wealth, grandeur, and status, but also—and surely, even more—for those much more ordinary members of a city or a national community who have to face up to a radical change of circumstances in their lives. And this, alas, in age after age.

ZION'S FINAL GLORY 4:2–6

The opening sentence of this passage stands in marked contrast with the closing verse of the preceding passage (4:1), and indeed of the whole of the proclamation in Isa 3:18—4:1. Whereas the earlier material spoke of a day, indeed a period of time, of deep calamity for the people of Jerusalem, now in 4:2–6 we have talk of a much renewed and purified city and community, and people of Israel. Just when this present passage is to be dated is subject to scholarly disagreement, and yet in a more general historical sense it clearly seems to come from a later time than the preceding passage. No doubt there are aspects of the ideal expressed in this passage, and the language used here does go some way to suggesting and indicating this, with its *spirit of burning* (v. 4), *cloud by day . . . fire by night* (v. 5), a *canopy* (v. 5), and a *pavilion* (v. 6). This is the sort of language that in the fullness of time would issue in what is called apocalyptic, material that in the book of Isaiah we find in chs. 24–27 and 34–35, namely, the use of language of a supernatural character, in which God is portrayed as doing what only God is able to do. See under chs. 24–27 below.

Verse 2 speaks of the future day when *the branch of the LORD* will become *beautiful and glorious.* Not only is that in large contrast from what has been the prophet's message about Judah and Jerusalem, but the Hebrew word *branch* would be taken up by other prophets to speak of the coming at some time of a Messiah (see Jer 23:5; 33:15; Zech 3:8) for the people of

Israel, thus expressed in English "branch" becomes "Branch" (i.e., Messiah). In the meantime (v. 3), instead of there being gross sinfulness in the city of Jerusalem, in the future there will be left there only those who are called *holy*, that is, those who belong to the LORD, who ever look to the LORD in hope and for guidance in their earthly lives. These people are those whose conduct and outlook are founded in their faithful relationship with the LORD.

We are hardly surprised, then, at what the following verse (v. 4) speaks about, namely the LORD having *washed away the filth of the daughters of Zion*, and by radical divine washing has cleansed Jerusalem of its *bloodstains*. This means that there will have been created by divine will and action a total renewal of the city of Jerusalem (v. 5). Further, this will be such a renewal of the city that in future days it will be fitted and prepared for, and moreover able to provide, shelter for its peoples from both rains and the sun. The word used in v. 6 that is translated in NRSV as *pavilion* is the same word that elsewhere in the Old Testament is used of the booth that would be employed by the person watching over the vineyard in the harvesting season, in particular guarding the precious products through the dark night hours (Neh 8:14); the present passage is about the transformation that will take place through divine action. So it is that a practice that had begun as the human protection of a harvest crop has become a celebration of the change the LORD God has brought about for his chosen people. Here—that is, in a spirit of faithful trust in the LORD—there will be granted a most adequate, even exalted, dwelling place for God's people, nothing less than *a pavilion, a shade by day from the heat, and a refuge and a shelter from the storm and rain* (v. 6).

David Stacey, in his commentary on Isa 1–39, in summary of what he has to say about this passage, observes:

> Whatever denunciations were necessary, the prophets preserved a glowing hope in the faithfulness of Yahweh. . . . The blessings are expressed in material terms because the material world is Yahweh's creation and it is in the material world that he acts; but it is a material world purged by the spirit of judgement. The initiative lies with Yahweh throughout and the end is not simply the protection of his people but the manifestation of his glory on Mount Zion.[17]

---

17. Stacey, *Isa 1–39*, 31.

THE SONG OF THE VINEYARD 5:1-7

Here, expressed in the medium of a song of a vineyard is a straightforward, and easily understood story of the work a person did to provide for themselves a good vineyard that would bring forth a healthy yield of choice grapes. And surely so it should have done, for after all, the vineyard was planted on a fertile hill, which NRSV translates *very fertile hill* (v. 1). He worked at the ground, he *dug* it—thoroughly—and *cleared it of stones*, planting *choice vines*, and moreover building a *watchtower*, presumably for those who watched over what were expected to be the precious grapes, and also dug out a *wine vat*. Yet what disappointment did that person experience at harvest time, for instead of their expectations from all this thorough, and presumably expensive, preparation, the vineyard yielded only *wild grapes* (v. 2)!

And thus the speaker changes the tone completely, speaking now not about someone else, an imaginary someone else, with his elaborately planned and built vineyard, but now to the actual people of the time who lived in Judah and Jerusalem, and inviting them to consider the plight of their vineyard owner, none other than God himself. Meanwhile they, the people, are themselves in fact here portrayed as being the vineyard, those who have had so much done for them, have been prepared so carefully and thoroughly for their present lives, and as it has turned out have failed to bear fruit, failed to live out their discipleship as the people of God (vv. 3-4).

Thus comes the judgement of the LORD upon the peoples for all their failures and shortcomings, and this is expressed in the bold and stark ways referred to in vv. 5-6, which must appear to be very harsh. Yet that is the point being made here; we are surely intended to understand that this is how the LORD God must feel about the people in whose history and present lives he has invested such love and trust, effort and guidance. In particular, this describes the situation of Israel's misuse of all the good provisions the LORD has made for their welfare in the land. Of course, if the LORD had really carried out his threats, and pursued such punishment and settlement with his people, then there would have been no continuing story, either in the book of Isaiah or elsewhere. Yet, in fact, this is a continuing story, about which there is still so very much to recount—not only for us to lament over, but also, by the grace of God, to rejoice over.

When the prophet Hosea contemplates the LORD's gracious provision and ongoing care for his people he is aware that humanly speaking there must be a deep tussle that ever and always takes place within the being of God: on the one hand, the divine sense of judgement upon his people; on the other, the overwhelming love and ongoing care he has for them. See Hos 11:1-9 in which we read in the concluding words of that great, indeed overwhelming, force of the divine commitment for the ongoing care and protection of his divinely called yet ever sinful people:

> How can I give you up, Ephraim?
> How can I hand you over, O Israel?
> How can I make you like Admah?
> How can I treat you like Zeboiim?
> My heart recoils within me;
> my compassion grows warm and tender.
> I will not execute my fierce anger;
> I will not again destroy Ephraim;
> for I am God and no mortal,
> the Holy One in your midst,
> and I will not come in wrath.
> (Hos 11:8-9)

Further, as far as the book of Isaiah is concerned, there is yet still something more to hear about one of the LORD's vineyards, that one being—or has become?—"A pleasant vineyard, sing about it!" (27:2; see on Isa 27:1-6 below.)

A SERIES OF WOE ORACLES 5:8-24

We have here a series of words of condemnation by the prophet, in each of which the first and crucial word is that of "Woe." In the Hebrew Bible the same word is used to describe funeral laments (see 1 Kgs 13:30), but more frequently it appears in the words of the prophets, and usually when there is a warning that doom and destruction are inevitably about to come. The form in which these expressions occur is usually "Woe to . . ." followed by some delineation of the sinful person or group, the human cause of condemnation, and concluded with a word of divine judgement—as indeed is to be found in the first of the "Woes" we shall consider below in Isa 5:8-10. A later "Woe" passage is to be found in Isa 10:1-4, and that will be considered when we reach that stage in the Isaiah book. We may perhaps understand this present collection of "Woes" in Isa 5:8-24 as having been deliberately placed thus so as to serve as a preparation for what is to come, namely the account of the divine call of the man Isaiah to be the LORD's prophet, in particular in the time of crisis for Judah and Jerusalem with the attack by Syria and Ephraim upon them, a time when truly they would need divine help and guidance. Yet before that series of historical events can be spoken about, there is perhaps the matter of some attention needing to be given to a number of serious outbreaks of sinfulness on the part of the people of Judah and Jerusalem.

The first of these "Woe Oracles" and the cause of the prophet proclaiming this *Woe* to his people occurs in Isa 5:8–10, and concerns what we might in our contemporary language call property speculation. Thus we read of those who join *house to house* and *field to field*, that is, a systematic and selfish appropriation of properties and lands, an appropriation that inevitably results in other, less wealthy, people being able to find space only for themselves alone, presumably, that is, without other family members (5:8). The dire and divine warning here[18] to those who have exercised such greed is that things will not work out well for them; rather they will experience finding themselves on their own in *large and beautiful* yet *desolate houses* (v. 9), and further, possessing *vineyards* that are yielding pathetically small harvests, a mere *bath*, a mere *ephah*, both measures of comparatively small quantities (the precise size being argued about by scholars) (v. 10). The immediate and physical cause of this calamitous situation is not spoken about; it could have been that the mere greed of the wealthy drove out other people, or it could have been warfare and invasion, but we are given no date of the occurrence of these events to help in such determinations.

The second Woe Oracle is of greater length than the preceding one, and concerns drunkards (5:11–17). There is in v. 11 a play on words to make clear what the prophet is concerned about: he is declaring "woe" to those who *rise early* (Hebrew *shakam*) in the morning so as to make an early start with their *strong drink* (Hebrew *shekar*). Further, we understand that in fact they are engaged in the same activity in the night hours. In the following verse (v. 12) we read of the employment of musical instruments in their alcoholic feasts, and at the same time their totally ignoring matters of the deeds and works of the Lord. Thus they are warned of the danger of an *exile* of divine judgement while so many of their peoples seem to be hungry and thirsty (v. 13). It is thought by a number of scholars that the following verses (vv. 14–17) make up an addition to an imagined original unit comprising vv. 11–13, being intended to emphasize, to flesh out, the approaching danger of *exile* unless there can be a change of emphases in individual lives, as well as in the corporate life of Judah and Jerusalem. Verse 16 makes it clear that the divine actions spring from the Lord's acts of *justice*, and come out of the divine *righteousness*. Yet there can be hope under the Lord for the future (v. 17), new life, even though it may be taking place and being lived out among the *ruins* of towns and cities.

---

18. Kaiser, *Isaiah 1–12*, 102.

The third woe is dealt with in verses 18–19, and is addressed to those who act in arrogance, and arrogant ways, both towards the people of Jerusalem and even towards the Lord God. Not only are those sorts of human leaders people of iniquity (v. 18), but they address the Lord God, none other than *the Holy One of Israel*, in arrogant ways. For this divine title and its usage in the Isaiah book, see above on Isa 1:4. However, here the Lord God is portrayed as appearing to be slow in executing his plans, and until the people see more divine action they will not be convinced (v. 19). Nothing is said in this woe about the particular danger the people court in their having such attitudes.

The fourth woe follows in v. 20, and concerns moral deviance, that is those *who call evil good and good evil*. This false naming of aspects of life inevitably leads to perversions of justice, and indeed, is a perversion of justice. One Old Testament scholar observed of this woe, "So underlying the fourth woe is the basic conviction that Yahweh punishes those who misuse their office or their calling for their own advantage and to the detriment of those who have no protection and no help."[19]

With v. 21 we come to the fifth woe, this one being spoken against those who are *wise in* their *own eyes* but who, so we are left to understand, are not so regarded by other people. That is, the judgement is also upon those addressed, those who are *shrewd in* their *own sight!*

In vv. 22–24 we have something by way of summary and conclusion of this gathering together of prophetic warnings about human words and deeds that have to be accounted in the sight of the Lord as leading to divine woes. With v. 22 we are back with those strong drinkers we read about earlier in the somewhat extended entry in 5:11–17. Once again these people are condemned (v. 22), as being too mighty in drinking wine, and too strong in the mixing of their drinks—both of these being too mighty and strong for their own and other people's good. Also spoken about again is the practice of bribery, and the habit of depriving the innocent of their rights (v. 23). This is followed by an extended verse that describes the great anger of the Lord God upon those sinners whose sinful deeds have been spoken about. Yet perhaps the greatest sin, and what is most seriously wrong with those who are called to be God's people, is what is expressed in the last verse here, they have *rejected the instruction of the Lord of hosts, and have despised the word of the Holy One of Israel* (v. 24b).

Within this collection of woe oracles there is a wide range of subjects, and clearly there were evidences for the prophet of the sinful goings-on of his peoples. There is therefore a variety of condemnations here, which at

---

19. Kaiser, *Isaiah 1–12*, 102.

first sight may seem to be off-putting for the contemporary reader, and yet a deeper consideration will surely reveal that here the prophet does still speak words to which we should pay attention: whether it is concerning joining house to house and/or field to field (vv. 8–10), or a too active search for strong drink (vv. 11–17, 22–24), or calling evil good (v. 20), or whether God's people today have rejected *the instruction of the* LORD *of hosts . . . and have despised the word of the Holy One of Israel* (v. 24b). And further, that this divine condemnation of human sinfulness also means both divine judgement and also human warning, as Roberts expresses it, "The judgment announced on these evildoers is that their root and fruit, that is, their future in its totality, the future they had hoped to secure by their wickedness, will disappear in the fire like chaff or straw, vanishing like dried-up rot or a puff of dust."[20]

JUDGEMENT IS COMING 5:25–30

After the preceding somewhat elaborate and extended delineation of the sins and the sinful goings-on in the lands of Judah and Jerusalem, it is hardly surprising that there now follows the serious warning that those peoples involved in the above sins are under the righteous judgement of the LORD. Thus we read in the opening verse of the (righteous) *anger of the* LORD (v. 25) being over the peoples for the reason that they have misused the gifts of the LORD, using them solely for themselves. This with its language of the *mountains* having *quaked*, and *corpses . . . like refuse in the streets*, surely seeks to alert us to a forthcoming divine judgement. For as yet, so we are told, the LORD's *anger has not turned away*, and that *his hand is stretched out still* (v. 25).

Yet now there is something new we are being told about. In v. 26 we read about the LORD calling a nation from far away who will come speedily to this Israelite setting and situation, and the language employed here is that of power, even aggression, of energy and weapons. Thus are we confronted with a series of words like *arrows, bows, horses, wheels, like young lions, seize their prey, carry it off, and no one can rescue*, in v. 28–29. This seems clearly to be a reference to the energetic activity of the Assyrian army under the leadership of the Assyrian King Tiglath-Pileser III (744–27 BCE), whose kingdom, centered in Mesopotamia, had a real military need to secure parts of its western borders, especially where the Assyrians might have been under threat from the Egyptian powers. Thus the Assyrian king came to be active in the lands of Israel and Judah and, as we shall come to see, in other

20. Roberts, *First Isaiah*, 83.

neighboring countries as well, no doubt needing to have them serve as "buffer states" between the heartlands of the Assyrian empire and any possible future aggression from the large country of Egypt.

What then we seem to be hearing about in Isa 5:26-30 is the activity of the Assyrian army, an army to which in succeeding chapters of the book of Isaiah we shall need to pay considerable attention. This army, and the leadership behind it, is here and elsewhere in this biblical book understood as being used by the LORD to carry out his divine judgement upon the sinful people of Judah and Jerusalem, about whose sins and shortcomings we earlier read (5:8-24). This Assyrian army is portrayed as being a seriously well-equipped force, complete—the present passage seems to be suggesting—with chariots (*wheels*) as well as *horses*, and further *bows* and *arrows*. Indeed, the whole tenor of the language employed in Isa 5:25-30 surely suggests a serious degree of aggression on the part of this army, one that will inevitably engender a real sense of fear in its enemies and any who would seek to hinder its progress. See especially what is said here in vv. 27-30.

The last verse of this passage has a definite sense of threat for all who may stand in the way of this mighty army, and perhaps to be noted is the ominous sense of danger that must have provoked the use of the words here concerning *darkness and distress*, and indeed with those certain new conditions whereby *the light grows dark with clouds* (v. 30). Yet there is very considerably more to come in this regard, for which we must turn to the following chapter of the Isaiah book and to those chapters that succeed its well-known and stirring account of the prophet's call to the divine service.

THE PROPHET ISAIAH'S CALL 6:1-13

It might have been expected that this account of the call of Isaiah the son of Amoz to his prophetical ministry would be placed at the beginning of the book of the prophet Isaiah, as indeed we find with other prophetic books in the Old Testament. For example, we read about the prophet Jeremiah's call at the beginning of the book that bears his name (Jer 1:1-19), and likewise with the prophet Ezekiel, the account of his call is spoken about right at the beginning of the Ezekiel book (Ezek 1:1—3:27). Yet here with Isaiah we do not read of his call until we come to the sixth chapter. Perhaps, in the case of the book of Isaiah, there is a good deal to say concerning the state of the nation of Judah, and about the style and quality of its religious and political leadership in recent years, and that these are the matters that need to be spoken about in the first place. Thus, the preceding five chapters of material have presented to us what we might term the "state of the nation" and also the conditions regarding the practising of the Yahwistic faith in Judah and Jerusalem. As far as the general state of the nation is concerned, it is clear that there has abounded, for a serious amount of time, what appears to have been gross sinfulness, this being manifested in a number of aspects of the national life. Hence, we find that the first chapter is about the divine judgement, yet also the mercy of the Lord upon Israel (1:1–31), this being followed by what it is that the Lord desires of his people (as opposed to what is actually being practised at present), and indeed also what is hoped for on the parts of the surrounding nations, namely that all may look in trust to the God of Israel about how life, both individual and corporate, should be lived (2:1–5, 6–22).

But sadly, as things stand in Judah and Jerusalem at present, here is a people among whom so many stand under the divine judgement (3:1–9, 10–15; 3:16—4:1). Further, though there can be talk of a latter-day glory of Zion (cf. 40:5), there is also that "song" that is to be sung, namely "The Song of the Vineyard" (5:1–7), which in parable-form speaks both of the care and work of the vineyard owner, and also of the sad and disturbing truth that the vineyard yielded not the desired grapes, but rather wild grapes (5:2). For the sad fact was that the Lord had expected from his people justice, but instead he had seen bloodshed; righteousness, but had heard a cry (5:7). This surely is a prophetic message about the divine judgement under which the Lord's people stand. Moreover, as we have seen, this parable of the vineyard is followed by another series of what have been called "Woe oracles," expressions of the divine judgement upon the sinful actions of the Lord's people. Is it not reasonable and understandable that in the completed book of Isaiah these oracles, stories, parables, these prophetical concerns about the social and religious lives of the Israelite peoples, should be set forth at the beginning of the work, and so provide the setting for—indeed the reason for the divine calling of—Isaiah the son of Amoz's call as the Lord's prophet in Judah "in the year that King Uzziah died . . ." (6:1)?

That is perhaps sufficient to say about the background conditions in the land of Judah and Jerusalem in those days around the time of the death of King Uzziah, and to understand that these matters needed some presentation in the literary setting prior to the account of the prophet's call to service in the Lord's name. Yet a further reason why the prophet's account of his call comes at this particular point in the book is surely due to what is to come, namely two whole chapters (presented predominantly in prose writing form, Isa 7:1—8:22) dealing with the crisis for Judah occasioned by the attack upon Jerusalem by a coalition made up of the neighboring countries of Syria and Ephraim (Israel), apparently seeking to seize control in Jerusalem. That coalition was not successful in its venture—apart, that is, from bringing a sense of danger and panic to the peoples of Judah and Jerusalem. Nevertheless, the long-term effect would seem to have been considerably more than that, in no small way through the appeal of the Judean king Ahaz to the Assyrian ruler Tiglath-Pileser III for help. Thus there came about the arrival in the land of Judah of the Assyrian forces, so bringing about a whole change in the conditions of life and activity for Judah and Jerusalem, as well as even more radical changes for the people of the northern kingdom of Israel. Henceforth, all these small nations and peoples would be under the influence, and ultimately the rule, of foreign empires: first, the Assyrians, who would later be defeated by the Babylonians, who would then reign for a period of history until the days came for the rise to power of the Persian Empire.

Thus it would seem that there is a real sense of logic in the placing of the account of the divine call to Isaiah between these two blocks of material we find in the book of Isaiah, that is *after* the background conditions of sin and failure by the Judean peoples have been detailed and set forth, and *before* the forthcoming political and religious crisis caused by the attack upon the city of Jerusalem by the combined armed forces of Syria and Ephraim. For with the latter the end result was that the lands of Israel and Judah would be under the Assyrian rule, and with that there had been lost any military and political independence for Israel and Judah, and perhaps above all in Jerusalem, the city of David.

This inevitably meant that Judah's people and leaders were moving into a whole new and wider realm. No longer would they be in the land making up a comparatively small and independent nation; henceforth they were becoming involved with—even part of—the mighty Assyrian Empire with its principal city Nineveh far away to the east, for the Assyrians needed certain "buffer states" in the west between it and the Egyptian political set-up. Thus, inevitably, were Judah and Jerusalem very much moving into what we might call a wider and larger political world, in which they would have to accept that they would henceforth be living not only with their traditional religious loyalties and devotions but also with what we would call new political considerations and judgements, for they were indeed moving into the settings of some of the world's great and mighty nations. In fact, coming straight after the narrative of the divine call to Isaiah to become the Lord's prophet, we are plunged straight into two chapters of prophetical and theological accounts and materials connected with the events of the so-called Syro-Ephraimite war.

The opening of the Isaian call narrative in Isa 6:1–13, immediately takes us into the exalted setting of what reads like the throne room of God; the Lord was sitting on his high and lofty throne, and that temple setting (we assume that of the temple in the heart of the city of Jerusalem) was only just sufficient to contain the divine robes—or perhaps merely *the hem of his robe* (v. 1), though the word translated in NRSV as *hem* can also mean *skirt*, even *seam*. Even so, the notion of such items filling the temple does suggest outstanding, remarkable, extra-earthly grandeur, indeed of remarkably extra-human dimensions. Further, we are told that there were *seraphim* standing over him (v. 2); *seraphim* are literally "burning ones," and again this indicate supra-human lives, with their six wings, two of which were to enable flight, two covering their *faces*, and two covering their *feet* (that last pair perhaps being a euphemism indicating the covering of their nakedness).

Meanwhile the *seraphim* were calling to one another (v. 3), thereby exalting the Lord *of Hosts* with their trisagion "*Holy, Holy, Holy*," and proclaiming that the earth is *full of his glory*. By *holy* there is indicated a real sense of otherness to the earthly world, without anything of profane reality; that which is imbued with a sacredness and purity, beyond comparison with anything earthly. Further, there is the perceived sense that there is something totally special brought about by the divine presence into the world, namely the divine *glory*. Indeed, *glory* for the Old Testament has become known and understood by some as the revealed presence of the Lord on earth, in the world. For the psalmist of Ps 19 presumably means that what we see of the night sky reveals the *glory*, that sheer incomparability of the works of God: "The heavens are telling the *glory* of God . . ." (Ps 19:1). In Isa 6:3 is the further thought that for those who have eyes to see, and hearts to appreciate it, *the whole earth is full of his* [the Lord's] *glory*. This "otherness" of the Lord in fact fills the whole of the world. It is thus hardly surprising that the following verse (v. 4) is about the strange, other-worldly events and phenomena that occurred when the Lord spoke; indeed, we are told there were shaking doorposts, and *the house was filled with smoke*.

This account then goes on to speak of the effects of this divine temple-sighting of the Lord by the prophet, in particular about it bringing forcibly to him his appreciation of his own sin, and the fact that so clearly both he and all his people are indeed sinful; they are people of *unclean lips*, and yet he, Isaiah, has seen no less than the *King* of the universe, *the* Lord *of Hosts* (v. 5). Thus the prophet feels his parlous state, he is such a sinful person, living in the midst of a sinful people, and *yet my eyes have seen the King, the* Lord *of hosts* (v. 5)!

Verse 6 then speaks of Isaiah having his lips cleansed through the actions of one of the seraphs, and the use of the glowing coal from the altar. Though the Old Testament does have a good deal to say about liturgies and actions for divine cleansing of sins, this particular rite is not spoken about elsewhere in the Bible.[21] Whether this rite was elsewhere known about in ancient Israel remains an unknown to us today, but clearly Isaiah was made well aware of what had taken place for him, for he was told by the seraph that his *guilt has departed and your sin is blotted out* (v. 7). This clearly leads on to the next stage (v. 8), namely the question being posed, we are told by the LORD, *Whom shall I send, and who will go for us?* This is followed by Isaiah's offer of himself for this task, *Here am I; send me*. Whereas when other people were called to the prophetic role there was first the protest that the person concerned could not possibly do this task, as was attempted by, for example, the young Jeremiah (Jer 1:4–6), here with Isaiah there appears to be neither protest nor hesitancy, but rather apparent willingness, *Here am I; send me* (v. 8).

Yet having secured the such-positive response of Isaiah to the divine call, we read about the LORD's informing Isaiah that it was going to be an exceedingly difficult task for him, Isaiah, to get a positive response from his people. Indeed, Isaiah was informed directly by the LORD that his ministry was to be characterized by the proclamation of a message that would inevitably, as we might say, fall on deaf ears. That is, while the people might listen to the message of the prophet they would not understand it (vv. 9–10). Presumably the thought was that they would keep going on in their old ways. They might be listening, they might be looking, but, alas, they would not be understanding the divine will and message. That is, the depth of the message they were hearing, and what they should be doing about it, were both alike beyond either their desire to understand or their agreement to adopt for their own lives.

It is very generally agreed that this is a difficult account to understand, in that it would appear that the LORD requires Isaiah to proclaim a message from God that the people would not even be able to understand let alone respond to positively! Perhaps it was intended to say to us that this is a divine message that the LORD knows his people will not in fact be able to respond to in any positive way. The prophet is being warned that his own task will be a difficult ministry to fulfil. Nevertheless, what it is that the LORD has been saying to Isaiah is what he, the LORD, requires of Isaiah, his prophet, namely the proclamation of the divine message with which to challenge his people. Indeed, and this is the ministry—difficult and demanding though it will inevitably be—to which Isaiah is being called.

Further, it is made clear to Isaiah that this will be no short-term ministry to which he is being called (vv. 11–13). Rather, here the news for the prospective prophet seems to be no better, for his message to his people is

---

21. See Thompson, *Greatly to Be Praised*, 201, 246–47, 274.

that things will have to get so much worse in Judah and Jerusalem, until there is nothing less than an empty city and empty homes, indeed an utterly desolate land (v. 11), from which the people will have been taken away. This was indeed what happened in the days of the Babylonian exile, but the situation was hardly as bad as that during the ministry of the prophet Isaiah (v. 12)! The calamity would come later. And what small evidences of civilization will be left will be so much smaller than what was there previously. Indeed, the divine message was that the sole remaining reality would be the mere stump of the *holy seed* (v. 13). Just what is meant by this wording is not clear, and the commentators on Isaiah are indeed stretched here in their understanding. The word *stump* suggests some remarkably small part of what might at one time have looked great and living, but now is looking dead and useless. Yet as stumps of trees can put forth growth, and can become large and living trees again, so surely is the prophet saying here that out of what one day may look like a final, ruined, and broken kingdom there could come renewal, new growth, indeed new life. Yet if that is to be, it will surely have to be grown in the things of the Lord, for indeed it is nothing less than the *holy seed* that is that *stump*.

Yet, we should not be forgetting the fact that this call to the man Isaiah to be the Lord's servant, in the particular ministry of being his prophet, is a call both to Isaiah all those years ago and also to so many individuals and nations ever since. There is portrayed in this account of Isaiah's call to ministry a real emphasis on the greatness of the Lord who is making these calls to his peoples to follow him, that he is a God who is indeed great, and further, totally "other than" the people of earth. Thus we read in Isa 6:3, *Holy, holy, holy is the Lord of hosts; the whole earth is full of his glory*. This matter of the holiness of the Lord was written about many years ago by Rudolph Otto in his remarkable work that became a classic, *The Idea of the Holy: An Inquiry into the Non-rational Factor in the Idea of the Divine and Its Relation to the Rational*. This is a writing about the "grandeur," the "sublimity," of the divine One. Otto said about this experience of the "*Mysterium tremendum et fascinans*" in Isa 6:1–13: "We meet it in an unsurpassable form in the sixth chapter of Isaiah, where there is sublimity alike in the lofty throne and the sovereign figure of God, the skirts of His raiment 'filling the temple' and the solemn majesty of the attendant angels about Him."[22]

---

22. Otto, *The Idea of the Holy*, 65.

THE SYRO-EPHRAIMITE WAR 7:1—8:22

These two chapters are taken up with what has been called The Syro-Ephraimite War, that is, the events that took place when, in the reign of King Ahaz of Judah, Rezin the king of Syria, and Pekah the son of Remaliah the king of (the northern) kingdom of Israel, mounted a military attack upon Jerusalem. They did not succeed, but what did happen—and this we know from the account that begins in 2 Kgs 16:5—was that Ahaz of Judah called for the help of the Assyrian ruler Tiglath-Pileser III, which in the longer term was not good for the independence of Israel and Judah. What this crisis for Judah also did was to draw forth from the prophet Isaiah a series of observations, prophecies, and narratives, much of this material being written in prose, though some of it is in poetic form. Some parts of this material are straightforward to understand, while other parts are more difficult to interpret. It is generally thought that this attack took place around 734 BCE, and on the part of Pekah, the king of the northern part of Israel, his assault on Ahaz's southern kingdom of Judah was something in the nature of a civil war. However, a good deal was to happen as a result of this comparatively minor war—as indeed we shall read about in some of the subsequent chapters of the book of Isaiah.

ISAIAH AND HIS SON 7:1-9

In Isa 7:1-2 we are told the basic facts about the war. Kings Rezin of Aram and Pekah of Israel laid siege to Jerusalem, the main city of the kingdom of Judah, in the days of King Ahaz, but did not succeed in their attack (v. 1).[23] We are then told that when Ahaz and those in the house and dynasty of the southern kingdom of Judah were informed of this, they were disturbed, indeed fearful—*and the heart of Ahaz and the heart of his people shook as the trees of the forest shake before the wind* (v. 2). It eventually emerged that the attackers were impotent, but even so they had succeeded in bringing about a serious sense of panic on the parts of king and people in Jerusalem.

In vv. 3-9 we go on to read of the prophet Isaiah's entry into this crisis. We are told that the prophet and his son, *Shear-jashub* (meaning "A Remnant Shall Return"), went to meet King Ahaz at a water conduit for the city of Jerusalem—presumably the king was inspecting the state of the water supply to his capital city in its state of siege. The prophet Isaiah's task was to

---

23. For further details of this attack upon Jerusalem see Irvine, *Isaiah, Ahaz, and the Syro-Ephraimitic Crisis*; Thompson, *Situation and Theology*. See also Clements, *Jerusalem and the Nations*, 53–65, Clements, "Written Prophecy: The Case of the Isaiah Memoir."

speak to the king with words of comfort, telling him that he should not be dismayed, as there was little strength in those two kingdoms that were attacking Judah and Jerusalem. Those who were attacking, though appearing angry—indeed, seriously threatening!—to the people of Jerusalem, were in fact, according to the prophet, *two smoldering stumps of firebrands* (v. 4). It appears that the enemy wished to conquer Judah and Jerusalem, and put on the Jerusalem throne their own nominee, *the son of Tabeel* (v. 6), about whom we know little else. And indeed, so the prophet assures the king of Judah, this plot *shall not happen, and it shall not come to pass* (v. 7), going on to say that one of these attacking kingdoms, Ephraim (i.e., Israel), will be *shattered, no longer a people* (v. 8).

What are we to make of the mention of this son of Isaiah, the one who accompanied the prophet in going to speak to the king, in particular, his name *Shear-yashub* (v. 3)? Presumably, the fact that we are given the name of the prophet's accompanying son, when we would not normally be given the name of such a minor character, or even told that the prophet took someone with him when seeking to deliver a word of the Lord, suggests that the name is in fact intended to be taken seriously. Presumably it was intended to convey some part of what Isaiah felt the Lord required him to say to king Ahaz. What might the intended message have been? Surely, the message must have been the positive one that there would not be total catastrophe for Judah, that there would be a real future, but a future for the kingdom's peoples in which its resources, its strengths, maybe even its confidences in itself and its leaders would not be as great as they had been previously. Indeed, the reassuring message was that a viable unit, a real population, would be emerging, surviving. The prophet was expressing the message, through his son's name, that *A Remnant Shall Return* (v. 3).

Then follows the rather mysterious prophetical word of Isaiah to Ahaz, king of Judah, *If you do not stand firm in faith, you shall not stand at all* (v. 9). Presumably, that is intended to say to the king that he is to have confidence, faith, and hope in God—so that thereby will he be given strength and hope for his leadership tasks. Further, he, Ahaz the king, would thereby inspire his people to have the same sort of faith and trust in the Lord. For truly, unless there is faith in the Lord God on the part of both king and people, there can be little hope of even continuing to stand (v. 9). In fact, they are all to *stand firm in faith*, or they will not *stand at all*. We assume that the prophet is saying that unless there can be on the part of the national leaders in Judah and Jerusalem a sense of deep trust in the Lord God, then—so the prophet seems to be saying in v. 9—they will be no better than their enemies, and no better able to defeat them. They will be like the people of Ephraim who are portrayed as merely looking to their weak earthly leaders for strength and hope (*The head of Ephraim is Samaria, and the head of Samaria is the son of Remaliah*). The prophet would seem to be saying that those two states, Ephraim and Samaria, which are seeking to bring defeat upon Judah and Jerusalem, are in fact as good as leaderless; they have no heads greater than their earthly kings, for indeed they do not seem to be looking to the Lord God for help. Let the king of Judah, Ahaz, be not like them, but rather let him put his trust and hope in the Lord God.

ISAIAH AND HIS SIGN OF IMMANUEL 7:10–17

We now consider the following verses, namely Isaiah 7:10–17, which continue to talk about what the prophet Isaiah had to say to the Judean king, Ahaz. No indication is offered regarding the matter of whether or not the giving of this message by the prophet followed on directly from the giving of the previous one, or whether, so to speak, we have moved on into a new setting and indeed at a later time. Yet perhaps the setting does seem to be different: we do not appear any longer to be inspecting the city water supply (as most likely we were in the situation depicted in Isa 7:3–9), but what is now being spoken about could perhaps have come from a setting in the royal palace. Certainly, it is once again the prophet addressing the king, and it seems to be about the same crisis for Judah and Jerusalem with the Syro-Ephraimite attack on Jerusalem.

However, when we come to study Isaiah's words about the sign of *Immanuel* (vv. 10–17) we find ourselves confronted with a baffling range of understandings and views on the parts of those who over the years have studied these words.[24] We read, of course, that King Ahaz said he did not wish to ask the Lord for a sign about what is presented as the siege of Jerusalem by Syria and Ephraim (Israel). However, the response of the prophet Isaiah was that regardless of what the king wished, or did not wish, about being given a sign, he was about to receive such a sign! Therefore, the king ought to listen carefully and cease annoying both people and God—presumably by his failure to ask for a sign, and perhaps thereby avoiding having to receive, and possibly act upon—the guidance of the Lord God in his and his country's ongoing political crisis (vv. 10–13).

The somewhat enigmatic Sign of Immanuel was to be that a *young woman* would conceive and *bear a son*, and would name him *Immanuel*. (v. 14) A considerable range of questions is presented to us by this apparently reasonably straightforward word, all of which have been studied by

---

24. For further details of these issues, see Collins, "The Sign of Emmanuel." See also Thompson, "Isaiah's Sign of Immanuel."

generations of Old Testament scholars and readers. But first we should take note of the fact that in Isa 7:14 the Hebrew word used means "young woman." In the Hebrew there is nothing here about her being a "virgin." It is later, when the Old Testament scriptures were translated into the Greek (called the Septuagint), that this word came to be translated *parthenos*, a word that means "virgin."

Then there are the *curds and honey* that the child Immanuel will be eating before he knows how to refuse what is evil and choose the good (v. 15). The child's eating of *curds and honey* suggests something in the line of good, even luxury, food, and would seem to be indicating a setting in a few years time. We seem to find something analogous in 8:1–4, when God speaks to Isaiah about the birth of another son (or possibly of the same son). God speaks of a time when the child knew what it was to say "My father," or "My mother," again suggesting a date a few years hence, say in two or three years time. The prophet was saying that by that time the enemy forces in the land of Judah and Jerusalem would have gone (7:16; 8:4), and the present crisis would be over. Further, in 7:17 there is reference to the king of Assyria's presence in the land of Judah—but that is a whole new factor, to which we shall return.

But what are we to say about the name of the child in Isa 7:14, *Immanuel* (literally "With Us Is God")? In particular, is this intended to be a hopeful sign (God is with us in support), or might it be something about the possibility of God's presence with his people to effect the divine judgement upon them? Surely it is the former. That is, it is the assurance that by the time this child *Immanuel*, "God Is with Us," is aged two or three, the threat of the invading forces against Judah and Jerusalem will have gone; in fact, those enemies' own lands of Israel and Syria will by then have experienced devastation. And moreover, by then, they, all of them—Israel, Judah, Syria—will have to be reckoning with the fact that the presence of the king of Assyria will be there for the duration in their lands, and that included the land of Judah. Such a happening surely meant that life in Judah would have to be adjusted accordingly (7:16–17), just as there had years earlier to be an adaptation and adjustment to life in Judah and Jerusalem in the days following the death of King Solomon, when Jeroboam departed with those northern tribes to found a separate and independent kingdom (see 1 Kgs 12).

Thus, overall the sign of Immanuel was intended to be a hopeful one for the people of Judah and Jerusalem: their foes in the coalition of Syria and Israel would have been defeated within a few years, but this would only work for the besieged people in Judah and Jerusalem if those people were willing to put their trust in the LORD God. They were not to be like their king, who uttered words that sounded pious—*I will not ask, and I will not put the* LORD *to the test* (7:12)—when in fact he was not himself able to put such trust in God and his divine purposes as this occasion of serious crisis demanded. Indeed, we may surely say that this whole incident of the attack upon Judah and Jerusalem by the Syro-Ephraimite military forces constituted a real test of the faith of both peoples and their leaders in Judah and Jerusalem to put their trust in the LORD. For as well as the sign of Immanuel being a hopeful sign, there is also the matter of it being in the nature of a challenge to the faith of those human beings who were being addressed.

Without doubt that is what this ancient account and story still has to say to Christian people who continue to read it—as indeed they are invited in the standard lectionaries during the season leading up to Christmas. For did not the promised Messiah live out, and proclaim as his central message, that in him God is with us, *Immanuel* (see Matt 1:23)? Yet that message, and indeed gift, is there in each Christmas season, either to be accepted, or indeed turned aside. Of course, the words and intentions of the Immanuel sign were for application in Isaiah's own particular historical moment and situation, whereas when we interpret it in the birth of the Messiah in the days of Herod the king, then we are applying it many centuries later. Yet we are surely still speaking of the same God, who in age after age is ever the God who is with us, our Immanuel, "God is with us" (7:14). Wildberger states the matter as follows. "The name Immanuel, intended as a sign for Ahaz and Israel, points to circumstances in which one can detect clearly the central message of the Old Testament. And what else did the Messiah demonstrate, in his own way, not only by means of his name but also by means of his deeds for Israel, if it was not . . . 'God is with us'?"[25]

COMING DEVASTATION 7:18–25

We now turn to the following passage in the Isaiah book, namely 7:18–25, a composition made up of four prophetical oracles that speak of a great devastation, vv. 18–19, 20, 21–22, 23–25. We are not told which land it is that is being spoken about. Is it Judah, with its capital city Jerusalem; is it Ephraim (Israel); is it Syria? Or could it be all three? We are not told, but perhaps most likely the reference is to Judah and Jerusalem, for that seems to have been the principal focus of concern of the prophet Isaiah, in particular at this stage of his ministry. Further, this seems to be a passage about the judgement of God on the people of Judah, and there does seem to be at least some connection with what we have read earlier in 7:10–17, for we do have here further references to those *curds and honey* (v. 22), and also to the

---

25. Wildberger, *Isaiah 1–12*, 318.

king of Assyria (vv. 18, 20). Each of these expressions of *woe* is preceded by the words *on that day*, vv. 18, 20, 21, 23, and it could well be that these various expressions of the coming devastation on Judah do come from different times, and maybe also even different authorship(s). Yet at the same time, it should be observed that this passage does follow on from the material about the prophet's sign of *Immanuel*, and is perhaps intended to flesh out and give some explanation for the fact that doom does threaten the land of Judah.

The first of these *woes* is in 7:18–19, and here the Lord is pictured as the one who will whistle for the *fly* and the *bee*, who represent, respectively *Egypt* and *Assyria*, suggesting a pestilential, indeed swarming, foe that will come upon the lands, though whether that is Judah, or Judah and Israel, or Judah, Israel, and Syria is not stated. The second *woe* is in v. 20 and clearly refers to the powers of *the king of Assyria*. Those powers are portrayed as being like a *razor* that will take off the *hair* from the *head*, *feet* (presumably private parts are intended), and the *beard*. Again, we are not told who the intended victim is, but perhaps once more we have to say that the possibilities are those suggested for vv. 18–19 above, and it would seem that what we are reading about here is a strong word of judgement, at least an act of humiliation.

In 7:21–22 is the third *woe*, and what is portrayed is a pastoral scene which is subjected to serious destruction and degradation, but neither attacker nor attacked is named. Yet here those *curds and honey* of 7:15 are making a re-appearance; however, here they are portrayed as making up the sole food of the few who are left in the (unnamed) land.

The fourth and final *woe* is in vv. 23–25, but neither place nor attacker is named. Clearly, however, there is fairly wholesale destruction in which *vines* will become *briers and thorns*, and worth virtually nothing. Indeed, such will be the prevalence of the *briers and thorns* that people will go around with *bows and arrows*. Further, on the land that used to be *hoed* there will be yet further *briers and thorns*, and now also in that part of the land there will be *loose cattle and sheep*. Altogether, a very sad and sorry state is here portrayed.

Thus in spite of the privileged place that the people of Judah, and even of Judah and Israel, had in the world, even so without care and attention to the will and purposes of the Lord those people could so easily descend into the sort of desperate situations that are so graphically portrayed in this short passage made up as it is of a series of *woes*. Regarding the last line of v. 25 Williamson says, "The emphasis . . . is not so much the advantage of having good pasture for the herds and flocks as the destructive effects of their being able to roam freely over formerly productive agricultural land."[26]

26. Williamson, *Isaiah 6–12*, 192.

THE SIGN OF MAHER-SHALAL-HASH-BAZ 8:1–4

We now have a passage in which the speaker, in the grammatical first person, is the prophet—as it was in the account of his call in ch. 6. Further, as it was with the sign of Immanuel, so it is with this sign, that what the prophet himself is doing is an action designed to express the word of the LORD that is to be given to his people. The intended recipients are clearly the people of Judah and Jerusalem. The sign is to assure them that the coalition of Syria and Ephraim (Israel) in all its military actions against them is doomed. This is to be proclaimed by the prophet, in particular through the birth of a child to his wife, the child being named *Maher-shalal-hash-baz*. The meaning of this name—and therefore the meaning intended to be conveyed through the birth of the prophet's child—is not totally clear to us, but most likely it is "Spoil Speeds, Booty Hastens." Clearly, this is a hopeful sign for the people of Judah and Jerusalem, as is made clear in the note in v. 4, namely that before the child can say either *My father* or *My mother* the wealth of Judah's enemies, in particular their appropriations of spoil in times of war, will have been stripped out of their capital cities, *Damascus* and *Samaria*, by none other than the *king of Assyria*.

The hopeful aspect of this sign for the people of Judah and Jerusalem is made even clearer by the prophet having made a *large tablet*, presumably to serve as a placard, which bore what were intended to be the readable words (we assume that is what the *common characters* of v. 1 is intended to indicate) of the name of the forthcoming son, namely, *Maher-shalal-hash-baz*, "Spoil Speeds, Booty Hastens"—and he even had it witnessed by the *priest Uriah* and also by a certain *Zechariah son of Jeberechiah* (v. 2). While there may be certain questions concerning whether the message of Isaiah in the Immanuel Sign about the Syro-Ephraimite War was one of hope or otherwise, this latest sign is much clearer. Here it is clearly stated that the LORD is with his people of Judah and Jerusalem, and is thereby surely committed to their future and their welfare.

This is surely a message of hope not only for those people of old, but also for those who in age after age seek in their different ways to follow this God, and to be faithful to him and his will. And this as certain events around us and in our lives take their course. Stacey speaks here of the prophet Isaiah not so much "giving information, still less pronouncing an opinion. He [the prophet] is caught up in the process of history and, by his words and actions, helps to carry it forward."[27]

---

27. Stacey, *Isaiah 1–39*, 63.

ANOTHER WORD ABOUT IMMANUEL 8:5-10

Here are further words about the same subject, the attack of the Syro-Ephraimite confederates upon the city and people of Jerusalem, and once again we are told that it is the prophet Isaiah who is speaking—and further speaking a word that was given to him by the LORD. However, what the prophet has to say is not entirely clear, not least because in v. 6 there is a question of translation, which does need to be faced up to as a decision about it affects the way it is rendered, as we can see in the footnote in NRSV.

The LORD is displeased with his people because they have become deeply disturbed over what should have been a relatively small matter (v. 6); they have panicked before those two small foes, Rezin and the son of Remaliah. Thus the prophet has spoken in picture language about the smallness of the foe being rather like that small stream that brought water into Jerusalem from the spring of Gihon; such are in the prophet's reckoning the dimensions of the Syro-Ephraimite attack upon Judah and Jerusalem, and it should not have caused such panic in the city. There is, however, a question for us about the Hebrew word found here, speaking of the Jerusalem people "rejoicing" in the attack, which all sounds rather odd, even inappropriate—rejoicing in being attacked? However, with a comparatively small change in the Hebrew letters of one word the familiar "melt in fear" translation comes about, rather than "rejoicing." This change is widely accepted, as we can see not least by the NRSV translators, who have added a footnote saying "Meaning of Heb[rew] uncertain."

Then comes the warning to king and people in Jerusalem: they should have faith in their LORD God, and not go panicking in the face of two very minor aggressors. If they are not careful they will bring the judgement of the LORD God upon themselves, which will come in the comparatively huge forces of the king of Assyria (v. 7), and will totally overwhelm the whole of the land of the promised *Immanuel*, that child whose name (*Immanuel*, v. 8) indicates "with us is God." There is surely being uttered here by the prophet the seriously probing question about what sort of faith there is on the part of the people of God in the face of a somewhat minor crisis for their country and its main city. Further, maybe, there is a similar challenge about faith and trust in the LORD by those who are reading this story in succeeding age after age—and in this regard, we should surely not be forgetting such people today.

Then in the last two verses (vv. 9–10) of this passage there is a certain change in what is being presented, because here it seems to be others, neighboring peoples and countries, that are being addressed. Their identities are not stated, but v. 9 speaks of *all you far countries*, suggesting that these further-away peoples could be those of larger nations. Thus the people of Judah and Jerusalem are to be encouraged by remembering the symbolic name of that child *Immanuel* (7:14), meaning *God is with us*. The prophet is assuring the people and their leaders that this surely is also applicable for future events, namely that their God will truly be with them. Let them learn from their recent past deliverances through the LORD that the same LORD will be with *them* in *their* future emergencies and conflicts. For the message that is surely for all ages of believers in the LORD God is indeed, *God is with us* (v. 10). Otto Kaiser in his commentary on Isa 1–12 says of the faith that the people of Isaiah's day and Christian people today share is this, "One characteristic of this faith is that it does not fade with future generations, because like their fathers, believers experience that God is with those who hope in him."[28]

TRUSTING AND OBEYING THE LORD 8:11–22

Here is another passage in which we hear of the prophet Isaiah's contribution to his peoples in their concerns over the crisis of the Syro-Ephraimite attack upon Judah and Jerusalem (7:1–9). In particular, here in 8:11–15 we read once again of the prophet's confidence in the LORD in the setting of this attack, and in particular that the LORD calls upon Isaiah not to be filled with fear like the people around him—*do not fear what it fears, or be in dread* (vv. 11–12). It is once again asserted that what the people should be doing is putting their faith and trust in the LORD (v. 13), and various aspects of faith and faithfulness are cited to drive the point home: let God be to them as their *sanctuary*, the safe place for their lives, even though meanwhile too many people are allowing the situation to be a *rock one stumbles over—a trap and a snare for the inhabitants of Jerusalem* (v. 14). Beware, says the prophet, for there will be many who do indeed *stumble*, who do allow themselves to *fall and be broken*, even *be snared and taken* (v. 15).

Rather, while this lack of faith is being manifest in Judah and Jerusalem, the prophet is required to be of a very different manner of life, and in particular to be a person of faith and trust in the LORD (vv. 16–22). Yet the language here suggests that the prophet feels himself to be very separated from his people. Isaiah, in seeking to fulfil his divine calling, has somewhat, and perhaps indeed inevitably, separated himself from them, for the reason that those people are not responding to his prophetic words and teaching about what the LORD requires of them. This was to be seen in particular in vv. 11–15 above.

---

28. Kaiser, *Isaiah 1–12*, 189.

Thus Isaiah takes some actions, and the first of these we read about is the sealing up of his "testimony" (v. 16), that is, what he believes is God's will for his people in this particular historical situation. Unfortunately, the Hebrew word which we translate "testimony" occurs only three times in the Old Testament, two of which are found here in Isa 8:16 (NRSV "testimony") and 20 (NRSV "instruction") in this very incident, and the other in Ruth 4:7. This clearly seems to be a word that in its first sense indicates a legal agreement, one that is used here by Isaiah to give written expression to what he has been proclaiming, namely that he has had a vital message from the Lord to his people, but one that alas at present they are taking insufficient notice of, if even any notice at all. To at least some extent they are those who are being "deaf" to the Lord's word. So Isaiah, as we would say, "puts it in writing," and has it formally preserved, while in the meantime he and his family will wait, remaining as *signs and portents* as to the will of the Lord God. They will continue to be witnesses to these matters of the Lord and his will as revealed through the prophet (vv. 17–18). Meanwhile there will be those of the people of Judah and Jerusalem whose wish will perhaps be to consult *ghosts* and their *familiar spirits that chirp and mutter* (v. 19), yet concerning them Isaiah proclaims sheer uselessness (v. 20). Further, a generally grim time on earth awaits such faithless ones: *only distress and darkness, the gloom of anguish*. Indeed, such people will truly be in *thick darkness* (vv. 21–22).

This is indeed an alarming state into which those who have failed to attend to the words and advices of the Lord's prophet have put themselves by continuing in their old ways, that is, not to be paying attention to what the Lord is saying to them. Further, maybe, as the people having thus sinned, judging by the reference to "king" in v. 21, so also was there prophetic condemnation of their king, Ahaz, who had shared the common panic and lack of faith and trust in the face of the national troubles. Both leaders and peoples had been called upon to have faith and trust in the Lord, but yet so many had failed, so that now, alas, the prophet feels he must be silent before his people, who indeed have thrust themselves into that *thick darkness* (v. 22).

John Sawyer in this part of his Isaiah commentary says about these verses, "The bewildering conglomeration of words and images could fit a national crisis, ancient or modern; they can be applied with equal poignancy to the personal crisis, spiritual, or otherwise, of an individual. In every crisis, says the prophet, true hope comes from the 'Lord of hosts, who dwells on mount Zion' . . ." (v. 18).[29]

---

29. Sawyer, *Isaiah*, vol. I, 95–96.

A GREAT LIGHT 9:1-7 [HEBREW 8:23—9:6]

Here is one of the Old Testament's most memorable passages, and not indeed without good reason, for it speaks of a coming one who will change much about the life of God's people, one who has been appointed and sent by the LORD God himself. That main passage runs in the English translations from Isa 9:2-7 (whereas in the Hebrew it is found in 9:1-6). Yet preceding is a link verse (9:1 in the English, 8:23 in the Hebrew) that provides an explanation of the significance of what follows in the context of where and in what sort of conditions Judah and Jerusalem are as a result of the attack made upon them by the Syro-Ephraimite confederacy (see above on Isa 7:1—8:22). The present passage in the Old Testament finds much acceptance in the Christian church, which uses it in its liturgies of Advent and Christmas worship. This is more than reasonable with its speaking of a coming leader, one who will bring the prospects of new and divinely given leadership and guidance to the people of earth.

Just who it was who composed this piece we cannot be sure. Yet it could well have been none other than the prophet Isaiah. Nor can we be sure about the historical occasion that drew out from the prophet this remarkable composition. I am not convinced that it can have been composed for the prophet's account of the Syro-Ephraimite war, for that rather minor affair can hardly have brought forth such a wide-observing and grand composition in the first place. Yet what is surely clearer is that this passage has been taken and placed in its present setting in the Isaiah book in a quite deliberate way, here at the close of the account of what has become known as the Syro-Ephraimite war, that is, the attack upon Judah and Jerusalem, under the rule of King Ahaz, by that alliance of Syria and Israel (Ephraim), being led by their respective kings, Rezin and Pekah. For the fact is that all these three kingly rulers were shown up in this comparatively minor military engagement to be exceedingly poor leaders of their peoples. Yet here in 9:2-7 is a very different message, for here we are now considering a vision of an ideal, God-given leader, a king who will bring light to the benighted and joy to those who are in distress, one who as well as being the *Wonderful Counselor* is nothing less than a *Mighty God* (v. 6). Thus is there here the promise of endless peace for the throne of David and his kingdom, with justice and righteousness *from this time onwards and forevermore* (v. 7).

This remarkable composition then, Isa 9:2-7, has been employed, along with an introductory verse that makes clear the setting to which it is now intended to refer, to close the account of this small and, it has to be said, poorly led war. Meanwhile, as we have already observed, there is a preceding account of the remarkable experience of the calling and commissioning of the prophet, of the revelation he was given in the temple in Jerusalem (6:1–13). Here we have surely two special and quite deliberately chosen passages to frame the prophet's account of the Syro-Ephraimite war, that is, to be at its beginning and its ending. What then, is the particular message of the words of this closing passage (9:1–7)?

Isaiah 9:1 (8:23 in the Hebrew text) proclaims the very upbeat message that the days for Judah of distress (NRSV *anguish*) and *gloom* are soon to be over and consigned to the past. The land of *Zebulun and the land of Naphtali* were both in the north of Israel, and would seem to be representing those territories and peoples who were at war with Judah and Jerusalem in the south. *Galilee of the nations* (the only occurrence in the Old Testament of this designation) perhaps refers to a province in the north of Israel carved out by the Assyrians after their activities there in 734 BCE, but which will now be made *glorious* by the Lord. What had been a region caught up in the conflicts of war and disagreements would now become again a place of peace.

In Isa 9:2 we are given, as it were, a summary of the changing circumstances for those peoples whose lands had been beset with strife and conflict: instead of their state of *darkness* there would be, rather, *great light*; for indeed a *great light* had shone on them. This theme of darkness and light is something of a theme in other parts of the Isaiah book too, used in the sense employed here, namely that the Lord can transform the situations of darkness and gloom that his people find themselves in, and enable them to move forward into light and hope. See Isa 42:6, 7, 16; 45:7; 49:6; 51:4. This theme of the divine promise of transformation of troubled and dark lives on the parts of Judah (and perhaps of Israel also?) is further to be seen in v. 3, here in the image of abundance being given by the Lord—days of successful harvesting of their fields, or even of military successes.

With 9:4 the imagery is that of success in battle, in fact, success as has been enabled by the Lord, so that no longer are the Lord's people under their prevailing oppressive conditions. Gone will be the *yoke*, the *bar*, the *rod*. Whatever these may in the first place have been referring to in the terms of military rule, in its present context they are being applied to the cessation of the Syro-Ephraimite conflict. Indeed, we are told that the enemy will have been *broken as on the day of Midian*. This reference is to the much-earlier military success of Gideon's forces against the Midianites on the plains of Jezreel as recorded at considerable length in the book of Judges (Judg 6:33—8:35). Indeed, Isa 9:5 expresses the promise that the soldiers' *boots* and their military *garments*, having completed their bloody tasks on the battlefield, will no longer be needed, and therefore will be *burned as fuel for the fire*.

In v. 6 we are told how this will take place. It will be enabled by the Lord through the human agency of a child who has been born, although spoken of as still being a child, yet one whose *authority rests upon his shoulders*. Further, he is accorded exceedingly special names, in particular four of them. He is to be called *Wonderful Counselor*; that is he will be a good and wise leader of his people, neither guiding them falsely nor making inappropriate choices or foolish decisions. His second name is to be *Mighty God*, that is, there would be someone in the nation's place of authority who was no mere human, but in fact nothing less than a real manifestation of the divine presence. The third name was to be *Everlasting Father*, or perhaps "Father Forever," that is one in authority who would ever and always have the welfare of all the people of the country as his deep concern. Finally, he would be named *Prince of Peace;* he would be his people's source of peace and harmony, of prosperity and well-being.

Verse 7 sums up the remarkable nature of this gift of the Lord to his people. They are assured of kingly and growing *authority*, and further, there is the promise of peace, indeed of *endless peace*. Yet more, these matters will be delivered *with justice and with righteousness*, not with undue aggression and force, but indeed in what amounts to an imitation of the Lord's dealings with his people in age after age. And this too on earth is to be forever, *from this time onwards and forevermore*. Moreover, we are told, there is a remarkable assurance, namely, *The zeal of the Lord of hosts will do this*. What is meant by this word *zeal*? One recent commentator has said about the biblical word *zeal* as it occurs in our present text: "It implies God's passionate commitment to the well-being of his people, and ultimately it is this which will ensure that the preceding outline of promised changes in their fortune is realized."[30]

Just whatever were the original setting and particular circumstances that brought forth what we must surely consider to be a remarkable written composition concerning the Lord's gift of a new leader for his people, we do not know for sure. What is very much clearer is that such a gift as is here talked about should have enabled the hearers to feel that they were no longer walking in darkness, but that they were now in true light, and more, that in their lives, both individual and corporate, their circumstances and fortunes had taken a dramatic turn for the good. Where this particular theological composition came from, and what were the special circumstances that brought it about we do not know, but it certainly was given an appropriate place and setting as a conclusion to the account of a fairly localized war experienced by Lord's people. It laid stress upon the fact that at the end of

---

30. Williamson, *Isaiah 6–12*, 405.

the day it was not what the humans had done, much less achieved, in their earthly and historic lives in the face of a national crisis, but rather what their LORD God had enabled them to do. It emphasizes that when those people could do no more, the LORD himself would bring a new situation into being for them. When we ask the question, "Who was this promised leader, this wonderful person?"—it has to be said that in the annals of what became the Old Testament scriptures there is no such named person. Some therefore continue to wait in hope for the fulfilling of these promises, while the Christians believe that these divine promises have been brought to birth in the gift of the child of Bethlehem.

Yet little, or none, of this will be found on earth apart from through the passionate concern of the LORD God. Thus, how vital is *the zeal of the LORD of hosts* spoken about in v. 7. Joseph Blenkinsopp says about this reference: "The final line, attributing this reversal of fortune to the zeal or passion . . . of Yahveh of the hosts, occurs in another anti-Assyrian context in the Isaian 'legend' (37:32) and has been added to the poem, perhaps, after all the exalted language about the ruler-designate, to dispel any doubt about the ultimate source of these great happenings."[31]

THE JUDGEMENT OF THE LORD 9:8-21 [HEBREW 9:7-20] AND 10:1-4

This passage is made up of a number of divine "woes," that is, expressions of divine judgement and condemnation upon the sins of various peoples and groups among the people of Israel and Judah. It very much continues the theme of the earlier passage, Isa 5:8-24, and that theme will still be there in the later passage 10:1-4. In two of these passages, Isa 9:8-21 and 10:1-4 there is a recurring refrain that speaks of the judgement of the LORD upon the various sins spoken about, *For all this his anger has not turned away; his hand is stretched out still* (9:12, 17, 21; 10:4).

The first word of judgement is in vv. 8-12 and would seem clearly to be expressing condemnation of the two countries whose actions led to the Syro-Ephraimite crisis as recorded in Isa 7:1—8:22 (see above for full details). Here the two nations that attacked Judah and Jerusalem, namely *Israel* (here also designated *Jacob*, and intended to refer only to the northern kingdom of Israel) and the Syrian kingdom (v. 8), are condemned for their arrogance of heart—presumably the sinful attitude revealed in particular in the actions of Israel in joining with another country to lay siege to some of their own peoples, in particular in the city of Jerusalem. The words in

---

31. Blenkinsopp, *Isaiah 1–39*, 251.

v. 10 about *fallen bricks* and trees (*sycamores*) may be reference either to the ravages experienced through engaging in warfare, or else to an earthquake (the possibilities of which have been discovered in certain of the local archaeological investigations). Whichever it is, it is interpreted here as the judgement of the LORD, and to this end the Israelite peoples are warned to be aware of possible dangers of *Arameans* and *Philistines*, foreign nations who had already wrought some damage in Israel (see 2 Kgs 15:8–10). Even so, the nations of Ephraim and Syria need to be aware of the continued judgement of the LORD upon them, *For all this his anger has not turned away; his hand is stretched out still* (v. 12).

The second word of judgement (vv. 13–17) also seems to be about the recent Syro-Ephraimite War, and appears in particular to be a condemnation of the northern kingdom of Israel, especially those individuals who were responsible for leading their peoples astray so that *those who were led by them were left in confusion* (v. 16). In spite of the fact that there were some relatively innocent peoples around, even so in view of the prevalence of the *godless* and the *evildoer*, the *anger* of the LORD was still upon them (v. 17).

The third word of judgement is in vv. 18–21, and takes up the language of a bush *fire*, which in its nature of being out of control seems to be reminiscent of the widespread nature of the Israelite sinfulness, so that not only have they been at war with Judah but they are also at war with themselves, in their own communities. One is reminded of some words of Ulysses in Shakespeare's *Troilus and Cressida*, "And appetite, an universal wolf, So doubly seconded with will and power, Must make perforce an universal prey, And last eat up himself."[32]

The last of this series of woes is in 10:1–4, and concerns those who commit the sin of making up decrees of earthly concerns and not those that have been divinely given, various of these being mentioned, such as imposing on the people *oppressive statutes* (v. 1), and showing no cares about *justice* for the *needy*, robbing the *poor*, and also failing in duties towards the *poor*, the *widows*, the *orphans* (v. 2). Let them be aware of the coming *day of punishment*; in their coming time of *calamity* they will find few places of help (v. 3), for it will indeed happen for them as for others, *For all this his anger has not turned away; his hand is stretched out still* (v. 4).

Hans Wildberger in his Isaiah commentary observed about the prophet of these verses, "He saw the frivolous nature of those who wanted to live a pleasure-filled life . . . He was shocked by the arrogance of the mockers and the self-conceit of the wise. He was most deeply upset that there were

---

32. I am indebted to Joseph Blenkinsopp (*Isaiah 1–39*, 219) for this quotation from Shakespeare, though unfortunately he cites it as coming from Shakespeare's play *King Lear* rather than from *Troilus and Cressida*.

leaders, in responsible positions, who misused their abilities by changing the laws in a way which would benefit them."[33]

For sadly, the words we find here in the ancient book of Isaiah, far from becoming outdated are still all too real, and moreover are evident in so many of our countries and communities in the contemporary world. Thus do the prophetic words still challenge us in our corporate lives, and in our individual personal lives.

ASSYRIA'S PRIDE 10:5–15

This is a passage with a single theme, namely the activities of the Assyrians in the lands of the Israelite people, about their employment by the LORD to effect his judgement upon the Israelites, and then of the Assyrians overstepping their calling, thus bringing about the LORD's judgement on themselves too, that is, upon the Assyrians. It would be generally agreed by scholars that we have here a number of separate pieces that over various times have been put together to create the present passage. For details about these matters see, for example, the commentaries of Clements and Blenkinsopp. Here we shall restrict our comments to what is the apparent meaning of the different parts of the passage.

Verses 5–7 are about Assyria being sent by the LORD to bring about the divine judgement on Israel, but unfortunately not doing that with the same mind and purpose as the LORD. It would have been more than reasonable for the Assyrians to have taken from the Israelites their gains of plunder in recent warfare, but Assyria is now overstepping the mark and seeking *to cut off nations not a few* (v. 7), by which is meant presumably to effect the utter defeat of nations like Israel and Judah. In fact, the opening word (v. 5) in the Hebrew of this passage is what traditionally has been translated "woe" or "alas," even as in NRSV, "ah," and which indicated a general expression of dismay, and is employed in places in the Old Testament as a lament for the dead, and sometimes also to indicate the sense of harsh criticism of the one being addressed. That is, we may expect some harsh things to be said in what follows.

Further, the words about the Assyrians taking spoil and seizing plunder (v. 6) are reminiscent—and maybe purposely employed here to be so—of that sign of Immanuel in Isa 8:1, *Maher-shalal-hash-baz*, "Spoil Speeds, Booty Hastens," which is to say that something of that threat is now being enacted. This is maybe being used here, both to warn the Israelites of the divine judgement that is still on them, but—and perhaps this is now the immediate

[33]. Wildberger, *Isaiah 1–12*, 216.

danger—the Assyrians have seriously overstepped their mark and the divine judgement on them is now awaited, and also in fact is actually taking place, for they have it in their hearts *to cut off nations not a few* (v. 7).

Verses 8–11 concern the coming fates of various cities that lie in the path of the approaching Assyrian army. In fact, the commanders of the Assyrian forces are behaving as if they were themselves kings—*Are not my commanders all kings* ? (v. 8). In v. 9 we read about Assyrian boasting over the cities of *Calno* and *Carchemish*. Both were conquered by Assyria, *Calno* being in Northern Syria, and *Carchemish* a Hittite city. So too did *Hamath* and *Arpad* fall to the Assyrians, and further *Samaria* (an Israelite city) and *Damascus* (a Syrian city). Thus does the Assyrian proudly proclaim his international conquests, and asserts that now his eyes are upon *Jerusalem and Samaria* (v. 11), contemptuously boasting about his powers as he further contemplates his planned conquests of the Judean Jerusalem, and the Israelite Samaria.

Verse 12 is in prose, and it is presented as something by way of an interruption in the Assyrian's prideful account of what he has done, and what he intends to go on and do. It seems that the Assyrian has not properly accepted what it is that the LORD God of Israel is now going to do, namely to *punish the arrogant boasting of the king of Assyria and his haughty pride*. Indeed, we do read in vv. 13–14 of the prideful boasting of the Assyrian, of how he thinks it is through his own strength that he has brought about whole areas of boundary changes as he has conquered further territories, and appropriated national treasuries of the numerous nations, with hardly a barrier or a protest in his way, or any hindrance to him. His foes are portrayed here as seeming to be as weak as a bird sitting upon her nest.

Yet v. 15 gives a different picture, indeed whole emphasis, for the point is being made here that behind human activity in the world there are in fact greater powers and purposes, just as behind tools such as axes, rods, and staffs there have to be human operatives. Surely, the ongoing message here to the readers of the Isaiah book is that though there may be very much that the human beings are able to do, and even to achieve, such results that do abide need the gifts of both the strengths and the blessings of the LORD.

LIGHT AND FIRE 10:16–19

These few but yet powerful words are about the king of Assyria, and from an editorial point of view they follow on from the previous passage concerning the rather arrogant boasting of that king. Indeed, there is a certain amount of discussion among the scholars of the Isaiah book as to whether or not the opening verse here (v. 16) does belong with the words that follow, or whether it should have been read with the preceding passage containing as that does a good deal about the Assyrian boastfulness. Thus there is some division among the commentators about where v. 16 should be placed and read, and further there is disagreement when the material here is to be dated. These matters will be found discussed in various commentaries (I suggest for useful possibilities see Clements and/or Blenkinsopp), but they do not need to concern us in our present context, and so I shall not discuss them. Suffice it to say that it does seem likely that these verses come from a time after the Assyrian rule over Judah and Jerusalem had come to an end, and possibly even a long time after that.

What these few verses are concerned with is the overwhelming pride of a certain ruler in his conquests of various lands, and it would seem most likely that in the present context in this part of the book of Isaiah this refers to the rule of the Assyrians over the Israelite peoples, that which took place between about 744 BCE and 605 BCE. The judgement upon the Assyrian ruler in the eyes of the Israelite writer here is that he (the Assyrian) has forgotten that he is not supposed to have been working for himself and his own gain, and in this way has acted arrogantly, indeed unforgivably arrogantly. Thus these few verses have words of warning for the Assyrian, as in that of the warning of a *wasting sickness among his stout warriors*, and the threat of a *burning* of his (the king's) glory, *like the burning of fire* (v. 16). Meanwhile, the LORD, *The light of Israel* (v. 17—the only occurrence in the Old Testament of this expression), will become a *fire*, and *his Holy One a flame*. Perhaps Ps 97:3-4 with its use of the words *fire* and *lightnings* that *light up the world*, so that *the earth sees and trembles*, helps us to appreciate this expression of the overwhelming presence and power of God in the face and threat of other powers and forces.[34] The expression *thorns and briers / briers and thorns* is found elsewhere in this part of the Isaiah book (see 5:6; 7:23-25; 9:18; 27:4), and here we can understand it as indicating ruin and destruction for the Assyrians. In fact, so much of what the Assyrian depends upon will soon not be there, namely, the *glory of his forest . . . fruitful land . . . trees of his forest* (vv. 18-19).

Here is a short and yet seriously powerful passage about the time-limitations of the forces of worldly empires, making the point that the human leaders of those forces must not step beyond their earthly callings and tasks. Here in this brief passage the empire concerned is the Assyrian. John N. Oswalt says about these verses,

---

34. For further details see Williamson, *Isaiah 6-12*, 547-48.

God is the ruler of the world, not Tiglath-pileser or Sargon or Sennacherib or any modern dictator. The hosts belong to Yahweh and they march at his call. For one who has seen the LORD high and lifted up, Assyria's vast army and suffocating glory meant little. Before the consuming reality of God, all human works are but tinder (v. 17). Although some are counted briars and thorns (cf. 5:6) while others are seen as towering forests, the differences mean little to a raging fire. Ephraim and Assyria go up together (cf. 9:17 [Eng. 18]), for both are an offense against him.[35]

Thus does the prophet Isaiah surely have a message not merely and alone for a setting long ago, but also for subsequent times, and on into the present, and surely indeed the future.

A REMNANT WILL RETURN 10:20-23

The writer of this short piece of text takes up the theme of "remnant," one that has been used a number of times in the preceding material, above all in Isa 7:3 where we read about Isaiah taking with him his son, Shear-yashub, whose name means "A Remnant Will Return." This was to meet with King Ahaz, and presumably the prophetical son's name was intended to be a serious assurance in the historical setting of the joint Syrian-Israelite attack, that for the people of Judah and Jerusalem all would not be lost, but that there would indeed be at least a remnant that survives the assault of this attacking army. However, we cannot be at all sure when it is that this new sense of the contemporary survival of at least the few spoken about in Isa 10:21 is expected to take place, and indeed further, what perhaps will be the (military?) crisis at that time. No dating is given in the present passage, and a whole range of possibilities to fill this gap has been offered by scholars over the years. Further, the expression in the Hebrew of v. 20 *on that day* is one that we find used by the Hebrew prophets as they warn people of future events. Yet in the present context, at the same time as the "warning" element of the word and expression, there is truly the spirit of hopefulness that at least a *remnant* (v. 21) will return, a people, or perhaps even just a group, who may make up only a few, but whose presence even so is real, and who do thereby constitute a real element of hope in the LORD in a time of crisis.

Whatever is the envisaged setting when these words will be appropriate, it will indeed be, as we are told in v. 22, one where there is *destruction*, there being a faint suggestion that this will be caused by human—presumably Israelite—sinfulness. Yet here also is the assurance that at the same time

---

35. Oswalt, *Isaiah 1-39*, 267.

there will be the survival of at least the few, *a remnant*, this in no small part being due to the fact that the divine love and concern of God will be present and active in the whole matter. Thus here is the talk of there taking place an overflowing with *righteousness*, even in a situation of decreed *destruction*, talk, that is, also of the Lord God. In spite of situations of *destruction* that will inevitably be taking place in certain settings and at certain times, we are being reminded here of the sheer importance of the *remnant* who seek in a sinful age and situation to practise the life of holiness, and to walk with the Lord (v. 23). Such remnants should surely be neither easily nor lightly despised in any age.

THE DAY OF MIDIAN 10:24–27A

The message here is one of hope and confidence for the people of Israel. Those people are addressed as *my people, who live in Zion* (v. 24), that is, residents of the city of Jerusalem. Yet presumably it is all the people of Judah and Jerusalem who are being reassured of a coming time of peace, the reference to Zion being to the capital city of those people, and thus intended to stand for the whole nation. Those peoples are being assured that the day of the Assyrians with their *rod* and *staff* aggressively employed to beat enemy people will soon be past and gone. Indeed, the Assyrians will cease to be acting as the Lord's agents for the infliction of the divine judgement upon the Israelites, and now the divine anger will be directed towards the *destruction* of those very Assyrians (v. 25). The reference in v. 26 to the Lord of hosts striking *Midian at the rock of Oreb* is a reference back to Isa 9:4, itself a reference to "the day of Midian" recorded in the book of Judges (Judg 7:25), and is a wholly positive message of great hope to the people of Judah and Jerusalem. The *burden* and the *yoke* upon them will be *removed/destroyed from your shoulder* (or *neck*) (v. 27a), they are here being assured.

Who the writer of this short passage was is the subject of considerable discussion in the commentaries. Perhaps there should not be read here what seems to be the characteristic new and original ways of looking at the traditions found in Israel's story as spoken about in the early chapters of the book of Isaiah. Rather, here we have various references to earlier parts of the biblical materials, which serve to assure today's readers that the traditional divine purposes continue. Further, the God who worked wonders of deliverance for his people in days of old was indeed continuing to be the God of his people's deliverance in age after age, and in no small way in the age and circumstances about which the prophet is now uttering his words. Brevard S. Childs speaks of "the promise of salvation for the remnant to serve as a word of comfort for every successive generation of the faithful, even when the threat of eighth-century Assyria has long passed."[36] Further, Brueggemann says, "Those who remember know about Egypt and about Midian, about Moses and about Gideon, and do not doubt that what has been can be again, by the mercy and power of Yahweh."[37]

INVASION . . . AND THE TREES 10:27B-34

We are confronted with some basic questions about the text at various points in this short passage, for there are considerable problems for us over the meanings of a number of the words. Further, some of what are presented as geographical details are not known to us. In the first sentence (v. 27b) we are not told who the "he" is, and the most likely possibility would seem to be that it is one of the Assyrian leaders, but which one depends upon when we think the passage is to be dated—which is another subject for discussion, but a discussion that will not be attempted here.[38] The Good News Bible inserted "the invader," the Moffatt translation "the Assyrian." Perhaps we do well to accept NRSV's "He." Further, the Hebrew does not have "from Rimmon" (v. 27b); that is a somewhat conjectural addition accepted by the translators of NRSV, while other possibilities have been suggested ("the north" is one, "Bethel" another). In v. 28 "Aiath" is presumably Ai, which was possibly the location near Beth-aven, east of Bethel, that we read about in Josh 7:2-5, while Michmash was in the north of Israel, to the south of Bethel.

In v. 29 the travel progress of what clearly looks like an invading army continues with reference to *Geba*, a place somewhat south of *Michmash*, and we hear of the trembling on the part of the residents further south in *Ramah*, while those of *Gibeah* fled. Verse 30 speaks of the crying out of people (*daughter*) of *Gallim*, and mentions *Laishah* (whose geographical setting we do not know), and *Anathoth*, the last named being a short distance to the north of Jerusalem. Meanwhile (v. 31) we read that the residents of *Madmenah* and *Gebin* (neither known to us) are in flight. So (v. 32) the Assyrian (for in all probability the army was an Assyrian one) halts at *Nob*, and *shakes his fist* (the threatening posture of the one who has come to attack) at *Zion*, that is *Jerusalem*.[39]

---

36. Childs, *Isaiah*, 96.

37. Brueggemann, *Isaiah 1–39*, 96.

38. For further guidance in these matters see Clements, *Isaiah 1–39*, 117–21; Blenkinsopp, *Isaiah 1–39*, 259–62.

39. For a map of the route of the Assyrians according to these verses, see Wildberger, *Isaiah 1–12*, 454.

And then, what happens next? We are not told. Has the mere presence of an aggressive army on the doorstep been enough of a threat to bring Jerusalem to decide that surrender would be the most sensible policy? Or does something of a divine presence have a real effect upon attacker and/or defender? We are not told. The story as we have been given it ends at the hill of Jerusalem, Mount Zion, and there is nothing more of an attacking, or of a military, nature.

What then are we to say about what follows, those vv. 33 and 34, telling as they do of the LORD God (*the Sovereign, the LORD of hosts*, v. 33) who will *lop the boughs* [of the trees] *with terrifying power*, cutting down the *tallest trees* and who will *hack down the thickets of the forest with an ax*? Further, *Lebanon with its majestic trees will fall*. Surely, two things are being spoken about here, and both of them are about the LORD God. First, there is clearly being set forth in human words something about the almighty power of the LORD God of Israel, whose strength and ability far outstrip any power and might of sundry, and indeed of all worldly armies. Then secondly, there is the wisdom of God, and his ever-wise decisions as to how he deploys and uses his power. Neither of those gifts is available to anything like the same extent and degree by any human power, however great may appear to be the resources of those worldly powers. Surely, the message here is that what these people of Israel need to do is to put their faith, hope, and trust in the LORD God of Israel and not in human armies, and humbly ask the LORD for his guidance in the particular situation they are facing. That is still surely a real message of guidance for the generations yet to come in similar situations of threat and danger to their own lands, their peoples, and their leaders.

THE KINGDOM OF PEACE 11:1–9

There is great change in tone here in Isa 11:1–9 from what we have been reading in many of the preceding verses, and even of some chapters. Here is a passage with a fulsome message of hope for the people of Judah and Jerusalem. And whereas the preceding passage used the image of trees to speak of those matters, and of those things of which Judah and Jerusalem needed to be rid, here in our present passage is the thrilling message of a new life. Indeed, the promise being spoken of here concerns nothing less than of a *shoot* coming *out from the stump of Jesse* (v. 1). This is surely intended to speak about a coming ruler of the line of David, the son of Jesse, and it leads on into a passage that speaks so confidently about a whole range of effects upon the realities of the lives and times of the Israelite nation and peoples in the days to come.

As perhaps can be imagined, there continues to be discussion as to the authorship of this passage, but a number of scholars believe that it did come from the prophet Isaiah, though again the matter of dating the passage is another subject of considerable and continuing discussion, as are also the matters concerning which crisis and what change of circumstances brought about this reassuring composition. What however is much clearer is the fact that here is one of the more frequently used Old Testament passages in the Christian lectionaries, particularly, in the Christian season of Advent.

In v. 1 the "tree" imagery is used to a considerable extent. The new *branch* which will come from the *stump of Jesse*, will be one that will *grow* from the old *roots*. That is, the "new" will be coming out of the old, as we might say, from the original. The author in this passage is making the point that the real hope for the recipient of this (presumed) gift of the Lord will be a king of the line of King David of old. We are well aware of the fact that in the reign of David all was not well, and that David had his foibles and his failings, and did commit some serious sins, but equally there were few Judean kings who achieved the successes that were wrought by David. In fact, perhaps the kingship of David was rivalled only by those of Hezekiah and Josiah—each of them being both good and successful kings, yet neither of them being perfect.

Perhaps then the important thing was that there came to be divinely given those much-needed gifts spoken about in vv. 2–3. Thus would be given a series of gifts to this forthcoming ruler, divinely bestowed by the Lord, that is, the Lord alone, and further, granted so that the king may be properly fitted for doing his appointed task of leading correctly and appropriately his people, the God-chosen nation. Thus there are spoken about here three pairs of gifts that this forthcoming ideal ruler and leader will be given by the Lord, namely, the spirit of *wisdom and understanding*, the spirit of *counsel and might*, and the spirit of *knowledge and the fear of the Lord*. These are divine gifts that are necessary for the king, and indeed for other important leaders, to be given, in order that those leaders may be enabled to fulfil their appointed duties. For here is a human leader who is given tasks that are beyond what most human beings could be expected to achieve. Yet an individual person does have to carry out these very things, these duties and responsibilities, for the reason that they are called to one of the supreme human offices and responsibilities, the kingship of the Lord's people.

The Hebrew word that is used to speak of these gifts is *spirit*, and it is a word that is used also, perhaps in the first place, to speak of wind, that force that cannot be seen, yet that can so definitely be felt. It may be a strong wind, one that while it is invisible, can effect such great changes. Thus is the word used in the Hebrew, which we usually translate as "wind," yet can also be rendered "spirit," and thereby it speaks of invisible powers, forces, abilities that may be divinely gifted in order to help people effect the will and desires of the LORD. Thus the promised one of the LORD will be so gifted in *wisdom and understanding*, and hence be enabled to think and act wisely when his *counsel* is called for, and also when his *might* may need to be employed. Then in v. 3 is the expression of the wish that he have a delight in *the fear of the LORD*, that is, that he may indeed reverence LORD, for it is through such a relationship with the LORD that he will be enabled to do the divine will, and in fact, thus in a practical earthly sense, henceforth be truly guided and empowered to serve his people (v. 4).

Verse 5 continues the theme and concerns of the vital ministry of this forthcoming king. However, the imagery changes somewhat here. Now the qualities and gifts of the coming king are spoken about in terms of items of clothing, illustrated through these items—that *the belt around his waist* may be one of *righteousness*, that is, may he do the correct, the right things, in his realm. Further, may he have that *belt of faithfulness*. What is being expressed here is the wish that such things may all be a real and vital part of his kingly character, his abilities and activities.

Verses 6-8 set forth what should be the results in the Israelite community when those preceding requirements as regards the national leadership are carried out and faithfully maintained. It would lead to conditions of peace and concord; indeed, there is something here in the nature of a promise of a perfect society in which there truly is peace. This would be effected by a sense of profound, indeed hardly believable dimensions of peace, in at least parts of the Israelite share of the creation. Thus in v. 6 there is the talk of, as it were, a reconciliation between the *wolf* and the *lamb*, between the *leopard* and the *kid*, between the *calf*, and the *lion*, and the *fatling*. Moreover, such a degree of peace in the natural world is being envisaged here that *a little child shall lead them*, that is the people of the LORD, the people of Judah and Jerusalem.

Further, the vision continues in the following verses, 7 and 8, with talk of the peaceful coexistence of sundry other animals, like the insects, and even with snakes (*the adder's den*); there will be peace and harmony between them on the one hand and human children on the other. Indeed (v. 9), here is the promise of a remarkable peace, with no hurting, never mind destroying, on all the *holy mountain*, presumably that is Jerusalem and Mount Zion. Yet this will not be merely because the human beings concerned have come to agreements (never mind anything that may take place between the members of the animal and insect kingdoms), but rather because of the surpassing benefit of the earth being *full of the knowledge of the* LORD *as the waters cover the sea*. Here surely is a remarkable vision of a truly God-given peaceful earth, and of an earth that has become a God-centered earth. There are parts of this glorious vision that will occur again in the Isaiah book and elsewhere, see Isa 65:25. Further, parts of Isa 11:9 are to be found in Hab 2:12–14. Moreover, the talk of the LORD's holy mountain in Isa 11:9 is the one occurrence of this expression in Isa 1–39, but it will recur a good number of times in chs. 55–66 of the Isaiah book (see 56:7; 57:13; 65:11, 25; 66:20).

This is surely a remarkable picture of the kingdom of Israel—perhaps it is intended to bring a series of chapters about strife and unrest (7:1—10:34) to a peaceful conclusion. Israel is here the divinely appointed kingdom now at rest and at peace, with harmony between the human beings, the animal world, and the insects all restored. There will be no more of the earlier spoken-about tendency to *hurt* and to *destroy*, but instead there will be peace, with good and fair governance, in fact, an *earth that will be full of the knowledge of the* LORD *as the waters cover the sea* (11:9).

Hans Wildberger writes about this passage:

> The gifts of the righteousness of God cannot become a reality unless they are given shape within the socio-economic sphere. The peace which this creates is not the "peace of the soul" for the believer, characteristic of one who survives in the midst of a wicked world, but can be attained only when evil is overpowered, which alone can guarantee that insecurity and fear can be repelled. The anticipated condition of salvation is irrevocably grounded within a knowledge of Yahweh.[40]

ISRAEL AND THE NATIONS 11:10–16

Most of the material in these verses of the book of Isaiah clearly comes from times after the Babylonian exile; that is clear from the various references contained within it; for example, in the talk in v. 11 about recovering the remnant of the people from Assyria, Egypt, and elsewhere. It is clear that with this passage we are approaching the end of this particular part of the book of Isaiah that has been dealing with religious and historical events for Jewish people prior to the exile. For after this short passage we have in chapter 12 a song of thanksgiving, and after that the beginning of a whole new section in the arrangement and architecture of the book of Isaiah, that is the section in Isa 13–23, namely a series of prophecies about foreign

---

40. Wildberger, *Isaiah 1–12*, 484.

nations. That is to say that here in the present short passage (11:10–16) we have something by way of a "summing-up" of the setting in which Judah and Jerusalem and all their peoples find themselves following on from the various events that are recorded in the previous chapters of the Isaiah book, culminating in the preceding passage, Isa 11:1–9, which spoke of a kingdom of peace following on from the previous days of strife, warfare, and sundry national internal difficulties.

Verse 10 speaks of a supposed time when so much will be the better for the people of Judah and Jerusalem. Yet more, those people will be acting in some positive role for neighboring peoples. The comment that the Judean people's *dwelling shall be glorious* suggests at least peace in their land, maybe also a sense of prosperity.

This leads on in v. 11 to the good news that the LORD will be involved in the task of gathering together that remnant of the Judean people who have been scattered to various places, in particular to *Assyria* and *Egypt*, but also into various other lands. The word *remnant* is used of those who will be thus gathered back together, a word that indicates the part of a nation, clan, or group that survives some catastrophe or other, and is thereby a real sign of hope for the present and the future. In its Old Testament usage this is the group that becomes a serious promise for various futures; each time it may be a small group yet it is real, and distinctive—like the group that survived the Flood (Gen 6:5—7:23); those who escaped from Egypt at the Red Sea (Exod 14:28); and indeed for the people of Israel in the days of Isaiah, whose own first son was named Shear-jashub, "A Remnant Shall Return" (7:3).

The thought is continued in v. 12, and here the raising of an ensign is spoken about, a flag, in NRSV a *signal*. This imagery is also to be found in Isa 30:17 and in both settings it is portrayed as indicating a rallying point for survivors of what has been happening, and what the people of Israel and/or Judah have been suffering. Further, in this verse peoples of both Israel and Judah are spoken of, and we are given something of a vision of a coming day when there will again be a gathering together of those who once were indeed one, a single and united Israelite people. This, we are told in v. 13, will be made possible by the elimination of ancient jealousy and hostility between *Ephraim* and *Judah*, and in such a way that when they are together these united peoples (v. 14) will be able to bring about endings to the threats of such peoples as the *Philistines* and *Ammonites*, and those of *Edom and Moab*. So also in v. 15 is there a sense of triumph over the forces of Egypt, which at one moment of history caused such problems for the Israelites, and further in v. 16 there is promised the provision of a *highway* from Assyria for the *remnant* left there, *as there was for Israel when they came up from the land of Egypt.*

Thus there is a remarkable promise here of coming times that will be so much better for the people of Israel and Judah. This will be one of the great themes of what will later come about for the people of Israel, and that is spoken of so thrillingly and eloquently in chs. 40–55 in the book of Isaiah (see for example, Isa 40:3). But there is yet a good deal more to be considered before we can come to that. First, there is a short psalm of praise (12:1–6) that the present historical events can now be looked back upon in a spirit of praise and thanksgiving, and then we have to consider a range of issues before we can come to the crisis of the years of exile in Babylon.

David Stacey in his Epworth Commentary on Isaiah 1–39 said about this passage:

> The Old Testament is sometimes embarrassingly down to earth. We tend to prefer "spiritual" solutions to our problems. The Old Testament reminds us that, if we are to be true to the Bible, our thinking must be practical and concrete, not simply theoretical. Finally, the great salvation is not simply for us, the chosen, and our friends. All the nations are invited in v. 10. This is only a hint, but it points to a theme in the book of Isaiah (cf. 2.1–4) that is breath-taking in its range.[41]

SONG OF THANKSGIVING 12:1–6

We have here a short song that clearly seems intended to be a concluding expression of praise and thanksgiving that a series of local and national crises for the people of Judah and Jerusalem in their national and international lives have come to an end, having been one way or another resolved. Thus for what has been recorded in the preceding chapters of the Isaiah book, at this point of resolution or completion, there is an expression of praise of the LORD to complete the account. Certainly, this material has the sounds and the emphases of some of the various types of psalms we find in the Old Testament book of Psalms.

In vv. 1 and 2 the speaker is an individual person, and the style of the writing appears to be that of a psalm of individual thanksgiving, the psalmist giving thanks that he is now at peace with the LORD. In v. 2 the writer reaffirms that he is dependent upon God for his very life, and that he has been brought through a crisis, or series of crises, successfully. Indeed, he confesses his dependence upon God: he *has become my salvation*. Although this is written as if it is an individual person who is thinking about these

---

41. Stacey, *Isaiah 1–39*, 95–96.

matters, it may be that the individual here (the "I") in fact stands as the representative person for a whole community, or part of a community.

In v. 3 with the talk of water being drawn *from the wells of salvation*, we appear to have an application of the thought and language found in Pss 114:8 and 116:13 (though in the latter the NRSV translates *cup of salvation*), which seems clearly to indicate the psalmist expressing his thanksgiving that his essential needs have indeed been provided for, and that those needs have been thus provided for by none other than the gracious provisions and mercies of the Lord.

Verses 4-6 make up a further expression of praise to the Lord, and the proclamation of the psalmist here is that God should be given *thanks*, that the people should indeed call on, and exalt his *name*, and tell other nations about the great things the Lord does, that is, *proclaim that his name is exalted* (v. 4). Telling other nations about the great things that the God of Israel does is not a major subject for the Old Testament—though perhaps the book of Jonah makes up a plea that God's people should *make known his deeds among the nations* (12:4). This matter is given further emphasis, particularly in v. 5 where the Israelites are not only to *Sing praises to the Lord, for he has done gloriously*, but also to *let this be known in all the earth*. Thus this expression of praise ends with the call for the people of Zion/Jerusalem to both shout aloud and sing for joy, for indeed great in their midst is *the Holy One of Israel* (v. 6), one of the frequent occurrences of this characteristic divine title employed in the book of Isaiah. See above, on Isa 1:4, p. 5 above, for the expression *Holy One of Israel*. In this way there comes in these words, which serve as a conclusion following the eventful first eleven chapters of the book of Isaiah, that title, that designation of the divine Lord God of Israel that is both so prominent and significant in this prophetic book. Indeed, Wildberger says at the close of his treatment of these verses:

> This psalm, Isa. 12:1-6, furnishes a conclusion for the first eleven chapters of the book of Isaiah. The redactor, who is responsible for the final form of this chapter, certainly had in mind that it would conclude with this vision of the future. One minute detail can show how reflectively he went about his task; at the very conclusion, he has placed the name which was so central to Isaiah's understanding of God: "the Holy One of Israel."[42]

---

42. Wildberger, *Isaiah 1-12*, 508.

II

Isaiah 13–23
Prophetic Words about Foreign Nations

FOR AN INTRODUCTION TO these chapters, which contain a series of prophetical words about some of the foreign nations of those times, see above pp. xxiii–xxiv.

The materials we are reading in this section of the Isaiah book are of a different nature from what has preceded them. So far it has been clear that the concern of the prophet—and of those other individuals whose voices we have been hearing in these texts—has overwhelmingly been with the peoples of Judah and Jerusalem, and of the northern kingdom of Israel. Here begins, however, a different series of emphases and concerns on the part of the prophet Isaiah, and perhaps also of other prophetical voices, namely issues concerning various foreign nations, those who in their different ways, and at their various distances from Jerusalem, had ambitions and concerns that did affect and influence the ongoing life of the people of Judah and Jerusalem. It would certainly seem that the individual, or the group, that was responsible for the arrangement of this section of the material is anxious at this stage to get us thinking about the place of the Israelite peoples in the wider world. It is as if those who had opportunity to make decisions about what should go into this work that became the Isaiah book did indeed see and understand that the people of Israel were moving into a wider world than they had known and experienced hitherto, and that perhaps mysteriously this was all part of the divine plans and purposes for the people of Israel. There is in the material that follows something of an invitation to the reader today to share in the worldwide and long-term perspectives of the faith that is proclaimed in the Old Testament, as well as in the New Testament.

Prophecies about Babylon 13:1—14:23

This is the longest of all these prophecies about the wider world in which the small states of Israel and Judah were set and which, politically speaking, were so deeply to affect, and to an extent dictate parts of, the internal lives of the Israelite communities, kingdoms, and peoples. These conditions of living under the rule of a major military power were indeed to color and direct the progress, or otherwise, of the people of Judah and Jerusalem. This covenant community, it should be remembered, were those who believed themselves to have been called into a special relationship with the LORD, indeed to have been charged to be nothing less than the people of the LORD in a world of growing non-Israelite foreign powers. It is as if the author responsible for these two chapters took Babylon as the first example to speak about because this major power was to affect profoundly the life of the southern kingdom of Judah, particularly how their corporate life was governed. However, it does have to be added that we cannot be sure of the precise historical moment(s) with which these oracles are concerned. A range of possible times and settings have been suggested, both for what read like the aggressive words and acts on the part of the Babylonian leader(s), and also the reasons for this activity; what the Judean leaders must have been engaged in or were threatening to carry out. Thus it is that we have to admit our ignorance of the precise historical background to what follows.

ISAIAH'S VISION OF BABYLON 13:1–22

In v. 1 we are told about the divine task the prophet was given by the LORD. The Hebrew word that in NRSV is translated *oracle* can mean "load" or "burden," and it would seem to be intended to indicate a sense of solemnity and seriousness about what the prophet is to speak to the people, and presumably in particular to their king and leaders. Further this message, this burden, this *oracle,* concerns Babylon, and no doubt that one name indicated to the audience a great and powerful overlord. Further, in the verses that follow we are given a series of bold descriptions of the power of this nation, and of the belief that they have been divinely called to what looks like an aggressive policy. Thus we are told in v. 3 about their divine call, while v. 2 (*On a bare hill raise a signal*) suggests a signal that the time had come when there should be action. Then v. 3 makes it clear that it is none other than the covenant LORD himself who is calling them (*I myself have commanded my consecrated ones*) and this in order to *execute my anger*. Moreover, vv. 4–5 speak and give some details of what looks like preparation for serious warfare, indeed for an onslaught, so we are told at the end of v. 5, *to destroy the whole earth*. This will surely seem to us to be somewhat exaggerated language, but it does have to be said that such hyperbole is a regular and characteristic feature of the writing in this part of the Isaiah book, and indeed of other writings in those sections of the Hebrew prophets that we call oracles or prophetical utterances about other nations.

As regards at least some of the foreign nations—and this certainly applies to the Babylonians—who were large and powerful, they appear to have believed that they needed to exercise a firm grasp upon such subject peoples as those of Judah and Jerusalem. No doubt this would be the approach particularly needed when the foreign nation concerned was one situated so far from the seat of power of the local nation over which it exercised power. Yet also, the faithful presence of the overlord was needed at times at that part of the outer rim of the empire by the local nation and its people. This helps us to understand the somewhat violent, even apparently overbearing, language of vv. 4 and 5, with even the suggestion that the *LORD of hosts is mustering an army for battle* (v. 4), and the talk here of *the LORD and the weapons of his indignation, to destroy the whole earth* (v. 5), which, while allowing for some understandable exaggeration, is speaking of the divine purposes. That is, the LORD's chosen people in Judah and Jerusalem are being enabled to serve the LORD and fulfil his will, for although in worldly terms their numbers were small and their political and military powers were severely limited, now they were being held in a strong divine grasp. Such we can understand was particularly so in these latter days when great and powerful nations inevitably predominated in the life of the world.

With vv. 6–8 the theme becomes that of *the day of the LORD*, a matter that we have earlier read about in the Isaiah book at 2:6–22, and also in Amos 5:18–20; Joel 1:15; and Zeph 1:14. In this type of Old Testament literature, what is being spoken about is usually the belief that one day there will be an outpouring of the divine judgement and punishment on the LORD's people, this being envisaged as an enactment of the LORD brought about by the sins of the people of Israel and Judah. It certainly sounds as if it is a serious visitation of the LORD, with its talk of *all hands will be feeble, and every human heart will melt* . . . (v. 7), while the following verse seems to be speaking about even more violent happenings for the people (*They will look aghast at one another; their faces will be aflame* [v. 8]), but no indication is given as to *which* people of *which* nation are envisaged.

Then in 13:9-16 we have a further, lengthy, and detailed treatment and explanation of what we have already been told in the preceding verses, vv. 6-8, except that now the divine judgement seems to be destined to fall upon a far wider setting. Now it is nothing less than *the earth* that will be made desolate (v. 9), and *sun* and *stars* will not be shining in their familiar ways (v. 10). Further, all this is envisaged as being the result of the *wrath and fierce anger* of the LORD, and the text goes as far as saying that this divine activity will have a *cruel* aspect (v. 9). This word, *cruel*, is a difficult one for us to deal with when used of an action by the Lord. The same Hebrew word can mean "fierce," and that would appear to be perhaps a rather more appropriate translation of it in this present context. What is being spoken about is certainly envisaged as being a serious act of divine judgement upon these sinful people, but we cannot be sure who those people were. It does, however, seem that it was some *tyrants*, for that word is used in v. 11, *the insolence of tyrants*. Yet just who these *tyrants* were is not stated—though there has been no shortage of scholarly suggestions. What, however, is more clearly set forth here is the great and dreadful judgement of the LORD God that is surely upon those who misuse their powers and responsibilities. In fact, many parts of humanity involved here appear to be spoken of: the *world*, the *wicked*, the *arrogant*, the *tyrants*. Thus there is to be a serious act of judgement upon all these sinful people, so that indeed *mortals* will be rarer than *fine gold, humans than the gold of Ophir* (v. 12). *Ophir* is spoken about a good number of times in the Old Testament as a place where gold is to be found, but we do not know geographically where it was, though, once again, there is no shortage of scholarly suggestions.

Clearly what is portrayed here is a most serious and thorough divine judgement upon peoples and nations. Indeed, as v. 13 expresses the matter, the LORD *will make the heavens tremble*, and further *the earth will be shaken out of its place*. These words about such dreadful happenings in the world are set forth concerning a punishment upon the sinfulness of humanity, and we should surely understand this as an indication that in the prophetic understanding of things there is a great anger and anguish on the part of the LORD regarding the gross sinfulness of the peoples of earth, and in particular on the parts of their appointed leaders.

This theme of the most severe divine judgement is continued in the following verses (vv. 17-22), where the object of the wrath and judgement of God is now upon no less than the Babylonian empire. Thus, clearly this is material that comes from a later time, for the Babylonians (also known in the Old Testament as Chaldeans) came to power after the demise of the Assyrian empire in 605 BCE, and only lasted until 539 BCE. However, the fate of this once well-regarded empire (*the glory of kingdoms*, v. 19) is here spoken about becoming *like Sodom and Gomorrah when God overthrew them* (v. 19; see Gen 19:24–28), suggesting serious religious and social failings. The Babylonian lands will become an unpopulated wilderness where none will desire to live (v. 20), apart from a number of wild and strange animals, including dancing *goat-demons*, otherwise called satyrs, goat-like creatures of corrupt wills (vv. 21–22). Such terrible times, the reader is warned, are close at hand (v. 22).

In addition to the words of Isa 13:1–22 there is more to be said by the prophet and his editors about Babylon, its sinfulness, and its fall in the following material (14:1–23), and therefore any comments about what we have read so far may be considered after we have studied that latter passage.

THE END OF BABYLON 14:1–23

Two nations are spoken about here. The first is Israel, and the prophetic message to the people is one of hope for the future. The second is Babylon, and concerning that we return to the subject of the preceding chapter, 13:1–22, yet the material about the fall of that empire will be expressed here in very different language.

First then we consider 14:1–2, where we find a comforting and reassuring word of the Lord to the people of Israel that their days of suffering are not to go on forever. In fact, life in Judah and Jerusalem is about to change radically, and into ways that will be so much the better for the Israelite people. This is a real expression of hope, although in all probability the time when this was written was in Persian days, for we seem here to be in the time of possibilities and expectations that we find expressed so clearly in chs. 40–55 of the book of Isaiah. Further, in v. 1 there is the expectation presented of the wish of other nations and individuals to join with the people of Israel, another theme of Isa 40–55 (see for example Isa 55:5), and further in v. 2 the assurance that there will be a reversal of fortunes as far as Israel and Judah's previous captors are concerned. Thus, when some of these things have happened, then will be the appropriate time for an expression of rejoicing on the part of the Lord's people over the total change in fortunes of their one-time captors, the Babylonians (v. 3). So it is that this is called a *taunt* against the King of Babylon (v. 4a); this is a word that is used elsewhere in the Old Testament in relation to the destruction coming upon Israel or Judah, but here it is as an expression of woe upon their erstwhile captors, namely the Babylonians, for indeed this *oppressor has ceased! . . . his insolence has ceased!* (v. 4). Indeed, the Lord has broken what we might call the "badges of office" of the Babylonians, namely *the staff of the wicked . . . the scepter of rulers* (v. 5), in this way bringing to an end their days of conquests and their victories *with unrelenting persecution* (v. 6).

Thus it is that the *whole earth is at rest and quiet*, with the result that there is the breaking out into *singing* (v. 7). Even the great trees such as *the cedars of Lebanon* can relax and be joyful, for they know that now there is no one who will come and cut them down, presumably either for military or building purposes (for example, we read in 1 Kgs 5:6–14 they were used in the construction of the great Jerusalem temple) (v. 8). Further, those who are in the underworld are now prepared to meet and greet the erstwhile great and powerful ones of life, in these latter days when they themselves are in *Sheol*, the place into which, in much Old Testament thought, those who died descended (v. 9). It would only be later that there developed in ancient Israel the thought and belief about a new life after human death, as we are able to read in, for example, Isa 25:8 and 26:19. But meanwhile all who are in Sheol—whether they had previously been among the great ones of earth or the most humble—will be saying, *You too have become as weak as we!* (v. 9).[1]

The account of the Israelite sense of release continues with further details, indeed, it has to be said, rejoicing. Verse 12 speaks about the great change of fortunes that have befallen the one-time conqueror, being spoken of here as if he were once like the planet Venus (*Day Star, son of Dawn* v. 12), a reference to the morning star, the "light-bearer" (which in the New Testament becomes an epithet for the Messiah, Rev 2:28; 22:16), but who is now *cut down to the ground*. The thought continues in the following verse, with its expression of overwhelming ambition to greatness of the onetime conqueror, *I will ascend to heaven*, followed by *I will sit on the mount of assembly on the heights of Zaphon* (v. 13). For the Canaanites, *Zaphon* was where their various deities had their dwelling (for others, it was Mons Cassius). Further, in v. 14 this boasting one, the one-time Babylonian ruler, asserted, *I will make myself like the Most High*. The title "Most High" had once applied to a Canaanite deity, though it was understood by the writers of the Old Testament to be an epithet for the Lord God (cf. Gen 14:19–20).

Yet all this changes radically in v. 15, for in this verse we are back to the imagery of v. 11 with its talk of the ruler being brought down to *Sheol*, here the word *Pit* also being employed to designate Sheol, as the word *Pit* is also used in Ps 16:10 and Prov 1:12. Humanity stare in some disbelief at this transformation of such greatness into such nothingness (vv. 16–17). Whereas normally earthly kings who have died *lie in glory, each in his own tomb* (v. 18), here in comparison is portrayed a very dreadful fate in the

---

1. While the English NRSV reads "as weak as we are," the American version omits the verb "are."

place of the dead (*the Pit, like a corpse trampled underfoot* [v. 19]). For as in earthly life this king treated his people—and surely the writer is thinking here of the late king's subject peoples—so also will that erstwhile Babylonian ruler be similarly treated in his death (v. 20). Further, not to be forgotten are the king's sons, who will also be slaughtered. This presumably is not so much a matter of revenge as a way of bringing it about that there may in future be better and more caring rulers of the peoples of earth (v. 21).

The final verses, 22 and 23, are in prose and make it clear that the subject of the preceding and seriously outspoken piece is intended to be the old kingdom of Babylon, and that the evil ruler was indeed Babylonian. In fact, since 14:4a here is the first verse that anchors the poem of 14:4b–21 to any particular historical setting, namely the fall of Babylon and the Babylonian empire. What we have in the poem of vv. 4b–21 is a composition in remarkably condemnatory words of the Babylonian empire, words that it would seem, must have come from the period sometime after its fall.

What are we to make of these words of condemnation in the poem in vv. 4b–21? Many Christian leaders of worship will not be sorry that this passage is not to be found in The Revised Common Lectionary, for it does indeed contain words, phrases, thoughts, and expressions that hardly conform with the command to Christians that they should love one another (see Mark 12:31–33 and elsewhere). It is in a style and language that though highly commendable as a piece of Hebrew poetry is at the same time difficult to read in Christian contexts because of its apparent sense of triumph over a fallen foe, namely Babylon. Yet, as Hans Wildberger points out to us, this in fact is a common wisdom topic, namely, "the judgment against the hubris of human beings who reach for the stars and break into a world reserved for God alone."[2] Perhaps it is indeed a fact that there can be peace for all on earth only as ruling tyrants are denied their powers and brought before the bar of judgement, maybe such judgement being effected either through the powers of human forces, or else those of the Lord alone.

DOOM FOR ASSYRIA 14:24–27

This short passage is about the fate of the Assyrians, who were for the peoples of Israel and Judah the great power prior to the rise of the Babylonians. We have already read in Isa 10:5–15 of the pride of the Assyrians, and of their having overstepped their calling to give effect to the Lord's plans for the people of Israel.[3] Here is a further word on the same subject, and it would

---

2. Wildberger, *Isaiah 13–27*, 75.
3. See above 46–49.

seem to have come from the prophet Isaiah himself, who here declares that the end, the demise, of the power and influence of the Assyrians is at hand. It is affirmed here that the Lord has a *plan—as I have planned, so shall it come to pass* (v. 24)—that it is about to be put into action, namely to break *the Assyrian in my land* (v. 25). This means that the Assyrian burden upon the Israelites will be removed, this indeed being part of those much wider plans of the Lord that in fact concern the whole world (v. 26). We have earlier heard of plans that the Lord God had in Isa 7:7–9, and later we shall come to more of these. See Isa 29:14; 31:3. Here in v. 27 the rhetorical question is asked, who on earth is there who will be able to foil this plan of the Lord God? As John Mauchline expressed it, "This is the regnant God of human history, whose is the kingdom, the power and the glory, to whom the nations are as a drop from a bucket and as the fine dust on the pans of a balance (Isa. 40.15)."[4]

BEWARE, PHILISTIA 14:28–32

Here we have another succinct oracle, this one concerning the Philistines, these people being the western neighbors of the people of Israel, and this will be followed by a much more extensive oracle about their eastern neighbors, the Moabites. We are told that the present oracle, concerning Philistia, was given to the prophet—it does seem to be Isaiah—in the year that King Ahaz died, in the terms of our own dating usage that is 715 BCE.

It seems that an unnamed enemy of the Philistines has been under attack and completely disabled—*the rod that struck you is broken* (v. 29). Perhaps that has been by an Assyrian king, either Tiglath-Pileser III (died 727 BCE) or else Shalmaneser V (died 722 BCE), but the Philistines are warned not to go into rejoicing, for worse is to come, *snake, adder, flying fiery serpent* being mentioned. But who or what was intended we do not know. Yet, the following verse (v. 30) appears to be expressing good and positive things for the Israelites, in particular for the poor and the needy, though the last two lines are difficult for they seem to be speaking of Israelites going back into troubles—famine and killings. This problem is a long-felt one, as can be seen in the footnote in NRSV, where the Hebrew in the Masoretic Text has "he," but the Dead Sea Scrolls, and the Vulgate (Latin Version) have "I." It is the latter reading that NRSV translators adopted, namely "I," that is God himself. Then in v. 31 the Israelites are to wail in their gates (the expected place for such corporate activities), and the Philistines are to prepare for the worst. The final verse (v. 32) expresses the great confidence, and place

---

4. Mauchline, *Isaiah 1–39*, 144.

of refuge in crisis, that all the Israelites—both rich and poor (*needy*)—can find in their city of *Zion* (Jerusalem). For this prophet, Jerusalem/Zion was a place of refuge and security.

CONCERNING MOAB 15:1—16:14

This is entitled in 15:1, in the translation of the NRSV, *An oracle concerning Moab*, but in reality these two chapters of the book of Isaiah (15:1—16:14) make up a whole series of prophecies about Moab and the Moabites, 15:1-9; 16:1-5; 16:6-11, onto which have been added some notes in 16:12 and 16:13-14.

What do we know about Moab? Unfortunately we know comparatively little about this nation which was a neighboring one to Israel, situated on the southern part of the eastern side of the Dead Sea. Still today we continue to be in considerable ignorance regarding the social and historical life of Moab in ancient times. Thus we are somewhat ignorant of much detail about this country, its people, leaders, and historical happenings.

The first of these poems is in 15:1-9, and is a lament for Moab, which we learn has suffered a disastrous defeat by an unnamed enemy. The towns *Ar* and *Kir* were the principal cities of Moab, and both have suffered in what sounds like a surprise and disastrous attack (v. 1). In v. 2 we hear of the laments of the peoples of other cities, *Dibon* and *Medeba*, this lamenting being in their temple. *Nebo* was the mountain where we are told Moses died (Deut 34). The baldness of the peoples suggests mourning in the face of their current tragedy, and putting on sackcloth (v. 3) for the same reason. Further, there were also peoples of other cities, *Heshbon and Elealeh*, crying out (v. 4). In v. 5 we read of our author/writer joining in the lamentation for the people of Moab. The waters of *Nimrim* (v. 6) were in the south-eastern end of the Dead Sea, so that further even apparently somewhat distant, desert areas were also made desolate. Moreover, this desolation took place right up to Moab's southern border, that is at the *Wadi* (Brook) *of the Willows* (v. 7). And the cries of grief and suffering sound out, in fact we are told that the peoples' wails go afar (v. 8), never mind the witness being borne by the *blood* in *Dibon*, a chief Moabite city as well as the name of a river (v. 9).

With 16:1-5 we have something different, which seems to read as if it is an intended response to what we have been hearing about in 15:1-9. Yet it is hardly a sympathetic response, but rather the suggestion that what should be looked for is a renewal of the rule in Moab of the line of David, as is made particularly clear in v. 5. When that is achieved there will be *a ruler who seeks justice and is swift to do what is right* (v. 5). This is made possible because this Judean, Davidic, ruler is spoken of as having a throne established in *steadfast love* (v. 5). This is a most significant Hebrew word (*chesed*) indicating loyalty, faithfulness, grace, and, perhaps in particular in this specific context, good kingship, the sense of obligation to the community for which a king would be responsible. Another Hebrew word of significance here is justice (*mishpat*): this new Davidic king will seek for justice (*mishpat*), a quality and a way of life and activity that above all brings about the good, right, and correct benefits, along with appropriate aims of life for the peoples concerned. Thus there is expressed the confidence that with this new Davidic rule there can be in Moab a place for the *outcasts*, and even *the fugitive* (vv. 3, 4). Further, there can peace, when *the oppressor is no more*, and *marauders have vanished from the land* (v. 4).

Nevertheless there is a rather different emphasis expressed in 16:6–12, as if it is following the theme of the 15:1–9 passage, maybe perhaps, as argued by Hans Wildberger,[5] reflecting a later assessment upon the Moabite way of life. Here there is once again talk about the *arrogance, pride,* and *insolence* of Moab (v. 6). The reference in v. 7 to *raisin cakes of Kir-hareseth* (that is the *Kir* of 15:1) would seem to be to offerings in fertility rites, which, for the Old Testament writers, is the seeking of false security, and further is actually forbidden for Israelites. Moreover, there is the warning here that the growth of vines is arrested, or at least they will be (vv. 8–9), but it is generally felt that those vines stand symbolically for the people, the inhabitants of Moab. Thus, there is the weeping spoken about in v. 9, the absence of *joy and gladness* in the land (v. 10), and an expression of prophetic sadness that these people have chosen such ways of life (v. 11).

With 16:12–14 it is widely agreed by scholars we are dealing with editorial matters added at later dates to the preceding vv. 1–11, the first of these being in v. 12, the second in vv. 13–14. There are different views about v. 12, perhaps the most satisfactory being that it is about the frequenting of temple and high places spoken of in 15:2, namely that the seeking of other deities will be of no help. As far as 16:13–14 is concerned there is the warning expressed here that the divine threat against Moab does still stand, even though its execution may be delayed a considerable time. Yet thus would end any present prosperity in the land of Moab.

Parts of Isa 15:1—16:14 make a reappearance in somewhat modified form in the book of the prophet Jeremiah (see Jer 48:29–38), among the collection there of that prophet's proclamations against the foreign nations. It would seem that in all probability the Jeremiah text is dependent upon the Isaianic, though perhaps the overall purpose of the Jeremiah version was

---

5. Wildberger, *Isaiah 13–27*, 145.

to present and emphasize an announcement of judgement, for other such passages expressing a hopeful spirit in the Isaiah presentation like Isa 16:1, 3–5 are missing in the parallel passage in Jeremiah.

Meanwhile, back in the Isaiah version we have been studying, the crucial message of hope for the people of the LORD is surely expressed in 16:14, *the glory of Moab will be brought into contempt*. Christopher Seitz says about these words, coming as they do from this extended block of material about Moab, "However terrible and haunting a lament went up from Moab in days past, the future is darker still. The Babylonian smoke from the north will soon descend upon Moab and 'those who survive will be very few and feeble' (16:14)." Brueggemann adds, "Mostly . . . this song of grief is not interested in blame. The costs and hurts are too massive and acute for moralizing."[6]

CONCERNING DAMASCUS AND EPHRAIM 17:1–14

There is something of a collection of prophetical words here that are about different historical events, but which have been brought together into this chapter of the book of Isaiah. Verses 1–3 are about Damascus, the main city of Syria, while vv. 4-6 concern the northern kingdom of Israel. These two nations in 734 BCE came together and attacked Jerusalem in what has become known as the Syro-Ephraimite War. Their attack was not successful, as we read in Isa 7:1—8:22, and it does seem that at least parts of the passage under our present consideration—either 17:1–14, or at least 17:1–11—come from that historical moment of crisis for the peoples of Judah and Jerusalem. The remainder of Isa 17, vv. 12–14, concern Assyria, the dominating national power at the time of the Syro-Ephraimite War.[7]

Verses 1–3 then concern *Damascus*, the capital city of Syria, the country to the north of Israel. In v. 1 there is the dreadful threat that *Damascus* is about to cease being a city, that it will become *a heap of ruins*, and it goes on to say that other Syrian towns will become deserted. In v. 2 the Hebrew speaks of the cities of Aroer, which was in fact a city of Moab, but which is not mentioned in the lament over Moab in Isa 15:1–9. Thus the NRSV, along with other modern translations, reads the Greek version (the Septuagint) here and renders it *her towns will be deserted forever*, speaking of their seriously miserable fate. Verse 3 makes the point that similar will be the fates of the kingdoms of Syria and Israel. Such for the writer here are described the

---

6. Seitz, *Isaiah 1–39*, 140; Brueggemann, *Isaiah 1–39*, 145.

7. For further on the Syro-Ephraimite War see Irvine, *Isaiah, Ahaz, and the Syro-Ephraimitic Crisis*; Thompson, *Situation and Theology*.

rather dismal futures of the lands of Syria and Ephraim in their anti-Judah and Jerusalem ambitions and warfare.

Verses 4–11 are about Ephraim, that is the northern kingdom of Israel, beginning in v. 4 with the threat of a forthcoming wasting disease, *the fat of his flesh will grow lean*, followed in v. 5 by the image of the standing corn in the field that will be seized, leaving the whole scene like that when an olive tree is beaten leading to there being precious few olives for others to harvest, the very thing that Israelite peoples were commanded not to do, as for example we can read in Deut 24:20 with its statement about provision for the poor—and similarly with *a fruit tree* (v. 6).

The result of all this is that the people of the kingdom of Israel will be left in a desperate situation (vv. 7–8), when they will have to turn to the Lord their God for help (*the Holy One of Israel*—for the Isaianic usage of this designation see above on Isa 1:4), no longer relying on their own artefacts and efforts. For indeed, those once strong people of faith in their God and their strong cities will be as good as back in the days when they first came into the land and had to deal with, and defeat, *the Hivites and the Amorites,* that is if having come out of the years in the wilderness they were expecting to find places for their homes in the new land (v. 9; see Josh 9:1–10).

In vv. 10–11, further, there is continued the theme of relying on other deities, turning to idolatry, and in particular there is here the condemnation of the making of religious gardens. It was believed that by a process of sympathetic magic the making of religious gardens would bring to the human beings involved real growth of life and fertility. This is to forget *the God of your salvation . . . the Rock of your refuge* (v. 10). Examples of such forgetting of the true God of Israel is also spoken about in other parts of the Old Testament (e.g., Deut 6:12; 8:11). Further, for other occurrences of the imagery of *the Rock* for the Lord see Pss 18:46; 31:3; 89:26. Even so, those plants in their prepared gardens may indeed grow, and blossom, maybe even with great rapidity, *yet the harvest will flee away*, all too soon, indeed *in a day of grief and incurable pain* (v. 11).

This chapter ends in vv. 12–14 with the great expression of confidence that the Israelites should feel in their own God as they have to face up to living among the nations in their world. For understandably there are great powers ranged against them that could be likened to thunder, *the thunder of many peoples*, as *they thunder like the thundering of the sea! . . . they roar like the roaring of mighty waters!* (v. 12). Yet the assurance is that the one referred to as "he"—which must presumably be the Lord God—will rebuke them with the result that they will flee away, in fact feeling themselves to be nothing less than blown away like *whirling dust before the storm* (v. 13).

Thus by the morning those who were such a threat the day before will be no more, indeed, *This is the fate of those who despoil us, and the lot of those who plunder us* (v. 14).

What we read in Isa 17:1-14 appear to be words of prophets, maybe coming from a number of different times, calling upon their people to have faith in their God, and to trust him in all sorts of varied and developing situations. Some of this material, as we have observed, does seem to have come from the time of the so-called Syro-Ephraimite crisis for Judah and Jerusalem. It may be that what have come down to us as some of the prophet Isaiah's words to his king and people in that now far-off time are presented in different words in the passage we have been studying. For the words here are surely for a later generation, and even further, they are surely of equal validity and beneficial assistance for our own age, and indeed of all earthly ages, "Take heed, be quiet, do not fear, and do not let your heart be faint . . ." (7:4), that is, in other such times of crisis or prospective crisis.

CONCERNING NUBIA 18:1-7

That land the Old Testament calls Kush (Cush) is otherwise known as Nubia, and it comprises a very large area being made up of much of modern Ethiopia, Sudan, and Somalia. Here in Isa 18:1-7 is the first of three oracles in the book of Isaiah (in chs. 18, 19, and 20) concerning the lands of Egypt and the neighboring nations.

In v. 1 the *whirring wings* would seem to be those of insects (the Hebrew says literally *pairs of wings*, what grammatically is called the dual form of a noun), suggesting that this land is one where many insects are to be found, while the talk of ambassadors being sent by the (River) Nile suggests that we are dealing with the land of Kush, as it is known in the Old Testament's Hebrew text (v. 2). Indeed, we go on to read that this land sends its messengers in boats made of reeds (*papyrus*) by *sea* (not necessarily travelling *by the Nile* as in NRSV), but just what they were going to report, or whatever is their present purpose is not stated. Further, at v. 3 is a somewhat mysterious verse, which some scholars think may be an addition (gloss) to an earlier version.

Yet what is portrayed in vv. 4 and 5 is a calm, quiet, and confident LORD God who counsels a like calmness on the part of his prophet, and presumably also of his people, as some particular earthly events take their course. Verse 6 seems to be suggesting that the LORD is acting as if he were a human gardener encouraging growth by pruning the maturing plants. In fact, it will be the birds and the animals of the natural world that will carry out this pruning operation, as it were, at the behest of the Lord (v. 6).

Then, finally, there is v. 7, what appears to be an expression of very great confidence on the part of many peoples, and expressed as such in the words of v. 2. Indeed, certain words of description we find in v. 2 are repeated in v. 7, generally the same Hebrew words being employed: a nation of *tall people*; *smooth* (skinned); *a nation mighty and conquering*. Nevertheless, the reference in v. 2 is to *ambassadors*, messengers, whereas in v. 7 it appears to be those who bring gifts. It is quite widely thought by scholars that v. 7 has been added at a later date, maybe speaking about the same sort of process of bringing gifts from the wealth of Egypt and Ethiopia as we read about in Isa 45:14.

Altogether, although this is not in any way a lengthy composition about one of the neighboring nations to the peoples of Judah and Jerusalem, yet it is one that raises in the critical mind a good number of questions and queries about both authorship and the dates of original writing and possible later additions, and even of geographical setting. Thus in the various commentaries on the Isaiah book, or parts of it, there are considerable differences of opinion regarding this short chapter. Yet perhaps the heart of the matter is there in v. 4 with its picture of the Lord looking down on all his peoples from his heavenly dwelling, *like clear heat in sunshine, like a cloud of dew in the heat of harvest*. Indeed, this could be the abiding message of this short passage, its essential message for the reader today being encapsulated in apparently later words of the prophet Isaiah, *For thus said the Lord God, the Holy One of Israel: In returning and rest you shall be saved; in quietness and in trust shall be your strength* (30:15). Yet also what presumably should neither be forgotten nor neglected is the further word about gifts being brought to the Lord of hosts from those people tall and smooth, presumably the peoples of Ethiopia.

EGYPT UNDER JUDGEMENT 19:1–15

These are verses about the divine judgement upon the land and the people of Egypt, and here the outstanding power and authority of the Lord God of Israel are made abundantly clear both in the opening verses (vv. 1–5), and then afterwards using different images in the verses that follow.

Verses 1–5 are expressed in highly dramatic wording, and speak of the extraordinary ways in which the Lord comes to the land of Egypt and how he deploys his almighty power. Thus in v. 1 we have the image of the Lord moving on a quick (NRSV *swift*) moving cloud, and that his clearly determined destination is Egypt. Elsewhere this type of picture and image of the LORD is to be found in, for example, Ps 18:10–12. Yet here in Isa 19:1–15 perhaps as well as there being intended the depiction of the power of God, it is also being averred that the LORD is able to travel very fast to here and there. Thus let all who might be accused of guilt be ready for his holy appearance! So also will the idols of Egypt *tremble*, and the hearts of the peoples *melt within them*. Is not this suggesting that there are things in the deities and peoples of Egypt about which they should feel a sense of shame, and further, a deep concern at the dramatic arrival in their midst of no less than the Holy One of Israel?

Verse 2 speaks of a further effect upon the Egyptian people, setting them in conflicts amongst themselves. Apparently there were in ancient Egypt times of internal division and strife, such as we read about regarding the particular events spoken of in our present text, *Egyptians against Egyptians . . . neighbor against neighbor . . . city against city*. Thus in some spirit, it would seem, of panic, these peoples consult their *idols and the spirits of the dead* (v. 3). A prophet such as Isaiah of Jerusalem would have expected these people to have consulted a greater One, or greater Ones, than idols and the spirits of the dead. Verse 4 speaks of the Egyptians being handed over to *a hard master . . . a fierce king*, and we do indeed know of such happenings over the centuries, but as we cannot determine the date of writing of the present passage, we cannot say who is here being imagined. The reference would certainly appear to be regarding a suggested change of national leader.

With vv. 5–10 we read of the effect of this divine judgement upon the River Nile, that river which was expected at all times to be in flow, constantly bringing water from far away, all through the central part of the land. Yet here was the threat that this supposedly ever-dependable river would in fact become *dried up* (v. 5), its *canals* becoming *foul* (v. 6), resulting in its fishermen and other workers, such as linen makers and *weavers*, finding themselves out of work (vv. 7–10). That is to say, the hardly believable becoming fact!

Verses 11–14 go on to consider a different aspect of the whole experience of this time of crisis for the Egyptian people. The issue here is the apparent inadequacy, even the sheer incompetence, in the decision-making, and also in the utterances, of those who were supposed to be the *wise counselors* and advisers to the political leaders. In fact, those who were supposed to be the *wise counselors* of the Pharaoh are now giving *stupid counsel*. These (v. 11) are the *princes of Zoan*, a place known as Tanis in the Greek, and situated at the north-eastern corner of the Nile delta, not too far from Sinai, and spoken of in various parts of the Old Testament (Num 13:22; Isa 30:4; Ezek 30:14; Ps 78:12, 43). Yet there is further incompetent leadership, manifested in the *princes* of both *Zoan* and *Noph* (otherwise known as *Memphis*), who *have made Egypt stagger in all its doings* (vv. 13, 14). Thus is *Egypt* indeed in a parlous state (v. 15).

Nevertheless, it does seem to be that it is the Lord, the God of Israel, who has brought about this dreadful state of affairs in Egypt, this country that was once a place of refuge for Israelite peoples, and—at least for one of the New Testament Gospels—becomes again a place of refuge for the new-born Savior (Matt 2:13–18). Yet in the days that Isa 19:1–15 is speaking about there is so much that is wrong and misguided in this same land of Egypt. In fact, "both the political and economic foundations of Egypt will collapse under Yahweh's judgment."[8]

EGYPT IN THE FUTURE 19:16–25

This passage—so contrasting with what has preceded—is one of the Old Testament's most remarkable writings, in that it speaks of a future for the people of Egypt strikingly different from what is presented in the preceding oracle (19:1–15). Rather than the preceding *Neither head nor tail, palm branch or reed, will be able to do anything for Egypt* (19:15), now we are reading, *On that day there will be five cities in the land of Egypt that speak the language of Canaan and swear allegiance to the* Lord *of hosts* (19:18). Hans Wildberger in his commentary says about the passage, "One is not far from Paul's 'to the Jew first and also to the Greek' (Rom 1:16),"[9] and not infrequently is that commentator on Isaiah of a good number of years ago, George Adam Smith, quoted in his observation of these verses that they "form the most universal and 'missionary' of all Isaiah's prophecies."[10]

This oracle is made up of five short pieces, each one beginning, *On that day . . .* , the first comprising vv. 16–17, and concerned—and having within its words a certain note of aggression on the part of the Israelite speaker—with the Egyptians, who will be *trembling with fear before the might (hand) that the* Lord *of hosts raises against them* (v. 16). Perhaps this piece comes from a time of political and military weakness on the part of Egypt, and goes on to speak of the Egyptian fear that there is what is called here a *plan* of the Lord of hosts against them. Thus there is imagined here (v. 17) a continuation of that sense of *fear* on the part of the Egyptians spoken about in Isa 19:1–4.

---

8. Roberts, *First Isaiah*, 260.
9. Wildberger, *Isaiah 13–27*, 282.
10. George Adam Smith, *The Book of Isaiah*, Vol. 1, 275.

The second piece is in v. 18 and speaks of five cities of Egypt where the people speak the language of Canaan (that is, Hebrew). Presumably, this usage of Hebrew will be for liturgical purposes, for indeed this passage goes on to say that regarding the Egyptians they will *swear allegiance* to *the* Lord *of hosts*. In all probability the reference in this verse to the city called the *City of the Sun* is to be understood as Heliopolis, the Greek form of that wording.

The third piece is in vv. 19-23, and is the longest of these five compositions. It begins by speaking of the establishing of an *altar to the* Lord in the center of the land of Egypt, and further, of a *pillar to the* Lord at the border, these artefacts being intended to emphasize the presence and successes of Yhwh, Israel's God, in the wide lands of Egypt. The people of Egypt can now rely upon the Lord God (of Israel) to protect them (v. 20). More than that: the Lord God *will make himself known to the Egyptians*, that is, the Egyptians will be enabled to have a real relationship with Israel's God; which is to say, the God of the Israelites will now be also the God of the Egyptians. Further, the Egyptians in their relationship with the Lord (*will know*—means "have a relationship with") will be making their worship with sacrifices and burnt offerings, and moreover, they will make *vows to the* Lord *and perform them* (v. 21). Thus will the Lord experience the people of Egypt turning to him, and he will indeed *listen to their supplications and heal them* (v. 22).

The fourth piece is in v. 23 and speaks about a *highway* between Egypt and Assyria, with apparently no shortage of people upon it travelling between the great nations to worship together. We are here given a remarkable and vibrant envisioning of two of the most influential nations of the world in ancient times living in peace, with all being enabled to traverse the highways between their respective main centers, between their great cities. This picture certainly suggests there being not only peace, but also the possibility of lively trade and exchange of goods between these people and their nations, not forgetting their joining in united worship.

The fifth, and final, piece is in vv. 24-25, and speaks about the apparent equality and good relationships between Israel, Assyria, and Egypt (v. 24). It is asked that there may be the Lord's blessing on all three: *Blessed be Egypt my people, and Assyria the work of my hands, and Israel my heritage* (v. 25). Yet how special is what Israel is called to be in this renewed earth, along with, in the very center of the world, the great nations of Egypt and Assyria, those who are indeed called to be nothing less than *a blessing in the midst of the earth* (v. 24).

We cannot be at all sure when the composition of this remarkable passage is to be dated, and further, who was responsible for it. Perhaps the Old Testament texts closest in theological sentiment would be some parts of Isa 40-55, and if authorship has to be considered, then that could be a likely direction for our considerations to take. That is, that the authorship could well be that of the Israelite prophet that Old Testament scholarship has named the Second Isaiah, the one who many scholars believe was responsible for Isa 40–55. Yet perhaps more importantly than that, as far as Christians are concerned in the living out of their faith, is that they prayerfully seek to be servants and messengers of the Lord, the one who indeed could make them, in their day and age, *a blessing in the midst of the earth* (v. 24).

This is indeed a remarkable passage, and what Wildberger has to say about it is singularly appropriate, namely, that the author here would seem to have been deeply affected by the spirit that shaped Deutero-Isaiah, that is, Isa 40–55, even if they are more caught up with speaking in cultic categories than the one who composed that material, going on to say that here:

> the knowledge that Yahweh is sovereign over the peoples is treated with utter seriousness—indeed, not only that he is the Lord over all peoples as a judge, but that he claims them as his own possession and puts them into the stream of blessings, which had been made visible to Israel at first, but which now would spread over the "heathen" as well. One is not far from Paul's "to the Jew first and also to the Greek" (Rom 1:16).[11]

EGYPT AND ETHIOPIA 20:1–6

This short chapter has similarities with at least some of the preceding Oracles against the Nations, such as those found in Isa 14:28–32 and 18:1–6, and yet at the same time there are some differences. Not only is there here the dating formula of v. 1, but in what follows there is also the acting out of the prophet's message in his going about naked and barefoot. As far as the matter of dating is concerned, we are told that what is being spoken about here is when Ashdod, one of the five main Philistine cities, was defeated by *Sargon*, the king of Assyria. This is generally regarded as 711 BCE. Further, this oracle does not concern the lands and dwellings of Judah and Jerusalem, but rather those of Egypt and Ethiopia (Kush/Cush), but it is perhaps a message that the people of Israel should be made aware of, namely the fact that such things are liable to take place in those lands where there are leaders and peoples who are not living faithfully under the lordship of the Assyrians. Perhaps there is a warning here that the people of Israel should take heed of such happenings in another kingdom.

---

11. Wildberger, *Isaiah 13–27*, 282.

In vv. 2–3 we read of the reasons for the prophet being naked, essentially to indicate the fate not of his own people but that of *Egypt and Ethiopia*. This we read about in vv. 3–4, *Just as my servant Isaiah has walked naked and barefoot for three years as a sign and a portent against Egypt and Ethiopia, so shall the king of Assyria lead away the Egyptians as captives and the Ethiopians as exiles*. Certainly, for the prophet to have acted in such a way must have been particularly demanding, not only for considerations of cold and warmth, but also the sense of personal shame about the act, as, for example, Gen 3:7 and 9:22 show was prevalent for those peoples of old. Further, we are told that this took place for the extended time of no less than three years (vv. 2–3). Presumably the walking naked actions were intended to convey the meaning that people were being warned of the danger that they could be taken away—*naked and barefoot* (v. 4), just like the prophet. That was, we are told, the particular danger that the peoples of Egypt and Ethiopia had to live with.[12]

The final verse (v. 6) speaks of *inhabitants of this coastland*, but the particular coastlands being referred to are not made clear to us. They could have been either Philistines or recalcitrant Judeans. Yet, as J. J. M. Roberts observes, it is likely that the prophet's message and warning to his own people, to their king, by then Hezekiah, was that they should not fall into the temptation to accept the invitation of the Philistines and the Nubians to join in an anti-Assyrian revolt.[13] Indeed, the essential message for contemporary readers here is clear, namely that all should put their trust in the Lord, in the one where real power and care for the people are to be found. Further, that is surely the ongoing and perpetually relevant message of this short chapter in the Old Testament book of the prophet Isaiah, namely that the real help in earthly life is ever to be found in the Lord God.

THE FALL OF BABYLON 21:1–10

From the point of view of critical biblical scholarship this is a somewhat demanding passage. That Isa 21:1–10 is about Babylon seems to be made clear in v. 9, with its *Fallen, fallen is Babylon; and all the images of her gods lie shattered on the ground*, but by whom, and when, the writing of this oracle took place is the subject of disagreement, and various dates have been proposed, some of these clearly later than the time of the ministry of the prophet Isaiah, therefore requiring non-Isaianic authorship. A further possibility that

---

12. For more about this matter of Hebrew prophetic symbolism, see Stacey, *Prophetic Drama in the Old Testament*.

13. Roberts, *First Isaiah*, 271.

has been suggested for this passage is that we have something in the nature of a "palimpsest," a writing to which later material has been added. I do not intend to discuss here the matters of the date and authorship of this passage, but for those who are interested and wish to pursue the matter I suggest consulting the works of both Clements and Blenkinsopp on *Isaiah 1–39* listed in the bibliography of the present work. Also on this chapter see Macintosh; *Isaiah XXI: A Palimpsest*.

Further, there is a very strong note and emphasis here on the power and might that is due to fall upon what is clearly (v. 9) *Babylon*, involving a *whirlwind* (v. 1) coming from the *Negeb*, the desert area to the south of Judah, which coming from the wild south will constitute a real sense of peril for those caught up in its trail, that is the Babylonians. The reassuring message of v. 2 for the people of Judah and Jerusalem is that rescue for them from the Babylonian power will be through the limited might of the small countries of *Elam* and *Media* (v. 2). In fact, artistic reliefs in Persepolis and Susa show *Elamites* serving in the armies of Cyrus the Persian at a later time. We are told that it was through the power and rule of Cyrus that those exiled people of Judah were enabled to return to their homeland, as we read in Isa 40–55. In this regard, see the mention of Cyrus in Isa 44:28; 45:1. This, of course, suggests a date of composition of the passage under consideration as being a good deal later than the time of Isaiah of Jerusalem, the "first" Isaiah. Meanwhile, a deep sense of amazement, even *anguish*, (v. 3) falls upon the prophet—presumably our writer here—as he contemplates such future events regarding the overthrow of a major world power of the day (v. 4).

Verse 5, then, seems to be suggesting that when this crisis fell upon the Babylonians they were engaged in feasting, the sort of activity perhaps being reflected in the account in Daniel 5. Meanwhile our prophet of the present passage speaks about posting a watchman (*lookout*) who will be on the watch for any such stirring events (v. 6), in particular for happenings that could well indicate the coming of horsemen and riders on donkeys and camels—could these be of an army and all its accoutrements and personnel? Thus let the watchman *listen diligently, very diligently* (v. 7). And indeed next we do read of the watcher on duty (v. 8), and then what was observed, this being an attack upon Babylon, and the shattering of *all the images of her gods*, which are now reduced to lying on the ground (v. 9). In v. 10 that individual, that *threshed and winnowed one*, sounds as if they must be a representative of the people of Judah and Jerusalem, now being assured of a truly positive change for the better, indeed the end of the aggressive foreign power that has earlier held them and so many others in thrall. R. E. Clements says of this final verse, v. 10, "In his concluding comment the prophet reveals the full depth of his personal interest in the judgment coming upon the people of Babylon."[14]

Thus is recorded in the Old Testament book of Isaiah some prophet's words about the fall of Babylon. Who the person—whether prophet, scribe, or editor—was is a matter about which we cannot be at all sure. Nor can we be sure about the possible growth of the passage, whether it is a palimpsest, having been added to at later stages after its first having been written. We can be sure and certain about none of these matters. But what is surely of greater import is this aspect, as it is expressed and presented to us in Oswalt's commentary on Isaiah 1–39, namely:

> But there is a word of hope in all of this judgment. The whole process goes forward at the word of Israel's God. History is not out of control, nor in the hand of some demon who wishes to destroy Israel. The shocks that had come and were yet to come could be endured so long as Israel could yet believe that it was God who was bringing her through the fire.[15]

PROPHECIES ABOUT ARABIA 21:11–17

We read here three oracles addressed to areas of Arabia, the first being *Dumah* in vv. 11–12. This was an oasis in the Arabian desert, being referred to in Gen 25:14, and spoken of here as one person addressed by another, the latter who is in *Seir*, a region of Edom, to the south-east of the Dead Sea. The individual being addressed is the watchman, who is asked *what of the night?* (v. 11) However, the answer the *watchman* gives seems hardly to be an answer at all, *Morning comes, and also the night* (v. 12), which is perhaps intended to mean that the time of suffering and difficulty will one day end, but that yet there is still a time of darkness, another *night* to be endured.

The second oracle is in vv. 13–15, and speaks about the desert oases of *Dedan* (v. 13) and *Tema* (v. 14), and what is being detailed here would seem to be the plight of travelers, maybe fugitives from situations of conflict. Such beings are also spoken about in v. 15, *For they have fled from the swords, from the drawn sword* . . . .

The third oracle is in vv. 16–17, and comes from the setting of *Kedar*, which was in Arabia, this being referred to in Isa 60:7 and Ezek 27:21. *Kedar* is here being warned that any glory it may have had, perhaps through caravan trading, will soon be taken from it, so that both its glory (v. 16) and its

---

14. Clements, *Isaiah 1–39*, 179.
15. Oswalt, *Isaiah 1–39*, 397.

weapons (*bows*, [v. 17], presumably either for defence or even aggression) will become *few*.

The dates and historical settings for these short passages and oracles are neither stated, nor are they clear to us. Those concerned with such matters can find them discussed by the commentators on these passages.[16] What however is made clear to us is the limited earthly time there is for individual nations to have their moments of power and influence, and to be the beneficiaries of their opportunities for business and trade. Yet above and historically beyond—both before and after—us all is the Lord God, who in the closing words of these three brief and somewhat mysterious oracles is portrayed as having *spoken* (v. 17), surely with the unuttered, the silent conviction and confidence, that thus also will he ever do.

COMPLACENCY IN JERUSALEM 22:1–14

In the immediately preceding chapters the texts have been progressing around various lands and peoples that neighbored Judah and Jerusalem. Now we come to the city of Jerusalem itself, and it is clear that what is being spoken about here is a city in a state of crisis, with some of its leaders making their exits from its midst (see v. 3). Presumably this is because they are observing that destruction is taking place all around them (v. 4). Further, it is clear that now it is the city of Jerusalem itself, the holy city, that is this city of destruction. This is made clear in references such as *He has taken away the covering of Judah* (v. 8), *city of David* (v. 9), *houses of Jerusalem* (v. 10).

What about a possible date of this *destruction*? It would be generally regarded as referring to one of the major happenings to Jerusalem, in particular to one of, either 701 BCE, or the later one of 587 BCE. The first of these (the 701 BCE possibility) seems to have the larger scholarly backing, and I am content to go along with that. In that particular year the Assyrian ruler Sennacherib laid siege to the major towns and fortresses of Judah, and thus Judah did indeed suffer major disaster, as we read in 2 Kgs 19. However, we further read, particularly in 2 Kgs 19:35, that in fact the Assyrian camp had urgently to be evacuated, and thus was Jerusalem spared, for what turned out to be about another hundred or so years until it was under serious siege once again.[17]

---

16. For these matters of dating here, I suggest the commentaries of Clements and Blenkinsopp could be consulted.

17. For these historical matters and the apparently associated chapters of the book of Isaiah, see the Introduction to the present work, xv–xvi.

What, then, we have in Isa 22:1–14 is in the main a lament over the situation of the besieged city of Jerusalem, yet the city that came to be relieved. However, in v. 1 we appear to have a somewhat strange opening statement, and perhaps the *valley of vision* (which presumably means the valley the prophet saw in vision) refers to what follows in v. 5, namely the experiences of *tumult and trampling and confusion*, and what looks like the city walls receiving a *battering*. Expressed here is what seems to be a real sense of there having been some misrule and failure on the part of Judean leaders, this being first expressed in v. 2, and then with v. 3 going on to speak of them making their escape from the besieged city and their own responsibilities. This causes great distress for the prophet, who, we read, weeps *for the destruction of my beloved people* (v. 4).

The somewhat distressing message of v. 5 is that there is more of this to come, a further crisis that will bring about *a battering down of walls*, presumably of Jerusalem; and *a cry for help to the mountains*, that is, we assume, an appeal for assistance from those Judean people who lived among the hills surrounding Jerusalem. If we are correct in regarding the present passage as reflecting the crisis of the Assyrian attack on Jerusalem in 701 BCE, the "more" of this crisis that is still to come could then refer to the later Babylonian siege of 587 BCE, which brought about an even worse situation for Judah and Jerusalem than that of 701 BCE.

With vv. 6–8a the account of Jerusalem's distress continues. We cannot be sure what is the significance of the references to *Elam* and *Kir* (v. 6), that is, on whose side were they in action? Were they seeking to assist in the Assyrian attack upon Jerusalem, or were they rather seeking to help in the defence of the city? Verse 7 seems clearer, and appears to be a reference to the very dire situation of the city, and that is presumably the significance of the expression, *He has taken away the covering of Judah* (v. 8a).

Verses 8b–11 continue to speak about the preparation for the defence of Jerusalem, making particular mention of the weapons of the *House of the Forest* (v. 8b), which was the armory of the royal palace, this being detailed in 1 Kgs 7:2–5; 10:17. Then further, in the city's defence are mentioned *walls*, for whose strengthening it seem that some *houses* had to be sacrificed (v. 10), and of course the supply and saving of *water* (v. 11a), a matter that had earlier been given good attention—see 2 Sam 5:8; 2 Kgs 20:20.

Yet what was missing amongst all these physical and necessary steps and preparations was the serious looking to the Lord for his help (v. 11b). But then, according to the account in Isa 22:12–14, there is to be a sense of "celebration" (of a resigned and desperate kind), for it appeared that the attackers of Jerusalem—the Assyrians—were going to be victorious, so that among the defenders, rather than *weeping and mourning* (v. 12) there was rather the approach *Let us eat and drink, for tomorrow we die* (v. 13b). Thus does the prophet pass on the divine word he has received concerning a long-term sense of judgement on the people of Jerusalem (v. 14). Yet in the meantime, while they have a certain sense of freedom before the coming judgement, let them celebrate while they can—that is, before the worst takes place!

Clearly this account is intended to speak of a crisis that deeply affected the people of Jerusalem, who are portrayed both as making their military preparations for the defence of the holy city of Jerusalem, but who seem also to feel that they are doomed to die in the face of the overwhelming power of the enemy. Yet they are not praying or mourning their desperate situation, and nor do we hear of them appealing for the help and assistance of their prophet of the Lord, or even more, of this prophet's Lord. In fact, the prophet is portrayed as being aware of this lack of religious concerns in this scene of Judean national crisis, and has the courage in the face of everything to warn his people that the word he, as their prophet, has received from the Lord is, *Surely this iniquity will not be forgiven you until you die, says the Lord God of hosts* (v. 14). This is the word of judgement that the prophet proclaims to his people in their time of crisis. Let this Jerusalem generation hear this word of the Lord. Further, let those today who in their present times read these words heed those words of warning that are perhaps being proclaimed, even to them, even in their own day.

SHEBNA AND ELIAKIM 22:15-25

This passage is one of that small number of texts contained in the writings of the Hebrew prophets that are about individual people, about those in particular who reveal certain human inadequacies and sinfulness in the discharge of their God-given duties. For other examples of this in the prophetic books see Amos 7:16-17 and Jer 20:1-6; 28:12-17. This emphasis on the inadequacies manifested by individuals applies only to the first part of this passage, namely vv. 15-19, verses that concern the steward Shebna and his misguided behavior. These verses are followed in vv. 20-25 with a narrative concerning another steward, but this time one who acted honorably and well, namely Eliakim. Though we are not told this, it does not seem unreasonable to regard Eliakim as having been appointed to take over the ministry and responsibilities of the steward Shebna.

In v. 15 Shebna is described as *master of the household*, and we assume that this must be the royal household in Jerusalem, which we also seem to be reading about in Isa 36:3; 37:2, and further in 2 Kgs 18:18 and 19:2. However, here in Isa 22:16 we are told that Isaiah was called by the LORD to go to Shebna and inform him that he had been found wanting, in particular that he had, so to speak, been feathering his nest for the future days and preparing for himself and his relatives a rather well-appointed tomb in a setting of high rocks. Thus some dreadful things are due to happen to Shebna (vv. 17–18), these being because he was a disgrace *to your master's house!* (v. 18). That is, Shebna will be pulled down from his post and associated responsibilities, because of his highly unsatisfactory conduct in his high office (v. 19).

Thus, in vv. 20–25 we go on to read about the new appointment of someone to take over those responsibilities that Shebna formerly had, namely *Eliakim son of Hilkiah* (v. 20). This means, among other things, that Eliakim will inherit the *robe* and *sash*, presumably items of formal dress intended to affirm his appointment to his new high office (v. 21). Further, he will receive *the key of the house of David*, this being placed upon *his shoulder* because of its size and weight, such being the dimensions and weights of certain ancient keys (v. 22). The text goes on to note further details in vv. 23–25 concerning the high and highly important office that had come to Eliakim, and eventually of the demise of those responsibilities—presumably as a result of the defeat of Judah and Jerusalem and the reality of the Babylonian exile (see 2 Kgs 25:1–12), and it is quite possible that they were added at a later time to the original text of the biblical book of Isaiah.

Yet certainly some of the words in this short passage about the high office in Jerusalem to which Eliakim was appointed are found to be quoted elsewhere, both in the New Testament, and also in certain Christian liturgies. Isaiah 22:22 we find quoted in Matt 16:19, when Jesus announced to Simon Peter that he will be given high office in the new kingdom of heaven, and thus will be given *keys of the kingdom of heaven*. The matter of the keys to heavenly fellowship and other matters are also spoken about in the book of Revelation (3:7). Further, *the key of the house of David* (22:22) makes an appearance among the antiphons of the church's Advent liturgy, *O clavis David*, and also in the Advent hymn from the eighteenth century, in the translation of John Mason Neale and others, "O Come, O come, Immanuel," in the verse that begins, "O come, thou Key of David, come . . . ."

The other issue that is treated in this comparatively short passage is the matter of faithfulness or otherwise in the holding of high offices, and fulfilling tasks in some of the most important roles in both national, and also international, life. How all too easy it appears to be that those who rise to high offices in national life find themselves forgetting to be servants of the people, and begin, as it were, to cut their tomb on high, being tempted to begin carving a habitation for themselves in the rock (v. 16).

TYRE OF PHOENICIA 23:1–18

We come here to the last of the collection of oracles against the foreign nations that we find in the Isaiah book, yet there are some difficulties that attend our study of it. In the first place, there is a whole series of problems with the text, which is quite simply difficult for us to understand in a number of places. Thus it is surely not without significance that there are a considerable number of different readings of words found in the Dead Sea Scrolls of this chapter, more than we find in our received Hebrew text. That suggests that those early copiers and translators found difficulty in dealing with the Hebrew text. In general terms in what follows I am content to go by the text we find in the NRSV, though as we proceed it will be seen that I do have a few comments to make about it.

The second difficulty we encounter with this chapter is to understand what is the historical setting from which it comes, and no less than four different periods have been suggested for this. Further, it is widely thought that this chapter does not come from the prophet Isaiah, but who it might have come from we do not know. Nevertheless, we should surely bear in mind that those who put together the various chapters and parts of what has come down to us as the book of Isaiah, in spite of these various difficulties, did include this chapter in their final work, and thus it is that we in our day and age take it and read it believing that there may be within it a biblical word for us today.

Verse 1 speaks of the past glories of *Tyre*, the Phoenician port on the Mediterranean coast. It had a name, a reputation, for its trading in ships with such places as *Tarshish*, which was most likely on what we know as the (eastern) Spanish coast, possibly close to present day Huelva. Yet now it has been attacked and plundered by people from Kittim, what is now called Cyprus (and so rendered in NRSV). Let the peoples of neighboring *Sidon*, a trading port to the north of Tyre, join in expressing sorrow at the fate of Tyre (v. 2). Further, also let those peoples of *Shihor*, a trading city on the River Nile, lament the loss of the contribution of trade in *grain* with the Tyrian merchants (v. 3). With v. 4 we are taken back in thought to *Sidon*, for the peoples there have suffered considerable losses with what has happened to Tyre. In vv. 5–8 we read of the call for mourning by the peoples both of *Tyre* and *Tarshish*, but especially it seems the author wished to stress the sense of overwhelming loss in the demise of *Tyre*; how can things like this happen in such a place, *whose merchants were princes, whose traders were the honored of the earth?* (v. 8).

In v. 9 something by way of explanation of the question is presented, namely, how can such a situation of tragedy be understood? The answer presented here is that all this does come from the LORD, who *has planned it—to defile the pride of all glory, to shame all the honored ones of the earth.* It does have to be said that many will not find this a wholly convincing argument to explain such a tragic setback for so many peoples, that is, to call to account a prevailing sense of *pride*. In a number of places in Isa 1–39 this language of the LORD planning (Hebrew *geʾon*) this or that matter is used (see also 5:19; 14:24–27; 19:12, 17; 28:29) and it indicates a divine response to human "pride," the over-inflated assessment of one's qualities and abilities. Yet the usage of such a word in the present context will leave the theological problem of how it can be that the God of love will allow that certain tragic things should happen to reasonably good-living people—and moreover be effected by none other than God? This is one of the great theological problems set before those who believe in a God of love. In fact, the Old Testament does present us with a range of possible answers, some being more convincing than others.[18]

The emphasis in v. 10 would seem to be that the sea-borne trade for Tyre is coming to an end with her having no harbor for the *ships of Tarshish* to use; in v. 12 there is talk about *Cyprus*, perhaps this having become a new place for the erstwhile traders of *Sidon*.

It does have to be said that in Isa 23:10–12 we do have some trouble making sense of the received Hebrew text, but we are helped by a number of differences found in the texts of the Dead Sea Scrolls. These are to be seen in the modern English translation of the NRSV. This is a good example of how in our Isaiah studies we have benefitted by the discovery by the Dead Sea of at least two copies of most of the book of Isaiah. Unfortunately, after this in v. 13 we have further difficulties. This is widely thought to be a verse added at a rather later date than the original Isaianic material surrounding it, and seems to be reflecting the time when Babylonians had taken over from Assyrians as the dominant overlord.

Then there is v. 14, which returns us to the theme of the opening verse, and presumably is intended to round off this oracle against a nation. However, while in v. 1 the *ships of Tarshish*, according to the original Hebrew, are to *wail* over the loss of *houses*, in some early translations this became "fortress," as in v. 14, where there is indeed talk of wailing the loss of their *fortress*. Whatever is the intended reading is, perhaps those concerned are being portrayed as being warned about the basic defences of their city, for thus their situation is parlous indeed.[19]

18. On this subject see Thompson, *Where Is the God of Justice?* and the comments of Roberts on this particular passage, *First Isaiah*, 301–2.

19. Note how in v. 1 NRSV reads *fortress* for the Hebrew *houses*, presumably to make the vv. 1 and 14 have agreement in wording *fortress*. Yet that may be felt to be

Verses 15–18 take us into the future of the life of the city of Tyre, and it certainly reads like a good future. This is spoken about as being in seventy years time. Further, whereas v. 16 speaks of that future life as being a turning away from a life dominated by trading, the dominant feature of the future here, alas, will be one of harlotry (v. 17), while the preceding verse speaks of *the song about the prostitute* (v. 16). Yet with v. 18 we read of the assurance that after these things are past there will one day be a new time of trading, but this will be one in which *her merchandise* will be dedicated to the LORD, and further, that supplies of *food and fine clothing* will be available in abundance *for those who live in the presence of the LORD*.

One cannot help feeling that this very positive ending to the oracle concerning Tyre is also intended to constitute an appropriate ending to this whole block of material in chs. 13–23 concerning the prophetical words about future days when there will be faithfulness to the will of God, days that will bring about full and appropriate provision for the people of the LORD. We can hardly avoid comparing this final picture in these Oracles of the Nations with that earlier picture we are given in Isa 2:2–4, which speaks about times when peoples of many nations will come to the mountain of the LORD, and ask that they may be taught how they should walk in the ways of the LORD. What we have in Isa 2:2–4 is surely a vision that one day many peoples will come to live lives of faith and hope in the LORD, as indeed we are given in the concluding verses of the Isaianic Oracles of the Nations, in particular in 23:18. Further, this is one of the themes that will be taken up in later parts of the Isaiah book, in particular in the material in parts of chs. 40–55, but it is also present where there is good news for a wide group of people, expressed, for example, in the vision presented in the third part of the Isaiah book (chs. 56–66) of the future house of the LORD, namely, *for my house shall be called a house of prayer for all peoples* (56:7b).

---

tending towards a wish to "even things out," whereas they are perhaps intended in v. 14 to come to something of a climax, namely that in v. 14 there is the talk of the *fortress* actually being *destroyed*.

III

Isaiah 24–27
Visions of the Future

FOR AN INTRODUCTION TO these chapters, which have a series of words concerning future times, in the particular style and language we find in parts of the Bible called "apocalyptic," meaning unveiling, uncovering, revealing, see above pp. xx–xxi. There in that introductory material are given some details about this particular type of biblical literature, and in an especial way about those parts presented in this style of writing that we find in the book of Isaiah. There is also something there in that introduction about the significance of the material in these chapters for the times in which they were written.

JUDGEMENT ON THE WORLD 24:1–23

With the opening verses (vv. 1–3) of this passage we are introduced to the theme of this chapter, and indeed to the whole of this section of the book of Isaiah (chs. 24–27), namely that the entire created earth lies under the judgement of the LORD, and that something quite dreadful is about to take place, this being that the LORD is to make a complete waste of—*make desolate* (v. 1)—the whole. Presumably, this will be effected by the LORD, here portrayed as the one who *will twist its surface and scatter its inhabitants* (v. 1). That sounds as if it is giving a warning regarding a coming earthquake, and that any humans who survive that catastrophe will have to go in search of dwelling places elsewhere. Further, this happening will have an effect upon everyone in the community, whether they are *people* or *priests*, *slaves* or *masters, maids* or *mistresses*, in fact, all peoples, all of them, will be affected by this catastrophe (v. 2). That is, all *the earth* will be dreadfully stricken, for the reason that it is none other than the Lord of all the earth—indeed, of the whole of the creation—who has spoken the appropriate word (v. 3).

Thus is the earth beset with these terrible happenings; v. 4 makes the point that as well as earth and world in a state of chaos, yet so also, according to the translation of NRSV, will *the heavens languish together with the earth*. The word here translated in NRSV "heavens" may not mean what we normally associate with that word; it is a different Hebrew word (*merom*) that is possibly intended to indicate high ground, heights. If that was intended by the writer here, the verse would perhaps then be indicating that all parts of the earth, from heights to depths, are in a state of having to *languish*. It is certainly difficult to believe that the prophet wished to say that it was the will of God that the heavens should *languish*.

In v. 5 there is emphasis on the sense of things having been *polluted*, this being caused by the *inhabitants*, those who have *violated the statutes, broken the everlasting covenant*. This seems to be intended to indicate that this part of the crisis is not due to what God has done, but rather is the result of the sinful activities and attitudes of the people of earth. Further, we may observe that it is certainly bold language being used here that speaks of *the everlasting covenant*, this also being spoken about in Gen 9:16; 17:7; Isa 55:3 and elsewhere, and surely intended to speak of God's eternal relationship with his people, and this in spite of the tendencies of those people to sin, and thus to be going away from the Lord. Yet, of course, here in Isa 24:5 it is emphasized that it is the human partners who have broken, failed to keep, what the Lord wished to be an *everlasting covenant*.

Thus we are told in v. 6 that due to this human sinfulness there is a curse upon the *earth*, such as is spoken about in Deut 27:15–26. This indicates what for the Old Testament is the seriousness of the relationship between the Lord and his people, and about the constant call for human faithfulness to the Lord, and to the keeping of his covenant relationship with his people. According to our present passage in Isa 24, a series of crises descend upon the people and their lives in the world, these happenings being caused by their human sinfulness. Thus we read about the crisis taking place and being experienced by so many at the time of the vine harvest (vv. 7–9), and the associated lack of the characteristic joy and celebration usually experienced at that time of harvest and thanksgiving (vv. 10–13).

With vv. 14–16a we have an expression of praise for the sheer greatness of the Lord, and thus we read of singing and shouting from western parts of the earth (v. 14) and the giving of glory in the east (v. 15), in fact, there are thus heard *songs of praise, of glory to the Righteous One* (v. 16a) from the very ends of the earth. Yet meanwhile the author of this account (or these accounts) speaks with a very different emphasis, for he observes that those who continue to deal treacherously remain. Indeed, we read here: *the treacherous deal very treacherously* (v. 16b). Further, the passage continues with a truly dire series of pictures, not only about the sinfulness of certain parts of the human population, but also about the exceedingly dire fate that they must expect to come their way (v. 17). Here the writer in speaking of the *terror*, the *pit*, and the *snare*, uses three Hebrew words, clearly intentionally put together, their similar sounds having a strikingly alliterative effect when read in the Hebrew, and all of them speaking of the coming judgement. This may all seem rather forced, even appearing to be using "over the top" language, but then, we are reading and dealing here with the language of apocalyptic, which is clearly intended to convey the picture of the situation for the people of God in days when some of their leaders believed them to be in the most serious of dangers.

This surely is also reflected in vv. 18–20, with its repetition of language concerning *terror* and *the pit*, and now also the *snare* (v. 18), these being followed by the statement about the opening of the *windows of heaven* (compare this with what is portrayed as the great flood in Gen 7:11; 8:2), and the very foundations of the earth trembling. The whole cosmic order seems to be portrayed as existing in a state of failure (v. 19), and nowhere does there seem to be any place of security for the human beings, for even the very earth itself is in a state of insecurity. The fact is that the earth has indeed little or no security, for its life is being infected, even dominated, by sinfulness, this surely being due to the ways in which the human beings are choosing to live (v. 20).

This whole situation is brought to a conclusion with what we read about in vv. 21–23, that is, with God's judgement upon both the hosts of heaven and also upon the human persons on the earth (v. 21), all of them being made prisoners of the Lord and under the divine judgement (v. 22). Even those bright lights of the whole creation, the *sun* and the *moon*, will feel a sense of shame (v. 23a), for before them, and also before *the elders* of the people of Israel, the Lord of hosts will reign on Mount Zion and in Jerusalem.

Indeed, before these elders, that is the human leaders appointed to lead the people in their lives on earth, the Lord *will manifest his glory* (v. 23b), indicating that he will reveal himself as he truly was, and is, and ever shall be. Indeed, this will perhaps be in the manner of divine otherness, as we are told it was for those elders of Israel with their leader Moses, at Sinai: "and they saw the God of Israel. Under his feet there was something like a pavement of sapphire stone, like the very heaven for clearness. God did not lay his hand on the chief men of the people of Israel; also they beheld God, and they ate and drank" (Exod 24:10–11). Then again, it could perhaps be compared with and illustrated by what we are told happened for the prophet Isaiah: "In the year that King Uzziah died, I saw the Lord sitting on a throne, high and lofty; and the hem of his robe filled the temple. Seraphs were in attendance above him. . . . And one called to another and said: 'Holy, holy, holy, is the LORD of hosts; the whole earth is full of his glory'" (6:1–3).

BANQUET ON MOUNT ZION 25:1–12

This is a remarkable chapter of the book of Isaiah, it being noteworthy for its profound expressions of confidence in the LORD God. The LORD's people on earth are called upon to rejoice in and to give praise to God for all that he has done in the life of the world, and in particular in the lives of his people, effecting divine works that have brought about great changes to the lives of those people; works and changes that unsurprisingly call forth much praise to the LORD from human beings.

Thus this chapter begins with the note of praise to God, in particular for all that he has done. Perhaps there is a feeling that this is the time, the season, for human praise and thanksgiving to be given to the LORD for now the people of earth can see what clearly had been the plan of the LORD formulated in ages long ago. Although what has happened has been taking place in the immediate presence of the people of earth in their particular earthly days, those were in fact works springing from divine *plans formed of old, faithful and sure*. Yet it is a fact that for the human beings concerned it has been only now in their present day that they have been able to see, and maybe experience, something of these *wonderful things* (v. 1b); ancient ideas yet only now, human ages after their divine formulation, have they come to be put into effect.

Verse 2 goes on to speak of the effects of these divine plans, and then the associated divine actions, that do lead to transformations—in a particularly negative sense for those aliens and their palace, which in fact through the divine acts will cease to be. Thus it will happen (v. 3) that even strong people will find themselves wishing to have an opportunity to glorify the covenant people, not understanding that the great changes for the Israelite peoples have in fact been the LORD's work. Verse 4 would seem to be referring to the ministry of the people of God towards those who are poor, or for those in distress, this being expressed in the language of bad weathers, and speaking of those who have themselves provided *a refuge to the needy . . . a shelter from the rainstorm and a shade from the heat*. Yet the verse makes clear that this is but imagery so as to express a place of help for those suffering *the blast of the ruthless*. Such imagery continues in v. 5, but also speaks of the divine stilling of the enemy activities—*the song of the ruthless was stilled*.

With vv. 6-9 we are led imaginatively, but very graphically, into a remarkable scene on a mountain where there will take place a great banquet, a great feast, one that is prepared for, and will be celebrated by, a wide range of peoples. The language of v. 6 certainly suggests that the good gifts of the Lord will not be just for Israelite peoples, but that rather this feast of rich food, will have been made *for all peoples* (v. 6).

The imagined setting for this celebratory meal is something of a cross between Mount Horeb (also known in the Old Testament as Sinai), which we read about in the book of Exodus (see Exod 24:9-11), and Mount Zion, the very center of Jerusalem and the heart of its life, and does remind us of such Old Testament passages as Isa 2:2-4; 45:14; 60:3-7; Pss 72:10; 96:7-8; Zeph 3:9-10. What we also have here is the assurance that under God there will be a resurrection of the dead, a matter, generally speaking, about which the Old Testament is somewhat coy, even hesitant. Yet there is a sense of confidence here about the acts, the power, and indeed the authority of the Lord God: *he will swallow up death forever* (v. 8). In the Isaiah book this matter is spoken about also in 26:19 and it speaks of the overwhelming power and authority of the Lord God. Indeed, as the German commentator Wildberger expressed the matter, speaking about the thought of the Isaiah book here: "the actual source of the idea of resurrection in the Old Testament is connected with the confession of faith that anticipates that Yahweh would rule without any limitations."[1]

This is one of only a small number of places in the Old Testament where there is confident talk of a resurrection of the dead. It is thought by a number of scholars that talk of life after death suggests that this passage will likely have come from times a good deal later than the rest of the contents of the book of Isaiah, for such a belief is not really attested in earlier biblical texts. We should remember that this life-after-death material occurs in a section of apocalyptic material, and such writings generally seem to come from fairly late times. For example, the contents of the book of Daniel, considered by most scholars to have been written in the second century BCE, seem to be referring to not dissimilar times. Even so, it can certainly be difficult to date materials that refer to such matters as life after death, along with other matters of thought and religious belief, as opposed to those that have an explicit historic linkage and setting. Nevertheless, what is being spoken about here is truly an expression of great confidence in what God

---

1. Wildberger, *Isa 13-27*, 533.

can do for the lives of his people in the time and the realm they will come to experience following their facing up to, along with the possible associated traumas of, death.

With vv. 9–12 we have two topics, the first being in v. 9 where we find an expression of thanksgiving to God for the deliverance he has brought to his people. Presumably this is referring to the deliverance that has been spoken about in the previous verses, and the suggested response in which the people are invited to be involved is to *be glad and rejoice in his salvation*. Verse 10 moves on to speak of the Moabites, and the sins they have committed, and the aggravations to the Israelites they have caused. Just what these were we are not told, but the fate for them being spoken of here is of being trodden down *as straw is trodden down in a dung-pit*. This would seem to be a reference to a cesspit, or a midden. Indeed, there seems to have been a somewhat longstanding hostility between Moab and the Israelites, as we see in such passages as Num 21:1—24:17; Judg 3:12–30; 11:26; Ezra 9:1; Neh 13:1, 23 and elsewhere. Further, it does look as if what is wished upon them here is a long period of suffering for the aggravations Israelites have suffered as a result of those Moabite attitudes and actions. The Moabites are warned in v. 12 that their dependence upon their high walls and fortifications are misjudged, and that the walls will be found wanting.

What we have in Isaiah 25 exhibits a range of issues to do with human life in the world, for not only is there here talk of the assurance of the Lord's presence and power with his people, both for their earthly lives and also for their earthly lives in the face of their physical enemies, that they may indeed experience physical strength sufficient to resist the powers of those enemies. Yet there is also here the assurance for people about their own personal and individual lives, in fact that they can be assured of a life beyond earthly life. The confidence being expressed is that after earthly death there can indeed be the assurance of a new and spiritual life. Thus this chapter has something of a gathering together of both the world of politics—in which there is concern with the matter of the city, with walls and military fortifications, and all such associated earthly issues—and also matters to do with the realm of ongoing faith and trust in the Lord. That is to say, what is also being set forth here is the assurance that these people may find through their trust in the Lord the promise of the reality of eternal life at the completion of earthly life. Moreover, it further needs to be affirmed that there is also to be found within this one chapter talk both of matters of religion and faith, and also those issues of what we would call political considerations. The double assurance for our lives of both of these aspects and issues continues to be a vital matter to so many people who live in the contemporary world all these centuries later.

Thus it is hardly surprising that in the current arrangement of biblical readings in the Revised Common Lectionary, over its three-year cycle, Isa 25 makes appearances no less than four times. Verses 1–9 appear once (on the 28th Sunday in Ordinary Time, but this in all three years of the cycle, A, B, C), while vv. 6–9 occur three times (two of these being on Easter Day, and one on All Saints Day). Christopher Sietz says, "The final unit of chapter 25 reflects the seriousness with which God judges any trace of human pride that threatens to undo his plan for a feast of grand proportions where all nations will confess him as Lord and give thanks for his salvation."[2]

NEW LIFE 26:1–21

In Isaiah chapter 26 we are dealing with two psalm-like passages, vv. 1–6 and 7–21, both of these expressing a real sense of confidence in the Lord, and also speaking remarkably positively of the future of the Lord's people and their land of Judah, and in particular of their capital city and religious center of Jerusalem. We consider these two passages, one at a time.

The first, vv. 1–6, is presented as a song whose theme is that the people of Judah and Jerusalem have a city, which we are told is a *strong city*, whose God-given strength is summed up in the words *victory like walls and bulwarks* (v. 1). This will truly be the work of God, a divine deliverance for the people of God, and for those people—that is, those people who are both and at the same time people of Israel and also people of God (*the righteous nation that keeps faith*)—the city gates will be thrown open (v. 2). In v. 3 we are told what the result will be for those who trust in God, those whom Blenkinsopp translated "those of trustful mind"; namely that they will be kept in perfect peace. (The fact is that biblical Hebrew does not have the grammatical comparative ["better"] or the superlative ["best"] of nouns, so in order to convey that grammatical sense it has to do things such as happens here, and simply repeats the one word [*in peace . . . in peace*], that is to indicate "perfect peace"). Thus does this *song* (v. 1) go on to say that clearly the obvious thing is that the city gates are to be opened for those people who make up *the righteous nation that keeps faith* (v. 2). These words remind us of the opening words of Ps 15, which ask who may dwell on the Lord's holy hill, and go on to speak of the style of life in the world that is pleasing to the Lord, namely to reverence the Lord and have a care for other people (Ps 15:2–5).

From the practical, earthly point of view, what is being spoken about here is fleshed out in the following verse (v. 4), namely that the most appropriate, indeed logical, way of life is to *Trust in the Lord forever*, for the

2. Seitz, *Isaiah 1–39*, 192.

believing one does indeed have in the Lord God *an everlasting rock*. Thus it will become clear that those who have the real power on earth are those who in earthly terms seem to be so weak, for the Lord has *brought low the inhabitants of the height* (v. 5); and indeed it will in fact be found, in general contradiction to what is deemed "success" in the life of the material world, that the real earthly strength of humans resides in *the feet of the poor, the steps of the needy* (v. 6), for the Lord has brought low those who appear in the eyes of the world to be those of power and authority (v. 5).

Then in Isa 26:7–21 we have yet another composition, this once again being presented in the form and style of a biblical psalm, one that very much looks to the future, from the vantage point of present life and conditions. The passage then, begins by considering the people's present situation, and calls upon them to walk their lives in the ways of the Lord, and asking further, as it were on their behalf, that God will *make smooth the path of the righteous* (v. 7). Yet the psalmist is aware of the presence of the Lord and the Lord's call to live in his ways, for there is ever before the earthly one the *judgments* of God (vv. 8, 9), that is, the call from the Lord to his people ever to live the life God desires in his people. With v. 10 the psalmist would seem to be grappling with the problem for religious people of their having continually to observe around them those who lead lives of wickedness, and who yet appear to gain the favor of the Lord. Thus the speaker voices the wish that they may experience the judgement of the Lord (v. 11). Even so, the prophet affirms that God will suitably and appropriately reward both the righteous and the wicked (vv. 12, 13), and speaks of ways in which the Lord does indeed reward both those wicked ones, and also his own faithful people, both individually and corporately (vv. 14–15).

The theme continues in vv. 16–18, even though at times the people seem to be having to wait a long period for what they may feel would be appropriate interventions of God to be effected. That is, until we come to v. 19, which would seem to be a real message of hope about life after death, and has occasioned much scholarly discussion. For in spite of what some say about this verse, it would appear to be speaking about a personal resurrection from the dead—a subject that appears in the Old Testament only rarely—rather than a national revival. This reference to postmortem life does seem to follow on from the preceding thought of 25:8, *he [God] will swallow up death forever*. Yet while no further details are given about this new life following on from earthly death, the writer seems clearly to wish—and to have the confidence—to pass on to the reader and hearer this great assurance, namely, that for the individual person there can in fact be the reality and gift of life after death.

The final two verses of this chapter (vv. 20–21) seem clearly to be about the matter of believers having necessarily to wait for the proof of the preceding assurance about life after death. This is a matter that in earthly terms a person cannot be sure about until they have reached that stage in their lives. Therefore, they do have to wait for it, yet wait in a spirit of hope and trust in the LORD, who indeed through his prophet has spoken about these things. So, they are told, *enter your chambers, and shut your doors behind you*, and this to be until the work of God's judgement (here termed *wrath*) has taken effect (v. 20). When that divine work is carried out there will be a time of revelation of what has been happening in the world; thus we are told, *the earth will disclose the blood shed on it, and will no longer cover its slain* (v. 21).

As we have already noted, there is indeed little said in the Old Testament about the whole matter of life after death, but here is one of those few places when we do read about it. Clearly, the writer here can give no details, yet what this person is able to set forth for us and for his readers in all ages is the assurance that in the fullness of time the ways of God will prevail, and according to the above passage there will be a revelation of what has been taking place upon earth. But nothing specific can be given by way of details concerning this possible future life, and who might possibly live that life. Perhaps our writer in his counsel to his readers to enter their chambers, shutting their doors behind them (v. 20), can go no further in explanation as to any details about this future life than can the writer of the book of Daniel with his advice, "But you, go your way, and rest; you shall rise for your reward at the end of the days" (Dan 12:13). One contemporary scholar's study of the subject of death and the afterlife in the Old Testament has this about the Isaianic passage under consideration,

> Here was the response to the yearning for some form of continued communion with God: "your dead shall live . . . and sing for joy" (Is. 26:19). Here was the breakthrough to maintain faith in traumatic times. The details of how, where and when this resurrection would take place, and with what consequences, are left unexplored—the belief itself was enough to begin with.[3]

PAST, PRESENT, AND FUTURE 27:1-13

With this concluding chapter, the block of material making up the so-called Apocalypse of Isaiah, that is chs. 24–27, comes to an end. Indeed here, in this passage, it is brought to a definite and very much God-centered

---

3. See Johnston, *Shades of Sheol*, 239.

conclusion. This material has been called "apocalyptic" because, alongside other writings in the Old Testament, it is about, and deeply concerns such matters as divine unveilings, revelations, both of the current and also of the future states of the world. Such we have been reading about in the preceding chs. 24–26 in the Isaiah book.[4]

Chapter 27 does indeed make something of a triumphant conclusion to the account of the particular purposes of the LORD that are set forth in this Isaianic block of apocalyptic material (chs. 24–27). Ronald Clements in his Isaiah 1–39 commentary helpfully emphasizes that this chapter sets out what he calls four eschatological impressions that God will bring about— that is, what is being spoken about in Isa 27 does concern end times.[5] Further, these are the end times when things on earth come into focus in accord with the desired ways and purposes of the LORD God. Clements understands these matters in this chapter as being spoken about under four headings, this schema having earlier been adopted by Hans Wildberger in his Isaiah commentary.[6]

> Isa 27:1 The slaying of the dragon
> 27:2–6 New song of the vineyard
> 27:7–11 Destruction of the fortified city
> 27:12–13 The great return

We consider each of these in turn. Isaiah 27:1 concerns the overthrow of the power of evil, what Clements calls the slaying of the dragon. The defeated enemy in this first part of this passage is called in v. 1 both *Leviathan* and also the *twisting serpent*, possibly (though not necessarily) suggesting that the author was drawing from two sources. *Leviathan* in the Old Testament generally refers to a primeval serpent who was a representative of chaos and rebellion. We read, among various other places in the Old Testament (see Job 41:1; Ps 74:14; 104:26) about *Leviathan*, and in particular about his defeat by the LORD in Ps 74:14. Indeed, the whole matter of *Leviathan*, of the *twisting serpent*, of *the dragon that is in the sea* is about mysterious forces of evil that are active in the material world, but that are in fact subject to defeat by the LORD God in his by far superior powers. This verse may well give the impression to many of its present-day readers that all this talk of sea monsters comes from and is only relevant to its ancient times and settings. However, in fact, such symbolism for evil and chaos is surely about the reality of so much that is to be seen going on in the world today. And we too can

---

4. On this Old Testament apocalyptic material see, for example, Rowland, *The Open Heaven*.
5. See Clements, *Isaiah 1–39*, 218–23.
6. Wildberger, *Isaiah 13–27*, 574–602.

draw comfort from the fact that the eternally superior power and authority in the world is the LORD God.

Then 27:2–6 concerns a new vineyard, about which there is singing. There has been an earlier spoken word about a vineyard in the book of Isaiah, in 5:1–7, a vineyard that had been found to be inadequate and something of a failure, such indeed that the LORD resolved it should be destroyed and abandoned. That talk was in fact about the failure of the people of Israel to be faithful and worthy people of God, and was therefore about the divine judgement that was upon them. This later vineyard (27:2–6) was clearly intended to be about a people of God many years later, and here now our author can envisage *a pleasant vineyard* (v. 2), which the LORD will ever constantly, *night and day*, guard and protect against harm. The LORD will in fact give constant care to it (v. 3). Even so, were it in future to fall into sinful ways, the divine judgement would be upon it (v. 4). Yet better would be that *peace* should be made between all whom the vineyard represents and the LORD (v. 5). Thus would come about great blessing for all peoples—*Israel shall blossom and put forth shoots, and fill the whole world with fruit* (v. 6).

Verses 7–11 it is very generally agreed are difficult, in fact one scholar says that, "No passage in the book of Isaiah is more difficult to unravel. The text is corrupt, the allusions imponderable, the links with the surrounding material obscure."[7] Already within the first verse we are not told who the "he" being spoken about is, but it would appear that it is highly likely to be God. Indeed, here the REB translation has inserted "the LORD" in place of the Hebrew "he." Further, we are not told whom he has *struck down* (v. 7). Not infrequently it is considered that those who have been killed are people in Israel, understanding this as having been an act of judgement for their sinfulness.

Verse 9 then fleshes out something of the Israelite former sins, and about this later judgement upon them. This judgement particularly involved the destruction of some of their aids to worship, like the stones of the *altars . . . sacred poles . . . incense altars* that are spoken about. Then in v. 10 to what does *the fortified city* refer? Again we cannot be sure, but Samaria is commonly suggested. However, we cannot be certain which historical destruction is being suggested. It could perhaps be that effected by the Assyrians in 722 BCE, for vv. 10 and 11 do read as if they are likely referring to the ruinous state of the destroyed Samaria. Nevertheless, of this, once again, we cannot be sure.

Verses 12 and 13 bring both the preceding verses—and indeed also the preceding apocalyptic-style chapters—to appropriate endings. Both of these verses are prefaced by the Hebrew phrase, *On that day*, as indeed are also the two opening verses of the whole chapter we are considering (ch.

---

7. Stacey, *Isaiah 1–39*, 164.

27). That is, there is real sense of the talk of a future day when there will be a raft of changes in the situation for the people of Judah and Jerusalem in their own lands.

Thus there is talk here of a gathering together of all the tribes of Israel (v. 12); presumably the language of *will thresh* is intended to suggest the separating out of the true Israelite peoples from those of other nations and persuasions. Alas, there is no talk here of wider and more comprehensively peopled communities. Nevertheless, this national gathering together is to be effected thoroughly, this being suggested by the language that the people of Israel *will be gathered one by one*. That is, following on from separations and divisions of peoples through warfare and strife, they are now to be reunited in their own homeland.

Then in v. 13 there is the talk of a great trumpet being sounded, by which the scattered will be called, summoned, gathered together from Assyria and Egypt, that is from both east and west, where they have been either lost or driven, or where they have searched for new life. Thus they are brought together, and hardly surprisingly the activity and the setting is that of the *worship* of the Lord, at that supreme place of worship, the *holy mountain at Jerusalem*. Hence, Clements says about this remarkably prophesied happening, "It will not be simply a return to the political independence and greatness of the kingdom of David, but will be a spiritual return to worship the true God in his temple in Jerusalem. With this strong note of hope the various assurances for Israel's future among the nations contained in chs. 24–27 is brought to a close."[8]

Yet this call to worship on Mount Zion also perhaps serves as a suitable ending for an even more extensive block of material in the Isaiah book, namely both that of the prophetical words about the foreign nations in chs. 13–23 as well as the visions of the future set forth in the apocalyptic material in chs. 24–27. Joseph Blenkinsopp observes that while we may regret the absence of the universalist theme in the concluding words of these two sections of the book, yet how much of a thoroughly positive nature and emphasis we do have. Thus he writes,

> One may regret the nonappearance here at the end of the section [ch. 18] of the universalist theme that emerges throughout it from time to time but, from the rhetorical point of view, the blowing of the ram's horn to summon the people no longer to battle but to the final liturgical assembly (cf. Zech 9:14) forms an appropriate conclusion to chs. 13–27.[9]

---

8. Clements, *Isaiah 1–39*, 223.
9. Blenkinsopp, *Isaiah 1–39*, 379.

IV

Isaiah 28–32
Isaiah and Judah

IN THIS SERIES OF chapters the focus is largely upon Judah and Jerusalem, along with something about those who are left in the northern kingdom of Israel with its main city of Samaria. Thus the following sections relate to a series of wider issues of life among the foreign nations. What might happen in more future distant times is somewhat turned away from here, and there is emphasis once again on how the people of Judah and Jerusalem should be living and ordering their lives and their ways at that present time. See further on these chapters in the introductory notes on p. xxv above.

EPHRAIMITE DRUNKARDS 28:1-6

Ephraim is the northern kingdom, otherwise known as "Israel," with its principal city of Samaria, and here the prophet has little or nothing good to say about its people and their leaders. It is generally felt that this is a prophetical writing from after the time of the so-called Syro-Ephraimite War, which took place when the northern kingdom of Ephraim (Israel) joined in coalition with Syria to (unsuccessfully) lay siege to Judah and Jerusalem.[1] Certainly here the Judean prophet seems to be critical about the northern kingdom, and in particular concerning its leaders. Further, it should be noted that this is not a straightforward Hebrew text, and in a number of places there are questions about what it is intended to be saying.

---

1. See pp. 31–40 above for more about the Syro-Ephraimite war.

The opening condemnation of this passage concerns the wine consumption and thereby the drunkenness of the leaders of Israel/Ephraim (v. 1). What a dreadful misuse of a fine valley is taking place when there are people (and their leaders—that is, we presume, what the word *head* is intended to indicate) who are *bloated with rich food, of those overcome with wine!* Thus is the appointed leadership of the people of Israel beset with inadequacy and incompetence, as well as totally inappropriate greed. Such is the understanding of the NRSV translators, and also those of REB; other translators—for example, those of RV and RSV—regard the reference to *head* being to Samaria, whose location was at the head of a valley.

With v. 2 the prophet speaks of the LORD God of Israel, who is all powerful, and certainly far greater and more powerful than those humans who are called to lead their people, Israel. Thus the LORD's coming on his people is likened to those apparently such strong forces of weather, *hail . . . tempest . . . overflowing waters*. The warning is that the LORD has this powerful strength, and thus in v. 3 it is *the drunkards of Ephraim* who are warned about what is to take place, namely the prospect of being *trampled under foot*. Verse 4 presents a further difficulty in translating: is the word *fig* intended to refer to the one who invades the country (so REB and NRSV), or is it to the city of Samaria? Both RSV and NIV think it should be understood as referring to Samaria.

Verses 5 and 6 are much more hopeful, and many scholars believe that they were added to the preceding words at a later stage, even perhaps after the time of the Babylonian exile. Further, they may also apply to the issues being spoken about in vv. 7–13 that follow. In both of these phrases the imagery employed to speak of the changed situation for the people of Jerusalem is that of *garland of glory* and *diadem of beauty* (v. 5). Further, the peoples of those future times are promised leaders who will bring about a *spirit of justice*, and also *strength to those who turn back the battle at the gate*, that is, those who will defend them from danger and attack (v. 6).

What a real assurance there is here of a positive and good future for peoples of Jerusalem and its environs. Moreover, these will be God-given gifts, in particular, the LORD giving divine strength to the leaders of the peoples and indeed to the whole of the nation. More, it is the promise that in the future the nation will be led by a better group of individuals than those the prophet regarded as that earlier cohort of drunkards (28:1).

FAILED LEADERSHIP 28:7–13

These verses continue the theme of the preceding passage, 28:1–6, though whether these present ones are intended to address the leaders of Ephraim as those of the preceding verses do, or whether these are now addressed to the leaders of Judah is not clear. Nor can we be sure about the dating of this passage. Yet it is certainly a very strong and prophetically deeply felt condemnation of supposedly divinely appointed religious leaders. Drunkenness is a very large part of the condemnatory charge, and in v. 7 we find the words *stagger with strong drink* occurring twice, and both are referring to the state of certain individuals among the religious leaders, in particular priests and the prophets (*priest and prophet*). Thus are these ones guilty insofar as *they stumble in giving judgment*. This is followed in v. 8 with the picture of very desperate and disgusting conditions left, presumably, by the priests who were eating those portions of sacrifices that were due to them after they had offered sacrifices on behalf of their peoples.

Verses 9 and 10 are set in the NRSV translation in quotation marks, these being a decision of the translators—Biblical Hebrew does not have quotation marks. Presumably the thought is that it is the prophet Isaiah who is saying these words, and thus expressing deep condemnation of, we assume, local priests and prophets, for having failed to carry out aright their duties, such that it hardly looks as if they are grown people (*those taken from the breast* v. 9). How can such people *teach knowledge . . . explain the message?* (v. 9). For they are hardly grown up, and indeed their talk is not adult talk, rather it is indeed all too like what has been called baby talk (v. 10).[2]

Yet, in v. 11 we read that there is a real word due to come to those we presume were the people of Judah and Jerusalem, a word that will come from a person with another language (*alien tongue*), but it will be a message of hope—*with alien tongue he will speak to this people*—and it could indeed be with an assurance of hope (*This is rest; give rest to the weary* [v. 12]). Yet the LORD's people will not listen, even though it would be for them a message of hope. Indeed, even to a message about *This is rest; give rest to the weary; and this is repose . . .* there is not the due attention, for we are told, *they would not hear* (v. 12). Instead, the message that they will hear and accept will be none other than their own talk, that which is akin to the talk of infants, that baby talk we heard about a little earlier in this passage (v. 13; see v. 10).

What we have been reading in this rather low-key, if not somewhat depressing, passage could be something that was spoken to the people of Judah and Jerusalem before the worst happened to them in 587 BCE and many of them went into exile in Babylon and elsewhere. Alternatively, it could possibly have been added later, during, even after, the exile, by an editor to these chapters, and thereby have been intended to serve as a very

2. This is suggested by Roberts, *First Isaiah*, 349, note f.

serious warning to later peoples that they should heed the word of the LORD to them, maybe one that comes to them through one of the God-appointed prophets sent to help them in such situations.

John Mauchline in his commentary says about these verses at the close of this passage: "So the scoffer, who, from afar off, tries to criticize the men of faith and the faith they hold, often fails to understand that all that he can learn of the faith is but a few childish ideas which he mistakes for the whole reality."[3]

MORE FAILED LEADERS 28:14–22

This is a not-dissimilar passage to the one preceding, except that whereas the earlier one was particularly concerned with Israelite priests and prophets in the north, here the subject is the political leaders in Jerusalem. Once again the prophet is pointing to strong grounds for the condemnation of the decisions and the actions of such people, as indeed is made clear in the opening verse with its summons to the rulers in Jerusalem, here referred to as "foolish speakers," NRSV *scoffers* (v. 14). Yet, we may ask, why are these leaders being addressed in this way?

This is begun to be answered in v. 15, the prophetical judgement upon the political leaders being that any covenant agreement they have made has in fact been a useless, even failed, one. For this has been in the nature of *a covenant with death*, that is something of the order of *with Sheol we have an agreement*. That is to say, they have made a relationship between themselves (along with their peoples) and the land of *Sheol,* that place where in general Old Testament thought humans go after their earthly death. It is highly probable that in fact the Jerusalem political leaders have made a political agreement with some earthly group, one that the prophet here cannot believe is any good and that will be of no real benefit, either for their peoples or for the nation. Thus, the prophet is saying that this is in fact a "deathly" agreement. For truly these political leaders have made *lies* to be the *refuge* for their people, they have *in falsehood . . . taken shelter*. Thus indeed the people are being led remarkably poorly.

With v. 16 we come across much more hopeful thoughts, presumably these being either the thoughts or the words of one of the prophets of the LORD. Here is the assurance that under the LORD there will be found in Jerusalem firm foundations: *I am laying in Zion a foundation stone*. Further, this is *a tested stone,* in fact, *a precious cornerstone, a sure foundation*. What is more, what remarkably powerful words does the prophet use to speak of

---

3. Mauchline, *Isaiah 1–39*, 200.

his assurance of safety for the people of Jerusalem, words that express the confidence that they will still prevail after earthly death? Indeed, *One who trusts will not panic*, even when earthly death is involved.

Verse 17 moves on to the imagined further details in the work on a new building—that is, in this particular situation, the renewed society. It will be built in *justice* and *righteousness*, that is to say it will have foundations of care for all peoples, especially the poor, the pursuit of doing those things that are right and proper, the ensuring that in this society there is a place for all sorts and conditions of people. It is a deep concern of the prophet Amos that these two matters should prevail in Israelite society, saying "But let justice roll down like waters, and righteousness like an ever-flowing stream" (Amos 5:24). At the same time in the vision of the future conveyed in this verse there is the warning that there will be no safe place for those who live by *lies*. Yet also, in v. 18 there is the assurance that in the renewed city there will be a true covenant relationship with the LORD, one that brings to the peoples security and peace, and further the assurance that the old *covenant with death will be annulled*.

Nevertheless, the reader is warned that alongside the divine assurance of the LORD's protection and care of his people, yet the earthly reality, alas, is that humans there may yet be subject to various worldly setbacks along with sundry other problems. We have already been told about the possibility of floods (vv. 17–19), while the talk in v. 20 with its references to *bed* and *covering* would seem to be voicing future concerns about accommodation, not only about its adequacy of size, but also its sheer basic provision. Therefore (v. 22), let those who do have adequate provisions in this regard humbly accept them with thanksgiving, because strange things could possibly happen to those who dwell in the *land*, or even those who live in other parts of the whole earth (for the Hebrew word for *land* can also mean "earth"). The talk would seem to be of possible coming tragedy. It is widely felt in scholarly circles that the thought here is that of a thinker living later than Isaiah and others in eighth-century BCE prophetical circles.

It should surely be noted that a number of the thoughts, phrases, and theological issues in this passage are taken up in the New Testament writings. In Paul's letter to the Romans we have the thought of part of Isa 28:16 adopted in Rom 10:11, the issue here being that of faith and trust in God. Then further, another thought expressed in Isa 28:16 is taken up by Paul in Rom 9:33, but here the *precious cornerstone* has become a "stone of stumbling" (perhaps some thought coming here from Isa 8:14). Thirdly, the *precious cornerstone* has in 1 Pet 2:8 become "a rock of scandal," what in NRSV is translated "a rock that makes them fall." What, however, we should note is that the Isaianic material was originally about matters that were definitely to do with issues concerning what we might define and describe as being both religious and political. The New Testament writers take them up purely for matters that we might wish to label "religious." One of the great values of the Old Testament material is surely about the fact that in many of its parts it does concern both of those issues, that it does indeed have a deep concern both for matters religious and also for matters political, that is, as we might state the matter, issues of faith and issues to do with the political state.[4]

THE GOOD FARMER'S WISDOM 28:23–29

This is a passage somewhat all on its own in the Isaiah book. There is nothing else quite like it in this prophetical text. It appears to be about farming techniques, but there is no mention of the fact that it is an oracle from God or something of that nature. Nor is its style at all typical of prophetical utterances and writings, but rather it is much more like a piece of wisdom writing. Somewhat inevitably, certain of the references to agricultural details and procedures are now of uncertain significance for us. Further, there must be a real question about the authorship of this short passage. It hardly reads like prophetical material, and in particular in the style of what we read elsewhere in the book of Isaiah. Thus there must be questions concerning whether or not it comes from the historical prophet Isaiah.

The passage is in two parts, the first being vv. 23–26. It would seem that we are being addressed by a sage here, a wisdom teacher, that type of writer we come across in an Old Testament book such as Proverbs. In this text, each of the worker's actions has its time and season, as in the first place the plowing of the field and the preparation of the land (vv. 23–24). Then are the seeds sown, each type of seed having its appointed place in the field, *dill . . . cumin . . . barley*, with *spelt* in particular being planted at the *border* (v. 25). This is believed to be the divinely ordered way for this task to be done (v. 26).

Verses 27–29 concern the continuing farming procedures at harvesting time, in particular with what has grown in this field. Indeed, there are different procedures applied to the various crops, and at different times. Further, such programmes and procedures have been determined by the Lord *of hosts* who thereby shows, indeed demonstrates, to those earthly people who will take notice of such things that the Lord indeed *is wonderful in counsel, and excellent in wisdom* (v. 29).

---

4. On these issues see, for example, Oswalt, *Isaiah 1–39*, 518; Wildberger, *Isaiah 28–39*, 45–47.

The message, surely, that this short passage is intended to convey is that what comes into being in the world, those things that come in accordance with the designs of the LORD God, the ever-knowing Lord of all, has an application too for those who seek to follow those ways and who do indeed endeavor to act in accordance with the LORD's times and seasons. They will surely find, in these matters in the natural world, some helpful examples of the LORD God's divine purposes and designs for them and their people in the world.

THE CITY PUNISHED AND DELIVERED 29:1-8

These verses are concerned with the city of Jerusalem, here called *Ariel*. In the Old Testament, this particular name is rarely used to designate a city, and only in the book of Isaiah. Here in 29:1-8, it is perhaps being intended to mean "the lion of God," or "the hearth of God." What is difficult to understand about this name is that at times it refers to a city that is under siege by God (as in Isa 29:1, 2, 7), whereas its usage elsewhere is of individuals, in particular those who will one day be rescued by God (as, for example, in Ezra 8:16).

At the beginning of this chapter (29:1, 2) certainly the theme as far as Jerusalem is concerned is that here is a city under attack by God, that is, *Ariel*, and, as if to make sure who is being spoken about, we are told that this is *the city where David encamped*. However zealously the people and authorities in the city may observe their religious practices and devotions (*festivals*) they will not succeed in avoiding this fate (v. 1). Still there will be distress for *Ariel*, *moaning and lamentation*, and indeed it will seem as if the city will be to God *like an Ariel*, that is, an altar-hearth—NEB translates it "fiery altar" (v. 2). Indeed, so we read in v. 3, Jerusalem will become a city under siege, it being none other than the LORD who is responsible for this attack. This will lead to a great sense of distress on the part of the people of Jerusalem, this being spoken about in a somewhat extended verse (v. 4). It is not easy to understand and to be sure about what is intended by the talk in this verse, whether it is to necromancy (see Isa 8:19) or simply an indication that it is to be buried as the debris of a once-besieged city. Certainly there is envisaged here a cry of a defeated people and their city, this coming from the depths of the earth.

Yet clearly all is not envisaged as being lost, for in v. 5 the enemy will be gone, this being brought about by the LORD God who has indescribably greater powers than do those who lay siege to his chosen city. Thus it is that the enemy is described in terms of *small dust* and *flying chaff*—and moreover these things, these great changes, can take place *in an instant, suddenly.* Further, this remarkably sudden change of situation is to be brought about, so we are told in v. 6, by the Lord of hosts himself whose activity and deliverance will be marked by *thunder and earthquake and great noise*, and a good deal else besides. The suggestion here would seem to be that this was believed to be the direct activity of the Lord, rather than any great military operation.

Verses 7 and 8 bring this passage to a fitting conclusion. First, in v. 7, in regard to the city of Jerusalem, again called Ariel: there is an enemy who fights against this holy city, and here the city is reported as being assured that this enemy will be found to have fled like *a dream, a vision of the night.* Meanwhile (v. 8) those who make up the enemy of Jerusalem—the city now being referred to as *Mount Zion*—will be like a hungry or thirsty person who dreams in the night of eating or drinking, but then wakes up still very hungry and thirsty. Zion's enemies shall not receive what they crave. It is surely intended here that the reader shall once more appreciate that frail human beings on earth suffer when they are seeking to be self-reliant. In marked contrast are the great resources and powers there are in the Lord God for his earthly people, that is, for those who call upon him to aid and help them in their troubles and labors.

Indeed, what a remarkable expression of hope this is for those who will put their trust in the Lord God. Wildberger makes the same point, saying,

> Isaiah 29:1–7 functions much like a key that opens the passageway into the overall message of Isaiah. Yahweh has to intervene until the city is totally humiliated, at least to the point that all the "presumptuous ones" and "powerful ones" are unmasked. Assyria is the tool that effects this humiliation of the proud ones. In reality, the water reaches the high-minded leaders of Jerusalem right up to their neck (see 8:7). But Yahweh does not want to obliterate and completely eradicate Israel from the annals of history. The dogma concerning frustrating the plans of the enemy that besieges Jerusalem is a sign and symbol of Yahweh's plans.[5]

NOT WISHING TO SEE 29:9–14

This paragraph falls into three individual pieces, vv. 9–10, 11–12, and 13–14. The first two are about the people's lack of spiritual perception, the third is presented as a word from the Lord to his prophet concerning the people, *these people . . . this people.*

---

5. Wildberger, *Isaiah 28–39*, 79.

In the first of these (vv. 9–10) the issue is presented as being a command of the LORD, concerning the people's amazement (*be in a stupor*), their apparent blindness, their (wineless) drunken state, their sleepiness. This last is particularly applied to the LORD's *seers* and *prophets*, who are thus unable to fulfill what the LORD requires of them; they are incapable of hearing the word of the LORD to them and unable to pass on any appropriate word from the LORD to his people. In v. 10 there is the suggestion that because of their wayward activities the *seers* and *prophets* cannot fulfil the will of the LORD.

Verses 11 and 12 are in prose and are presented as a follow-on comment by the prophet to what has been spoken of in the preceding two verses. There is the criticism of the LORD's servants in their local communities who cannot pass on the desires and calls of the LORD to his people because those people quite simply refuse to read what they have received, and further also profess inability to read.

Finally, vv. 13–14 are about more deep-seated spiritual matters on the part of the people, the issue being that while people may say the correct things, they do not put them into effect. Thus they do not truly give praise to God, because while they may be able to utter the right things to the LORD, in fact their hearts are far away from God, and therefore their actions are somewhat inevitably not what they should be, and certainly not what the LORD wishes.

We may take note of the fact that in Paul's Epistle to the Romans we have a quotation of one of the verses here, Rom 11:8 quoting Isa 29:10. Further, John Mauchline in his Torch Commentary on Isaiah 1–39, about this passage says in regard to people's worship of the LORD becoming formal and then even hypocritical:

> [R]eligion for them does not mean a living experience but a code of conventional practice which is part of the tradition into which they have been born. This traditional inheritance, which might have prepared the people to enter into the realities of religious faith, has been accepted as something to be formally honoured and as efficacious in itself—a process which can be illustrated frequently in human history.[6]

BETTER DAYS IN THE FUTURE 29:15–24

This passage begins with two verses (vv. 15–16) concerned with the issue of people wishing to hide their deeds from the LORD, and then goes on

---

6. Mauchline, *Isaiah 1–39*, 204.

(vv. 17–24) to speak about a promised coming salvation in which many things in the life of the Israelite community will change so much for the better.

Verses 15 and 16, then, make up a prophet's expressed "woe" to those people who wish to hide their secret plans (NRSV *a plan too deep for the* L<small>ORD</small>—v.15). This, in fact, is a course of action concerning which the people involved are assured of failure. Not only can they not keep such things secret from the L<small>ORD</small> (v. 15), but also, says the prophet, this is a course of action that in fact is an attempt to turn things upside down (*shall the potter be regarded as the clay?* v. 16). The prophet seems to be saying that this is what is happening with the politicians. Their policies are in reality nothing less than wrong. Instead, what they should be putting forth are laws that are acceptable to God.

Then from v. 17 onwards the whole tone of this passage becomes much more hopeful. For here there emerges talk of Lebanon becoming a *fruitful field*, and even that this *fruitful field* will become so very plenteous—where once it was scrub land, in the future it will be a place of worthwhile plenteousness, what can be referred to "a reversal of fortune in the future."[7] R. E. Clements speaks of these verses as being akin in thought to chs. 24–27, saying that "this is an expression of post-exilic eschatology, closely bordering on apocalyptic."[8] Thus there is expressed here a real note of hope for the future for the people of Israel.

Further, with v. 17 there is a fulsome notice of the future fertility of the earth; the land of Lebanon will become a *fruitful field*, and indeed even coming to be regarded as *a forest*. Lebanon had been noted for its cedars, and there are a goodly number of references in the Old Testament to them; an abundance of earthly growth, along with the renewal of nature for the future, is now being assured for Lebanon, and presumably therefore also for the neighboring Israel. The following verse (v. 18) speaks of another renewal, that of individual people, with the *deaf* hearing and the *blind* seeing. Are these restorations to be understood in a physical or a spiritual sense? It could well be that both of these are in mind. In v. 19 there is a general state of improvement in the situations of many members of the Israelite society being spoken about, in particular *the meek* shall find a new joy in the L<small>ORD</small>, *and the neediest people shall exalt in the Holy One of Israel*.

In vv. 20 and 21 there is the assurance of the end of two further groups of people, this time both of people who could be those who are actually members of the Israelite society, namely *the tyrant* and *the scoffer*, and those

---

7. Blenkinsopp, *Isaiah 1–39*, 407.
8. Clements, *Isaiah 1–39*, 241.

alert to do evil. Verse 21 would seem to be about those who would seek to use and work the Israelite legal system purely for their own personal advantage.

Concerning vv. 22–24, some scholars regard these as having been added at a later date to the preceding material. This could possibly be correct, and Clements sees the reference to Abraham as having come from the post-exilic age, this being a time when there was a re-awakened interest in that patriarchal figure.[9] Whatever may be the truth of that particular matter, what we do have here is a prophetic assurance—either from Isaiah or a later prophet—of a whole change of situation and fortunes for the people of Israel. The peoples' renewed lives in their lands will bring about an end to the feeling of shame on the part of Israel (v. 22). Rather, there will be praise for the Holy One of Jacob, awe for the God of Israel (v. 23). Further changes are being promised here: those *who err in spirit will come to understanding*, while *those who grumble will accept instruction* (v. 24).

Here indeed is a message of great hope for the people of Israel. There is a prophet's call to Israelite people and leaders to consider their past and to appreciate again the guiding presence of the LORD with his people in age after age. Indeed, Joseph Blenkinsopp expresses the matter thus: "that Abraham was redeemed out of Ur as Israel was to be redeemed out of Egypt and, in due course, out of Babylon (33:10; 51:11)."[10] It was not without good reason that Hans Wildberger in his Isaiah commentary headed his work on Isa 29:17–24 with "The Great Reversal."[11]

A REBELLIOUS PEOPLE 30:1–5

As the book of Isaiah begins, so it now continues, that is, with the theme of the people of the LORD rebelling against their Lord (see Isa 1:2–6). In particular the aspect of rebellion that is specifically spoken about here is the people's failure to trust in the LORD God, this leading the people to go once again to Egypt for help. Both *Zoan* and *Hanes* (v. 4) were Egyptian cites. At certain times, Egypt had been of assistance to the people of Israel, but here the people, along with those of their leaders, are regarded by the prophet as sinning in their appeal to Egypt for help without consulting the LORD, that is, *without asking for my counsel* (v. 2). Thus, what we have here is rebellion against both Judah's earthly ruler (Assyria), but also against the LORD God. The result of this sin will be a lack of assistance for ruler and people, *neither*

---

9. See Clements, *Abraham and David*, 61, 70 88. See also Blenkinsopp, *Isaiah 1–39*, 410.

10. Blenkinsopp, *Isaiah 1–39*, 410.

11. Wildberger, *Isaiah 28–39*, 103.

help nor profit, but rather *shame and disgrace* (v. 5). Thus, these actions will please neither worldly leaders nor the divine Lord.

The dating of this incident has been much discussed, and it is widely felt that it could be reflecting the situation for Judah and Jerusalem in the period from 705–1 BCE following on from the death of the Assyrian ruler Sargon II in 705 and the establishment and rule of Sennacherib. Such a time might indeed have presented the opportunity for some rebellions on the parts of subject peoples. Yet for our prophet here, the perceived real and unfailing source of present help, and future hope, is ever in the Lord God of Israel.

THE SOURCE OF REAL HELP 30:6–7

It may indeed be wondered what this short piece is about, whether its concern is with the animals of the Negeb, or rather with Egypt's worthless help. While both are spoken about, in fact it appears that the primary concern is with the issue of where the real power and might for the people of Israel are to be found. The obvious answer is, of course, in and from the Lord God of Israel. It is widely felt by biblical scholars that these short verses come from around the same period of history as the preceding verses, that is from the time 705–1 BCE when there were changes of leadership in the kingdom of Assyria, and thus the possibility, maybe, of the dawning of better days for the people of Judah and Jerusalem.

The *Negeb* was the arid, desert region south of Judah, one that would have to be traversed by those who wished to go to Egypt, and vice-versa. It was not surprisingly the haunt of wild animals, some known to us (*lions, lionesses, vipers, donkeys, camels*), but others obscure, like, for example, the *flying serpent*. Yet this is where some humans think that the real *riches* are to be found, those *treasures* to be carried on the *humps of camels* (v. 6). The being *Rahab*, literally meaning "strong one," was a mythical monster that for Israelite peoples personified powers of misrule and chaos.

All of this appears to be intended to say that the prophetic message here is that in such beings and forces as have been mentioned there is no power to help Israelite peoples. Rather, while it is not actually stated in these verses, it is implied that the people's real help in fact is, as ever, to be found in the Lord.

WRITTEN PROPHECY 30:8–17

It is difficult to know what we should regard as distinctive sections of the material from v. 8 onwards in this chapter. Different scholars divide up these verses variously, and the way they are regarded here in this present work is only one of several possible arrangements. Nevertheless, a majority scholarly view would be that this is further Isaianic material that comes from the same historical time as the preceding passages, namely that of the changing of the Assyrian monarchy between 705 and 701 BCE.

The content of v. 8 with its talk of *Go, write it before them on a tablet, and inscribe it in a book*, reminds us of other such instructions in the book of Isaiah, in particular 8:1 and 8:16. Nor should we forget the command to the prophet Habakkuk, *Write the vision; make it plain on tablets, so that a runner may read it* (Hab 2:2). Here, once again, is clearly material that has a real degree of importance for the people of Israel, and that well deserves to be committed to writing. Presumably the contents of this passage (30:8–17), is the word of the LORD for the prophet, and thereby for the people of Judah and Jerusalem. We have already noted that different scholars and students divide up these verses (8–17) in a variety of ways. The assumption in the present work is that the written word of the prophet Isaiah himself is what we have in vv. 9–17 of the present chapter.

Verse 9 concerns the attitudes of the people to the requirements of the LORD, in particular that they, as adults, are in fact behaving in rebellious ways, as indeed the book of Isaiah makes clear to us with its note in the opening verses about those who *are a rebellious people* (1:2). That is, presumably those people who have not attended to the will and commands of the LORD, and have gone off in their own ways. In fact, they have acted as if they were children, rather than adults, and have not attended to *the instruction of the LORD*, presumably as that was communicated to them by prophets, priests, and Levites. Further (v. 10), what these people really desire is that such peoples as *prophets* (those who convey and interpret the will of God for the people) and *seers* (those who interpret dreams or visions) are proclaimers of matters and issues that the people wish to hear about, rather than what God desires, or even needs, to say to them. Thus, alas, it is that the people say, *speak to us smooth things, prophesy illusions*. That is to say (v. 11), the people no longer wish to hear about *the Holy One of Israel*. On this name, this designation, of the LORD God, and its prevalence in the book of Isaiah, see above on Isa 1:4.

In vv. 12–14 we have the prophet's response to what the people are saying, and associated with that their attitudes to the LORD and his will for them, concerning those matters that have been spoken of in the preceding verses. Thus in v. 12 we read again of the written word (what has been inscribed of the LORD's will on a tablet), in particular that it has been rejected, and that rather than obeying those words the people have put their trust *in oppression and deceit*, and moreover have come to *rely on them*. Thus they have opened the way for all sorts of calamities and destructions to take place in their midst—breakages, collapses, sudden crashes (v. 13). And such has been this scale of destruction in their society that, in the language of a smashed potter's vessel, it was discovered *that among its fragments not a sherd is found* . . . (v. 14).

With v. 15 we have a summing-up word about this whole false approach to matters of life and faith, and what the prophet has to say to the people of his day. Some scholars put this verse as the first of a new short unit running to v. 17[12] while others regard it as belonging with the preceding unit, thus making a more complete whole unit of vv. 8–17. In fact, v. 15 makes up one of the truly memorable verses of the book of Isaiah, with its message about the real need of those seeking help in life. This help is discovered in *returning* to the LORD and finding *rest* in him, for there those who do so will find the *saving* help they need and seek. Moreover, it will not be so much in frenzied activity, but rather *In quietness and trust* that they will find their real *strength*. Yet sadly, so the prophet feels, the people have *refused* to make such a search. At one level, this comment seems to relate to the factor of the people's earnestly seeking help for their lives—and no doubt, military help—outside their homeland. Yet the prophet here is directing, or re-directing, them to that real strength and help that they will surely find in the LORD God, a much greater help and strength than they can find in their own frantic activities. Yet sadly, it is these very things of faith that the people of Judah and Jerusalem have in general been neglecting, abandoning, forsaking.

Yet still, so the prophet is saying in v. 16, the people want some more evident and quicker ways of getting things done, and thus there is the talk of their wish, maybe even determination, to *flee upon horses* and *ride upon swift steeds*. That sadly is surely about the determination on the people's part to flee from Jerusalem, with the result that the remaining group in the city will be small indeed, *like a signal on a hill* (v. 17).

At this point in the book of Isaiah it may be appropriate to recall the words of the prophet Isaiah in the days of crisis, when Judah and Jerusalem were under siege by the forces of the Syro-Ephraimite coalition, and when the prophet called upon his people and their leaders to have faith in God and to put their trust in him: *If you do not stand firm in faith, you shall not stand at all* (7:9b). John Sawyer says of this passage,

> The prophet sees them [his people] fleeing for their lives, pursued by the Assyrians and, in an image exactly parallel to 1:8, he sees Jerusalem, alone of all the cities of Judah (36:1), standing forlorn on top of a hill, like a flagpole. Yet it is Isaiah's vision of "the peace

---

12. So, for example, Clements, *Isaiah 1–39*, 248.

that passes all understanding" that gives us hope in difficult times if only, unlike his first audience, we listen and "return."[13]

SALVATION COMING 30:18-26

This passage begins with a verse of promise, one that does appear to follow on from what has preceded, that is, a time of troubles and crises. Yet here there is given an assurance of hope for the people of Judah and Jerusalem. Scholars are divided as to whether or not this passage does follow, from a historical point of view, from what we read in the foregoing (30:8–17), some feeling that this is clearly the prophetic presentation of a time of real hopefulness after the preceding talk of so much crisis and calamity for the populations of Jerusalem and Judah. However, other scholars think that these words cannot have been spoken so soon, or at least not until a good deal of time later. The approach taken in this present work is that this is a real expression of hope for the future of those above-mentioned people who have experienced deeply troubling times.

Verse 18 does read like a profound expression of hope for the people, this being made clear through such words as, *the* Lord *waits to be gracious to you*, and more, *he will rise up to show mercy to you*. Further, there is the great assurance, *For the* Lord *is a God of justice*, and therefore his people can in confidence await the Lord's bringing upon them much better times than they have recently been knowing. Yet, as ever, they may have to wait for the due time for the fulfilment of these promises, as indeed the Lord *waits* for the due and appropriate time for his actions.

With v. 19 we seem to be moving into material presented in prose, and for much of the time these verses are taken up with what amounts to a fleshing out of the preceding expressions of hope. Thus in this present verse there is the assurance of the absence of weeping in the future in *Jerusalem*—here also called *Zion*—and even if there is the sound of the people's *cry*, there is also the assurance that the Lord will *answer* it. Further (v. 20), should there be the experience of having to live with *the bread of adversity and the water of affliction*, yet the Lord, here spoken of as their *Teacher*, is the one who will be revealed to them in their sight. Moreover (v. 21), they will be guided in their lives, in the ways they take, hearing, so to speak, *This is the way; walk in it*. Thus (v. 22) will these people have such confidence in the Lord, which will result in their wish to defile their *silver-covered idols* and their *gold-plated images*, saying to them, *Away with you!* Such aspects of idolatry were

---

13. Sawyer, *Isaiah*, Vol. I, 249.

indeed totally unacceptable in Israelite society, and the argument here is that now with all this so-evident divine leadership and guidance the people will have absolutely no good need of such things.

Further, these people can be assured also of good things happening in the agricultural sphere. There will be rain in due season, and thus will fine produce come forth from the earth. Further, *cattle* will be able to graze in very adequate lands and fields, even *oxen and donkeys* being supplied with more than abundant food for their particular tasks (vv. 23–24). Yet also, there is talk of hill and mountain *brooks* running with water, and a somewhat mysterious reference to a day of great slaughter *when the towers fall* (v. 25). That last mentioned happening would seem to be speaking of the end time, the time when God's victory over the forces of evil would be complete. Finally in v. 26 we read of the making complete of all things worldly, a time when the purposes and ways of the LORD would be brought to their destined completion. The *moon* will shine as the *sun*, and the *sun* become that much brighter. Meanwhile for the affected people of earth in these cosmic happenings there is the promise that *the* LORD *binds up the injuries of his people*. And for any who are affected in the flesh by these mighty acts, there is the promise of the healing of their wounds.

This is far from being in the language of full-blooded Old Testament apocalyptic thought. That is, this is not the Old Testament language of the end of the world. Rather, this is surely about a sense of the renewal of nature and of the whole of the natural world. Thus will come about for these peoples that sense and reality of deep peace and concord in the world, surely all that is intended and represented by the Hebrew word "shalom," that sense of being safe, uninjured, at peace.

DIVINE JUDGEMENT ON ASSYRIA 30:27–33

There is in this passage a complete change of emphasis and tone from what has preceded. Thus, and somewhat inevitably, those changes have brought about questions regarding the authorship of this passage, and in particular whether or not the same person could have been writing this material as the one who authored the preceding passage. For the fact is that these present verses (30:27–33) portray a God *burning with his anger . . . his tongue is like a devouring fire* (v. 27). Not surprisingly scholarly opinion is divided on this issue of authorship, and yet Wildberger, having examined these verses in his ever-thorough way, believes that they could come from the Isaiah we know elsewhere in this book. Even so, he admits to a few places here, and also certain words, that do cause some difficulties and challenges to that viewpoint.[14] The approach in what is said here is that essentially we are dealing in this passage with Isaianic authorship, but with full acknowledgement that there are certain particular difficulties for us in what is being presented.

The theme of this passage concerns the anger of the LORD God upon the Assyrians, and the presence of this theme must come to us as some surprise in view of the ways in which, in the preceding writings and thought of the Isaiah book, Assyria is portrayed not infrequently as being the earthly power who gives effect to the will and the ways of the LORD God. What, then, is it that now the prophet has to say about the LORD God and his purposes on earth, and in particular in regard to his people Israel?

The first two verses (vv. 27-28) are set out in NRSV in poetic form, though whether it is poetry is questionable. What these verses are speaking about is the anger of the LORD, expressed by the words *burning with* his *anger*, with his lips expressing his *indignation*. Further, concerning the LORD, *his tongue is like a devouring fire*. This is in v. 27, but it is not until the following verses in prose that we learn of the object of this divine anger, namely the Assyrian (v. 31). This has a certain degree of strangeness and surprise about it, as previously in the book of Isaiah Assyria has been portrayed as acting as a force for good, being in the nature of Yahweh's agent on the earth, one who in a particular way is called upon to effect the LORD's judgement upon his people Israel. However, here we are given the impression that Assyria has used too much force, and at that for his own purposes, and thus both the anger and the judgement of the LORD has come upon Assyria and its leader. Verse 28 speaks further about this burning anger of the LORD, thus *his breath is like an overflowing stream*.

The imagined scene in vv. 29-33 would seem to be that of an Israelite religious festival, in particular one that is celebrated in Jerusalem. Thus, there are songs as the people set off for Jerusalem, *to go to the mountain of the LORD, to the Rock of Israel* (v. 29). The ensuing scene in Jerusalem (v. 30) is expressed in the familiar language of an Old Testament theophany account, that is, an occasion when we have a real manifestation of God to one or more human beings. For examples of such happenings, see Exod 19:16-25; 24:9-18. Yet what we are reading about here is no peaceful thanksgiving occasion, but rather a terrible occasion where there is the deep expression of the anger of the LORD (v. 30) against these particular imagined "pilgrims," that is the Assyrians (v. 31). Though this is not stated, presumably the LORD's complaint against the Assyrians is that in their calling to fulfil certain duties and acts supposedly for the LORD God, they have totally overstepped

---

14. For this issue, see Wildberger, *Isaiah 28-39*, 189-94. Clements understands this passage as being a part of what has been called the Josianic Redaction, for which see above xxi-xxiv.

the mark and gone too far, deploying far too much violence, and no doubt acting so as to serve their own interests and concerns. Thus presumably it is that they have called down upon themselves the judgement of the LORD God, with the result that they find themselves *terror-stricken* (v. 31).

In the final two verses of this passage (vv. 32–33), we are certainly presented with the account of a serious judgement of the LORD upon the Assyrians. Verse 32 appears to be speaking about an act of judgement with its *staff of punishment*, and this apparently to the accompaniment of *timbrels and lyres*, two of the various musical instruments the Old Testament speaks about.[15] It does have to be admitted that this appears to be a somewhat strange joining together of the instruments of divine judgement and earthly music. Then further, in v. 33 there is talk of a *burning place*, called in the Hebrew *tophet*, a place to the south of Jerusalem, and meaning place of burning, a location that at certain times had been used for ritual infanticide and sacrifices (see 2 Kgs 23:10; Jer 7:31–32). This place of burning is now, we are told, made ready for *the king*, which we assume is the Assyrian king. "The implication" says J. J. M. Roberts, "is the total destruction and fiery death of Assyria."[16] J. Blenkinsopp adds, "In this instance, and in the last sentence of the book (66:24), this cultic setting provides the lurid backdrop for the final overcoming of evil."[17]

NO HELP IN EGYPT 31:1–9

The theme here is one spoken of earlier, in 30:1–5, namely that it is futile for the people of Judah and Jerusalem to go to Egypt for help in their difficulties occasioned by threats from the Assyrians. Thus, this is another of the so-called Woe Oracles, beginning with the Hebrew word *Hoy* "Woe," "Alas" in NRSV (v. 1). This is a Hebrew word found mainly in certain speeches of prophets, often to announce and warn the people of an impending act of divine judgment and destruction (e.g., Isa 5:8–10; Mic 2:1–5).

It is widely accepted by scholars that this is the message of the prophet Isaiah, rather than of a later writer, and the themes are indeed familiar. That is, Judah is relying upon the Egyptians. Being dependent upon Egyptian *horses* and *chariots* and *horsemen* (v. 1)—the heavy military hardware of their times—they are looking to human sources and resources for the provision of help for their troubled situation. This is not at all looking in the

---

15. For the Old Testament's references to musical instruments see Thompson, *Greatly to Be Praised*, 120–22.

16. Roberts, *First Isaiah*, 400.

17. Blenkinsopp, *Isaiah 1–39*, 424.

correct place for the real help of which they are sorely in need. What, of course, they should have been looking for was the *Holy One of Israel*. That is to say, they failed once again to *consult the* LORD (v. 1), indeed, to put their trust in him. The designation of the LORD God, the *Holy One of Israel* is common in the message of the prophet Isaiah; for further details about this expression see above on Isa 1:4.

In v. 3, there is the affirmation that the search on the part of the Judean people and their leaders in the direction of Egypt for help, for military help, is seriously misguided. The prophet avers that those in *Egypt* are no more than other human beings. In fact, there is nothing special about either those people, that is the Egyptians, or their *horses*! All the LORD has to do is, as it were, to *stretch out his hand* and these imagined helpers will fall. Moreover and tragically, in such a situation both Israelites and Egyptians *will stumble . . . will fall, and they will all perish together.*

Then when we turn to the following verses, vv. 4-9, we can certainly read into them a real sense of assurance that the power of another great nation, this time Assyria, can be broken, and that is through acting in accord with the will, guidance, and strength of the LORD. There are alternative ways of reading this passage, and grounds can be uncovered for questioning the Isaianic authorship of it, but these are not being pursued here. Rather, authorship of Isaiah of Jerusalem is accepted, the passage being understood as expressing a positive response to the troubles spoken about in the preceding vv. 1-3.

Verse 4 may seem somewhat expressive of violence on the part of the LORD God, in its speaking of him *As a lion or a young lion growls over its prey*, but this is concerned to express the conviction that there is more than the strength of the lion in the LORD, and truly that he, the LORD, will be fully able to save his people. Additionally, this power and care of the LORD for his people is spoken of in v. 5 in terms of the God's bird-like hovering over the city of Jerusalem to *protect and deliver it*, to *spare and rescue it*.

Then the prophet's words are directed to the issues of the faith and attitude that the people of Judah and Jerusalem should adopt in the face of this divine and personal help from the LORD God (vv. 6-7). Indeed, these people of God are to *Turn back to him whom you have deeply betrayed, O people of Israel* (v. 6). Earlier in the Isaiah book there are prophetic calls of this sort to the people to return in sorrow and penitence to the LORD God (see for example, Isa 2:20; 17:7-8; 30:22). Here there is also the specific call to turn away from any consulting of their *idols of silver and idols of gold* that they themselves, sinfully, have made for their own use (v. 7).

In vv. 8-9 the subject changes to the *Assyrians*, in particular to their fall from power, and that this will be caused not by human planning and activity, but rather by an unstated force. This is presumably to be understood as being effected by and through the initiative and almighty power of the LORD God. Certainly in v. 9 this turn of events is spoken of by the LORD as effecting his will. Verse 9 also portrays God's great powers being applied in the very setting of Jerusalem: the LORD, *whose fire is in Zion, and whose furnace is in Jerusalem* (v. 9). So, there is mention here not only of the almighty power of God, but also about it being activated through certain earthly activities and ceremonies, all by earthly people, and all in earthly settings. Yet all is done in the spirit of looking to the LORD as the divine enabler of their activities.

There is surely being portrayed in this passage the very different powers and resources that are ready and available for both Egyptians and Israelites, but how very different they are, particularly in their powers and effects. On the one hand are the Egyptians, by earthly standards a very great and powerful nation, and yet about them, says the prophet, *The Egyptians are human, and not God; their horses are flesh, and not spirit* (v. 3). As such, they are fragile and vulnerable. On the other hand are the power and eternal resources available for the Israelites, namely, *the LORD, whose fire is in Zion, and whose furnace is in Jerusalem* (v. 9). In this passage there is made a contrast between the powers of Egyptians and Israelites. The fact is that the Israelites are called upon, and expected, to depend upon their LORD God to give them the strength and powers for their tasks. Even further, the same could be said of the contrast between the powers of Assyrians and Israelites. Moreover, such can surely go on being believed, and moreover, expressed with confidence, by those who put their trust in the LORD.

Walter Brueggemann says about this passage and its references to various nations:

> This brief chapter exhibits a firm grasp of geopolitics. It also reflects discerning psychological insight into the way in which militarism takes on a life of its own as a theological reference point. Our reading must pay close attention to both the geopolitical and psychological distinctions that are operative. Both, however, are finally in the service of theological affirmation. In the end, with due attention to detail, Judah, Egypt, and Assyria—every part of the map—must come to terms with "the Holy One of Israel" (v. 1). There is no viable alternative. Every attempt at an alternative ends, inevitably, in humiliating disaster."[18]

---

18. Brueggemann, *Isaiah 1–39*, 252.

KINGDOM OF RIGHTEOUSNESS 32:1-8

Here, it may be said, we are moving from one extreme to another. Having had a series of compositions concerned with the "woes" of the people, we now move to prophetical words about the ideal of kingship and those features and qualities that make up the picture of the ideal king in Jerusalem. What are the vital qualities the king must have if his reign in Jerusalem is to be acceptable to the LORD, and to be of true benefit to the people, city, and nation of Judah?

The author appears, so to speak, to plunge into the subject, speaking of two very basic considerations concerning the place and the role of the king in the life of the nation and of the individual people therein. Thus the first word is *See, a king will reign in righteousness, and princes will rule with justice* (v. 1). In the Old Testament the words "righteous" and "righteousness" are about correct and good things taking place in the life of the community. The king's responsibility is to rule in ways that are right, not incorrect or sinful; ways that will bring about fairness and reasonable shares, provisions, and protection for all the people. These are the qualities that make up *justice* and *righteousness*, and they further constitute one of the main responsibilities of the ruling king, namely that there is *justice* and *righteousness* in the land, and further that such are available for all the people. Where those qualities are not present, where they do not prevail, it becomes the responsibility of the king to act in ways that will change things for the better. The *princes* are presumably those members of the royal family who are not kings, or specifically ruling at that time, but who might be expected to do so in future days. May they, in their turn, rule in justice.

Kings reigning in such ways will bring about conditions that are here set forth in the four imaginary and imaginative pictures presented in v. 2. These are expectations of there being appropriate and helpful and saving actions for those beset with earthly troubles such as conditions of *wind* or even *tempest*; may there be help with water supplies in a *dry place*; and may there be that needful shelter and strong support of a *rock* in a troubled land, what is called here, a *weary land*. These of course are poetic ways of speaking of sundry earthly problems in which people may one day find themselves. Verse 3 goes on to speak of the ongoing blessings for the people who have *sight* and *hearing*, presumably intended to be referring to their seeing and hearing of the divine presence in their lives and their land. Compare Isa 6:10.

Verse 3 expresses ongoing concerns with human sight and hearing, in particular that they will be functioning, functional, and useful. With this we may compare Isa 6:9-10 and 35:5. Further, in v. 4 is an expression of the wish for good *judgment*, and the gift of good speech, so that there may neither be over-hasty judgements nor the indistinct use of words. What is especially needed is the absence of foolishness and villainy on the part of Israel's future leaders (v. 5). Meanwhile v. 6 is about not forgetting those who have particular and basic needs, here illustrated poetically in the crises of those who are *hungry* and *thirsty*. Verse 7 is about scheming leadership, such leadership that is of no help to people who are in particular need of help. Yet, v. 8 affirms that there can be a real acceptability—as well as of need—of those who *plan noble things*, and who take their stands by the side of *noble things*.

Blenkinsopp says about the theme of this passage, "A basic postulate is that the primary duty of rulers and the ruling class is to protect the rights of the poor and to prevent their exploitation by the powerful and wealthy."[19] Here indeed is a picture of the ideal of the Israelite king as perceived in the Old Testament. For a good deal of the time, as certainly we gather from reading the accounts in the Old Testament's books of Kings and Chronicles, the Israelite kings failed singularly in carrying out their responsibilities to maintain justice and righteousness in their realms, especially in the lives of those who did not have the power and authority to ensure those things for themselves. The responsibility of the Israelite king to care for the least well-off in his realm was one of the issues laid out in certain of the so-called Royal Psalms, for example, Psalm 72:

> For he [the king] delivers the needy when they call, the poor and those who have no helper. He has pity on the weak and needy, and saves the lives of the needy. From oppression and violence, he redeems their life; and precious is their blood in his sight. (Ps 72:12–14)

A WARNING AND AN ASSURANCE 32:9–20

There are two subjects dealt with in this passage. The text, unfortunately, lacks total clarity about where the change takes place, but it would seem to be the most satisfactory to regard the two parts as vv. 9–14, understanding it as being concerned with the issue of women who are able to live their lives at ease, and then vv. 15–20, about a spirit from on high. Even so, this division of themes is not completely obvious, for the above arrangement does mean that the second of these begins in the middle of a sentence. Though these

---

19. Blenkinsopp, *Isaiah 1–39*, 430.

two passages follow a hopeful word, what we are dealing with now does not have the same degree of continuous prophetic confidence and hope.

Verses 9–14 are addressed to those who are called *women who are at ease*, and *complacent daughters*, both being called to listen to the prophet's voice (v. 9). They are warned of the forthcoming failure of both *the vintage* and *the fruit harvest* (v. 10), the same sort of troubles that are spoken about earlier in the book of Isaiah at 24:4-13. Here the women are called upon to lament and to put on sackcloth, and to lament the loss of good fields and fruitful vines, for at the present time there is the unhelpful growth of *thorns and briers* (vv. 12–13). Further, it is indeed all the people of the community who are in trouble, including their leaders. Thus community and leaders are spoken about in v. 14, where there is talk both that the (royal) *palace will be forsaken*, and also *the populous city deserted*. Even *the hill and the watchtower* will become dens for wild asses, and a pasture for flocks.

This does read as if it is a time of serious crisis for king and people of Jerusalem, and maybe also for other parts of Judah. That is, these verses portray a very desperate situation that Jerusalem and its surroundings have fallen into. In fact, it reads as if it could be about what happened in the crisis of 587 BCE when the Babylonians successfully seized control of Jerusalem and the surroundings, but this is not stated here. Further, there is not any reason given why an enemy should have wrought such havoc on the Judean capital city. Wildberger in his commentary says, "The end of Jerusalem is never stated in such an unconditional and absolute way even in Jeremiah. . . . It is idle to speculate about where this threat originates and why the author of vv. 9–14 thought it was coming."[20]

With vv. 15–20, we have a definite change in both tone and content from those of the preceding verses, as it were, the change taking place in the midst of a sentence in the texts that have come down to us. Thus, instead of the threats we have been reading about and the words of judgement and condemnation, now there is a real message of hope. Thus there will be the transformation of the earlier spoken-about wilderness conditions into the reality of there being *justice* and *righteousness* in both *wilderness* and *fruitful field* (v. 16), and that *righteousness* will bring about *peace . . . quietness and trust* (v. 17). Further, the people will be able to live in *peaceful habitation, secure dwellings, quiet resting places* (v. 18).

Verse 19 with its definitely downbeat emphasis has puzzled commentators over the years, and its presence at this point is very difficult to justify, for the following, and final, verse (v. 20) returns to the theme of the preceding verses, and speaks once again of life in a peaceful land, in which there are not

20. Wildberger, *Isaiah 28–39*, 254.

only happy peoples, but also free-ranging animals. Indeed, Richard Coggins in his commentary on Isaiah in the *Oxford Bible Commentary*, says of this verse, "The whole passage ends with a 'beatitude,' comparable in form with those found in the New Testament, in the Sermon on the Mount (Mt 5)."[21]

---

21. Coggins, "Isaiah," 461.

V

Isaiah 33–39
The Center of the Isaiah Book

WE HAVE COME HERE to chs. 33–39 of the book of Isaiah, that is, to the closing chapters of what has been called by many biblical scholars the first part of the book, namely chs. 1–39, which are in the main about situations, along with prophetical words concerning them, that lead ultimately to the Babylonian exile for the people of Judah. The story is then taken up some decades later in chs. 40–55 and after that, and apparently at a later stage (or stages), in chs. 56–66. Yet it is becoming clear in scholarly circles that there are aspects of the thought and the language of chs. 1–39 that are taken up and used in the following chapters from ch. 40 onwards. Further, the chs. 33–39 that stand between chs. 1–32 and then chs. 40 onwards have become frequently referred to as those that are at the center of the book, and it is these that we shall now be considering. For further introductory material to these chapters, see the introduction at the beginning of this work, pp. xxv–xxvii above. First, we must turn to Isa 33:1–24 and seek to understand its significance as what some have called the "hinge chapter" of the book of Isaiah, that is, the "hinge" between chs. 1–32 and what follows from ch. 34 onwards.[1] Further, there will also be some consideration as to why some of us believe that this chapter is presented to us as being in the style of a liturgy.

---

1. See Sawyer, *Isaiah*, Vol. II, 4.

FROM VISION TO LIFE AND WORSHIP 33:1–24

First we ask what this passage appears to be saying, and then we will go on to assess where and when it might possibly have been intended to have use, and be used, and then further consider the matter of its possible authorship, whether or not it is from the prophet Isaiah.

Verses 1–6 begin the chapter speaking of it being a "Woe oracle," though this is not made clear in NRSV with its *Ah, you destroyer . . .* , whereas the Hebrew is perhaps better rendered "Woe, destroyer . . ." (v. 1). This word "Woe" ("Ah") we have come across earlier in the book of Isaiah. See above, in particular Isa 5:8–24 and what is said by way of introduction to that passage. Yet who is the particular destroying one being spoken about in v. 1? It is not stated. What is clear is that person condemning the *destroying one* is in fact speaking in the name of the Lord. It is further clear that the one who is being threatened with destruction is clearly Jerusalem, and here, the destructing one, Jerusalem's adversary, is warned that in fact they will be destroyed: "When you have ceased to destroy, you will be destroyed" (v. 1). Further, the unnamed destroyer makes a thorough job of his destroying, and moreover, in being *treacherous* (v. 1). Thus do the afflicted people call upon the Lord for his help in this crisis, to be their support (*arm*), their *salvation* (v. 2), being confident that the sounds of divine activity will cause the enemy to scatter (v. 3). In fact, it will be as if the enemy is consumed by *locusts* (v. 4). For truly, while the Lord may be far away, yet he will make sure that in Zion, the earthly city, there will be *justice and righteousness* (v. 5). Further, there is the assurance here that on earth there will also be *stability* and *salvation, wisdom and knowledge*. Indeed, the people of Zion are reminded that in fact their greatest treasure is their *fear* (that is, "reverence") *of the Lord*, that is their worshipful acknowledgement and worship of the Lord God (v. 6).

Thus, we read in vv. 7–9 of a deep sense and feeling of lamentation on the part of the people of Jerusalem. While we can surely appreciate the note of mourning (v. 9) in this passage, the identity of the *envoys of peace* of v. 7 is not clear to us. Nevertheless, what is much clearer is that normal life seems to be at an end, at least for the present; after all, *the highways are deserted* (v. 8), and *the land mourns and languishes*, while normally fertile places like *Lebanon, Sharon, Bashan*, and *Carmel* are going through a variety of experiences of bad times (v. 9).

Yet there follows in vv. 10–13 a real expression of hope, for it is the Lord who will arise and change the situation, his *breath* being like a fire that will consume the enemy. The word for *breath* in the Hebrew also means "wind" and indeed "spirit," and that last is perhaps what is intended here, namely that this sad situation will be changed by none other than the LORD God, through the medium of his spirit (v. 11). Further, all peoples—both those who are far away and also those who are near at hand—should take notice of what God has done in the past, and what he has the power to do once again, now in the present situation (v. 13).

With vv. 14-16 the thought of the passage moves forward to something different. We are told that *the sinners in Zion* (Jerusalem) find themselves *trembling*, and the understanding would seem to be that this will be occasioned by their wish to enter the temple in the city of Jerusalem (v. 14). It is widely felt that the envisaged setting here is of the liturgy of the people's entry into the temple, such as we read about in Pss 15 and 24:3-6.[2] Thus the people are called to be very humble for they are made to realize again that the only truly worthy ones are *those who walk righteously and speak uprightly* (v. 15). It will be such people who will be enabled to find a secure *refuge*, and receive their much-needed food and drink (v. 16).

And what a vision it will be that these people will be granted (vv. 17-19)! Speaking surely of the LORD God (the divine king) this is the one they will see in his *beauty*, and in the vastness of his divine kingdom (v. 17). How different from mere earth will be all that is experienced in this vision. We should surely take notice of the fact that the Hebrew in v. 17, in speaking of the human "seeing" the king in his beauty and vastness of presence, uses instead of the usual verb for seeing, *r'h*, the verb *chzh* (see), a verb that generally is used of prophecy, and further, usually about something special in what is seen—as here, with the divine king in his beauty. And what a change this brings about for those who see such a vision! How small do their seeing experiences of the things of earth now seem, for truly how small do these so-familiar earthly things appear to be once even a mere glimmer of the greatness and the glory of God has been revealed to a human person (vv. 18-19).

Thus comes, finally, to the one experiencing these mighty and wondrous things (vv. 20-24), further wonders to be seen, and once again the Hebrew verb is not the usual one for "see" (*r'h*), but rather as in v. 17 the verb *chzh*, and perhaps intended here to indicate, "seen in vision." What is being seen appears to be envisaged here as no longer the earthly city of Jerusalem/Zion in its current state, but now the city as the LORD wishes it, and which he will indeed make it, a place of quietness and peace, a setting where *the LORD in majesty will be for us a place of broad rivers and streams* (v. 21). Further, there can be the assurance that there will be no major shipping, aggressive or otherwise, upsetting the peace of Jerusalem (v. 21). Rather there

---

2. For details of this liturgical thought and practice see, Day, *Psalms*, 60-61.

can be the assurance that it is the LORD who in his glory and greatness will be the true saving one for the city and its people, he will be the true Lord of his people. Expressed in worldly terms, he will be all of *judge, ruler, king*, truly the one who will indeed *save* his people (v. 22).

Then in v. 23 we have a further reference to shipping, but we can assume that it is not to be taken literally. Perhaps what is intended here is the assurance of the sense of security, with freedom from those who would come and plunder the LORD's holy city. Rather, Jerusalem will truly be the secure home of those who otherwise might be under threat of strife and also of divine judgement, for *the people who live there will be forgiven their iniquity* (vv. 23b-24).

It is exceedingly difficult to be sure about a possible historical setting for this chapter. The commentators on it come up with a wide and exceedingly varied range of possibilities, and so I suggest we do not seek to proceed on such lines. Rather, I wish to suggest that it is much more likely that this chapter was intended to be a liturgical piece, rather than a prophetic composition and proclamation concerning a particular historical setting. That is, we have in this passage a series of theological pieces that we also see in other Old Testament compositions, not least in the biblical book of Psalms. Thus we have a woe oracle (vv. 1-6), an assurance of divine saving activity (vv. 10-17), a temple entrance liturgy (vv. 14-16), a vision of God (vv. 17-19), and a vision of the peaceful city of Jerusalem (vv. 20-24). That is to say, what is offered to God is the current situation of suffering in Jerusalem (vv. 7-9), and what is sought from him is the assurance that he is aware of the difficulties of his people and will take positive actions for them (vv. 10-13). The people are trembling as they contemplate their sinfulness, yet receive assurance of the LORD's care of them (vv. 14-16). This is the LORD seen in vision (vv. 17-19), and further there is the vision of peace and hope for the people of Jerusalem (vv. 20-24).

Thus it is that Joseph Blenkinsopp can write about this chapter, "The poem therefore ends with the assurance of ultimate salvation, expressed in terms designed to recall traditional and primordial Israelite realities and beliefs."[3] Such is the first of our three pieces at the center place of the book of Isaiah.[4] Moreover, the significance of this particular chapter is that it seems to some of us to be in the form and style of a liturgy, and that thereby it conveys to the reader through its words, images, and writing, an invitation

---

3. Blenkinsopp, *Isaiah 1-39*, 447.

4. See above pp. xxv-xxvi for the significance of the issue of three pieces of text at the center of the Isaiah book.

to the reader/hearer to travel in thought between the present situation of the people of Judah and Jerusalem on to a new life of peace, hope, and freedom.

Then, it is surely appropriate to make the observation, as I did in my earlier article about this chapter,[5] that one of the characteristic features of the book of Isaiah is that at crucial moments in the whole work, we find ourselves reading of liturgical events and issues, or at least reading texts that display the language of liturgy. Thus in that early introduction to the general state of religious laxity and failure there is a censure regarding false worship (1:10–17); the crucial visionary experience of the prophet comes from the place and setting of worship (6:1–13); the closure of the early block of material in ch. 12 is set forth in the form of thanksgiving and worship. Further, liturgy can be found also in the later parts of the book of Isaiah in, for example, a series of hymns and praises in 42:10–13; 44:23; 49:13; 52:9–10. Moreover, in 63:7–64:12 there is a corporate lament prayer. Thus, it is hardly surprising that at the particular crucial moment between an old order and a new one, we should find the prophetic message expressed in the present chapter in the words and the style of a liturgy of worship. And moreover, a liturgy that ends with an assurance that one day there will be true healing of the people ("And no inhabitant will say 'I am sick'") and real forgiveness of sins (v. 24). That is, there is something of a "bridge" being spoken about here, a bridge between an old order of life and a new one of renewed faith and life and hope.

Judgement and Salvation Chapters 34 and 35

It is widely agreed, though not unanimously, by scholars of the book of Isaiah that these two chapters belong together, and further that in all probability they do come from later times than those they write about. Further, they make up the second of the three parts at the center of the Isaiah book (chs. 33–39), and they are particularly concerned with the divine punishment of Edom (ch. 34) and the contrasting glorification of Mount Zion in Judah. Moreover, these chapters are expressed in the language and the style of what has been called apocalyptic, an example of which we have already encountered in chs. 24–27 in the book. Yet these two collections of apocalyptic materials in Isaiah are not such "advanced" apocalyptic as we find elsewhere in the Old Testament. See pp. xxiv–xxv above for a summary of the characteristic features of apocalyptic writings.[6]

---

5. Thompson, "Vision, Reality and Worship: Isaiah 33," 332.

6. On these two chapters, see also the study of Miscall, *Isaiah 34–35: A Nightmare/A Dream*.

JUDGEMENT ON EDOM 34:1-17

This chapter is about the judgement of God, particularly upon Edom. Thus a series of ancient empires are called together by the LORD, as if they are to hear of the divine complaints about them regarding their conduct in the life of the world, but it is Edom and its sinful ways and failings that are the real objects of the LORD's anger. That is, it is Edom that is presented here as the most seriously sinful nation, and all the world is called upon to consider what the LORD has to say about these peoples (v. 1). Yet we are not told just what the particular sins of Edom are, and anyway *the* LORD *is enraged against all the nations* (v. 2), and it is made clear here that a grim fate awaits not only the Edomites but in fact *all the nations*. Thus, there is the warning in v. 3 that *the mountains shall flow with their blood,* while in the following verse there is the warning that *All the host of heaven shall rot away . . .* (v. 4). Perhaps that is a suggestion that a great change will even come over the skies.

In v. 5 the nation of Edom comes to the fore, and there it will remain for much of the rest of this chapter. Edom was a near neighbor to Judah and Jerusalem, but it seems that relationships were not generally good. The judgement upon the Edomites spoken about here is in fact presented in a number of images. The first is in vv. 5-7, comparing the LORD's attack upon the Edomites with the sword to the slaughter of an animal for sacrificial purposes. Indeed, it could almost be that the slaughter of the people of Edom is portrayed as being part of an animal sacrifice. Then in vv. 9-10 there is talk of unquenchable fires in that land which will go on night and day, so that the one-time city of theirs will become something of a smoking, ruined place.

The result of all this will be a land only fit for animals and birds, *the hawk and the hedgehog . . . the owl and the raven*, and further made by the LORD a place of *confusion*, of *chaos* for the humans who would otherwise live there (v. 11). Indeed, that land is portrayed as something akin to what there was in the earliest stage in the creation of the world. As in Gen 1:2, with its talk of "formless void and darkness" (Hebrew *tohu, bohu*), so in Isa 34:11 we read of the land of Edom reduced to *tohu, bohu—confusion* and *chaos* in the translation of NRSV. Indeed, this kingdom will be named *No Kingdom There*, and its princes and nobles will be as if they were not in existence (v. 12). Rather, *thorns, nettles, and thistles* will be growing there, for this indeed will be a suitable land, even a good land, for the birds and the animals. Further, this will make a real resting place for *Lilith*, a night bird, one in the Old Testament only spoken about here, something of a demon (v. 14). Nor should this land be forgotten as a suitable place for the homes and breeding places of the *owl* and the *buzzard* (v. 15).

We do not know what *the book of the* LORD, spoken about in v. 16, is. Maybe the point being made here is that the matters the prophet is talking about, and the coming situations and fates of the people they are referring to, are sure to take place, and are therefore required to be recorded in writing— and above all to be taken seriously. If anything, the final verse, (v. 17), is even more difficult for us to understand, unless it is intended to indicate that it has indeed been by divine will and purpose that the land of Edom has been taken away from the human beings and given to the animals, for their particular lives and uses. The expression *cast the lot for them* is perhaps to refer to the sort of allocation of cultivable land that we read about in Ps 16:6 and Mic 2:5.

This is certainly a difficult chapter for us to read, notwithstanding the fact that it may have been speaking about a particularly troublesome nation whose dwellings were so close to those of the peoples of Judah and Jerusalem. We are reminded that in his book on Isaiah 34 and 35, Peter Miscall refers to the former chapter as possibly the picture of "a nightmare." Equally, we may perhaps wish to add, just how many other nations are there in the world in age after age that are troublesome to the LORD, not forgetting our own nations in our own times? Perhaps there is the call here to acknowledge how fortunate we are indeed, insofar as we are still allowed and enabled to stay here on earth, on those parts of the earth we regard—hopefully humbly—as our lands?

RETURN TO ZION 35:1-10

This remarkably hopeful-sounding passage reads as if it is something that has some sort of relationship with the material that we read in Isa 40-55, and so indeed over the years it has been regarded as closely associated with, or even as a part of, the material in chs. 40-55.[7] In this present work this passage is perceived as being part of the second section of the three-part bridging materials (chs. 33 + 34-35 + 36-39), that lead the reader on from the earlier to the later parts of the Isaiah book, in particular being associated with ch. 34 as the middle part of those three compositions at the center of the complete book of Isaiah.

The emphasis here in Isa 35 is on a truly blessed future for the people of Judah and Jerusalem. Indeed, the picture in 35:1-2 is of growth and blessedness in those areas that had not previously seen such apparent prosperity. In this way, as well as the appearance of gladness (presumably, growth) in the

---

7. For an example of this approach, see the work of Smart, *History and Theology in Second Isaiah*. As far as the above mentioned work of Miscall on Isaiah chs. 34 and 35 is concerned, the latter chapter is referred to as "a Dream."

wilderness and the *dry land*, further *the desert shall rejoice and blossom, like the crocus* (NRSV) (v. 1), that is possibly asphodel or desert crocus. Thus, there will be abundant growth where previously there was desert, and this wondrous event is pictured as accompanied by joyful singing on the part of the rejuvenated land. Further, there will be new life appearing in Lebanon, Carmel, and Sharon, because those observing these things are seeing nothing less than *the glory of the* Lord, *the majesty of our God* (v. 2). With this we may compare what we read in Isa 40:3, 5; 60:1, and see that what is being spoken about here is a real message of hope for the future of Israelite people.

With v. 3 we move on to consider the human beings who will hopefully draw strength from these changes in the natural world. Thus may *weak hands* be strengthened, and *feeble knees* be made firm. Meanwhile, for those who may feel that such happenings betoken changes for the worse, such as have been experienced in the past, this time they are not to *fear*, or be of *fearful heart* (v. 4); rather, they are to be assured that their God is coming for their good, their welfare, *He will come and save you* (v. 4). Thus will come about for the human people involved—who in the past have endured sufferings and various losses of freedom—the invitation to be strong, and not fearful, for this is their own God who is coming to them; let their God open the blind eyes and the deaf ears (v. 5), and may all be ready to *leap* and *sing for joy* (v. 6). They are here surely being called to be ready for radical changes to take place in their midst, acknowledging that there will indeed be radical things brought about by the Lord God, such as that *waters shall break forth in the wilderness, and streams in the desert . . .* and other quite amazing transformations. Thus, sands and thirsty grounds will be transformed into useful water-bearing areas, while other less-useful regions will be made into what look more like wastelands (v. 7).

We are not told where the highway spoken about in v. 8 runs from and to, but we assume that this is a reference to the one spoken of in Isa 40:3–5, that is, from Babylon to Jerusalem and surrounding areas. It will be called *the Holy Way*. Of course, the desert area between those places will still be there, and perhaps in reality the talk about the highway in this verse is to be understood, as Blenkinsopp points out, as "a metaphor for passage to the new age about to dawn."[8] That is, here is talk of the Lord having a new future for his people Israel, and here he is providing ways for them to be taking it up and engaging in it. Further, there is the promise of safety in all this, for it is the *redeemed* who *shall walk there* (v. 9), and there will be *ransomed* (v. 10) people who walk on it. Moreover, this they will do with *singing* and

---

8. Blenkinsopp, *Isaiah 1–39*, 457.

everlasting joy. In fact, *joy and gladness* will be the order of day, no longer *sorrow and sighing.*

A number of commentators on this passage make reference to the similarity with Isa 51:11, a verse that is a message of hope of later years and speaking of the return of the Lord's people to Zion after their years of exile in Babylon. Richard Coggins says, "The final verse [35:10] is virtually identical with 51:11; the two uses may be seen as a kind of refrain, in each case bringing a hymn of triumph to a joyful conclusion in the restoration of Zion and its community."[9]

The Isaiah Narratives, chapters 36–39

We now have in the book of Isaiah some very different material from what we have read previously in this biblical work. It is largely in prose, and much of it is parallel with textual material we find in 2 Kgs 18:17—20:19. That is, it covers a period of Judean and Jerusalemite life in which a very great deal is happening. In the first place, in around 605 BCE, the Assyrian rule in Judah and Jerusalem, and elsewhere, came to an end when the Assyrians were defeated by the Babylonians, who became the major rulers in that part of the world until about 539 BCE.

Meanwhile, in 587 BCE, the end of normal Judean and Jerusalemite life came to a time of enormous change when a proportion of their peoples were taken away into captivity in Babylon. That was destined to last for around fifty years, that is until a time when a further change of national leadership in Babylon enabled, even encouraged, subject peoples to return, under certain conditions, to their own lands. Thus, there is a real and significant purpose for the presence of chs. 36 to 39 in the book of Isaiah, for they carry on the account ended by the Judean defeat and deportation by the Babylonians into a further era. That was the historical period spoken about in the book of Isaiah from ch. 40 onwards, by which time the Babylonians had been defeated by the Persians, and when under those last-named there opened-up whole new possibilities for the people of Israel, under certain conditions, to go back to their promised land of Judah and Jerusalem.

We do not come across elsewhere in the book of Isaiah a similar occurrence of the sort of writing that we find in chs. 36–39, for indeed what we have here is in the language and the style of the books of Kings. Thus it seems to be most likely that the material we have in Isa 36–39 did indeed have its origin in the books of Kings. However, there are those who maintain

---

9. Coggins, "Isaiah," 462.

that these chapters have their origin in the Isaiah tradition.[10] Whatever the authorship and source of origin of this material, clearly it has been used by the editors of the book of Isaiah to speak of that historical time leading up to the siege of Jerusalem and its fall in 587 BCE, and to the life for these defeated leaders and people in Babylon and elsewhere.

Yet at various points in this account, assumed in this present work to be coming from the books of Kings source, there can be observed the additions of certain extra materials. It is also clear that certain portions of the account in the 2 Kings text are omitted in Isaiah. The possible significances of these various additions and omissions will be spoken about as we come to them. As far as the remaining text is concerned it is clear that what it does do is to carry the reader over from the narrative covering the "Assyrian" background (chs. 1–35) into that covering the biblical material having a "Persian" background (chs. 40–55). Yet further, while we study this material in Isa 36–39 we are still in fact in the setting of the Babylonian background, that is, exilic, background.[11]

JERUSALEM IN DANGER 36:1—37:8

This long passage states what was the great crisis that beset the cities of Judah, including Jerusalem, perhaps in particular Jerusalem, in the year 701 BCE. We are told that in the fourteenth year of the reign of King Hezekiah of Jerusalem, King Sennacherib of Assyria laid siege, and indeed captured those places (v. 1). However, for us there is a certain complication in our sources of information about this happening, because we also read about this in the books of Kings, in 2 Kgs 18:13—19:8, yet these two accounts are not always in agreement. Thus, because the Kings account is thought likely to have come from an earlier time than the Isaiah one, and also thought to be the one on which parts of the Isaiah account were based, the Kings account has been called Account A, while that in Isaiah, Account B. The Assyrian account of the same event certainly reads as if Sennacherib made a good haul of various items—and human beings—from Jerusalem, saying, "I made to come out . . . 200,150 people, young and old, male and female, innumerable horses, mules, donkeys, camels, large and small cattle, and

---

10. The case is set out in particular in the detailed work of H. G. M. Williamson. See *The Book Called Isaiah*, 184–244.

11. For further details about these chapters of the book of Isaiah, see the introduction to the present work, xv–xviii above.

counted them as the spoils of war. He himself I shut up like a caged bird within Jerusalem, his royal city."[12]

We read in the following verse (36:2) about the king of Assyria sending the Rabshakeh (an officer of the invading Assyrians, having either military or political responsibilities, or both), and the suggestion would seem to be that he was to be in charge of things for the Assyrians in Jerusalem, and it would further appear that Jerusalem officers such as Eliakim, Shebna, and Joah were appointed henceforth to report to him, and to serve under him (36:3).

Then in 36:4 we read of the Assyrian officer, the Rabshakeh, addressing the captives in Jerusalem, appearing to encourage them to accept this new leadership, but the fact is that his speech to them is filled with references to issues that we find are spoken about in the book of Isaiah. Indeed, it has been pointed out that what we have here is what we find elsewhere in ancient historiography of putting such speeches into the mouths of leading characters in the story, such as we find in Herodotus, Thucydides, and even in the New Testament Acts of the Apostles. Thus we have here in the Rabshakeh's speech a series of quotations of what have come down to us as words of the prophet Isaiah, in particular what we read in Isa 10:8-9, 13-14; 19:1-15; 30:1-5.

In Isa 36:4-10 the Rabshakeh is portrayed as addressing the people of Jerusalem, and first he speaks about their reliance upon help from Egypt (36:5-6), pointing out that Egypt is *a broken reed of a staff* (36:5), and will therefore be of no help to them, for *Such is Pharaoh king of Egypt to all who rely on him* (36:6). Then, the Assyrian makes reference to Hezekiah's removal of high places and altars (36:7), which indeed we do read about in 2 Kgs 18:3-7, yet that kingly action was taken in Jerusalem as part of an attempt to centralize the cult, and make sure that what was done in worship was correct and in accordance with regulations. In Isa 36:8 there is the Assyrian suggestion that they, the Assyrians, could help the Israelites with horses, so that the Israelites could have mounted troops, but then, we do not hear of the Israelites having mounted troops, so what use would the horses be? The final argument of the Assyrian Rabshakeh was that he had been sent by none other than the Lord God to effect the divine judgement upon Jerusalem and the surrounding countryside, destroying both of them (36:10).

The conversation then continues in Isa 36:11 with a request from the Jerusalemite leaders Eliakim, Shebna, and Joah requesting the Rabshakeh to express himself in the Aramaic language, rather than Hebrew, that is to use the language of diplomacy rather than the common language. Thus hopefully, ordinary Jerusalemite peoples would not understand what was being

---

12. Thomas, *Documents from Old Testament Times*, 67.

said, and what was taking place. The Assyrian response was resoundingly negative, pointing out that all would be affected by what would be taking place, the ordinary people in singularly most unpleasant ways (36:12), and so, presumably, they ought to be able to understand what was going on, and what were the issues involved.

Thus begins the Assyrian Rabshakeh's speech, which we are told was in Hebrew (*the language of Judah*), and in a loud voice, and which religiously yet arrogantly called on the people to *Hear the words of the great king, the king of Assyria!* (36:13). He goes on to speak of not allowing Hezekiah to deceive them, the people, for Hezekiah will be unable to deliver his people from this military crisis (36:14). The Rabshakeh rants on in this manner, claiming that the result of all this will be that Jerusalem will be given into the hand of the king of Assyria. These people of Jerusalem should be putting their faith in the great king of Assyria, whose spokesman goes on speaking in this tirade, in ways that for the Hebrew leaders, especially the religious ones, must have been regarded as a great display of arrogance, both religious and also political (36:15). Yet still the Assyrian speech goes on, making an offer of peace and prosperity, reading as if that will take place first in Judah and Jerusalem, and then later in the land of Babylon, a land, they were being told, where they would find and benefit from such great plenty (36:16–17).

Already the people of Jerusalem had been informed (36:15, 18) that they were not to let their king Hezekiah mislead them, and now again they are given the same Assyrian message (36:19), this time inviting them to take note of the fates of various other nations: Hamath, Arpad, Sepharvaim, and also, it had to be said, Samaria, the old northern kingdom of Israel, which had earlier fallen to the Assyrians. Where, asks the Rabshakeh, was your Lord God, on those occasions? (36:20). Thus the people of Jerusalem were told to be silent—and so we are informed they were (36:21). Meanwhile, those three Jerusalem leaders, Eliakim, Shebna, and Joah, came to King Hezekiah with their clothes torn, and reported to him the words of the Rabshakeh (36:22).

King Hezekiah, on hearing the grim news for his city and people did three things. First, he tore his clothes, as had his officers earlier; second, he covered himself with sackcloth (a covering for humans, used in times of distress and mourning); and third, there in Jerusalem he went into the house of the Lord (37:1). That last action we assume was to pray to the Lord about the grim military and political situation. Further, the king sent certain of his national officers to the prophet Isaiah, with instructions to call upon the prophet to make his own prayers for his people and city in this time of crisis (37:2–4). We read of prophets making their prayers for other peoples in such settings as are spoken about here, in 1 Sam 12:19, 23; Amos 7:2, 5; Jer 7:16; 14:11.[13]

In Isa 37:5–7 we read about the visit of King Hezekiah's servants to the prophet Isaiah, to seek his advice and counsel in his having received the words from the Assyrian king. What is Hezekiah to do? *Do not be afraid* is the counsel of the prophet (37:6), for the fact is that very soon the king of Assyria will hear that certain things will be happening back at his home base that need his attention there; thus very soon he will leave Jerusalem (37:7). In fact, the death of Sennacherib did not take place until later, but clearly some people on the Jerusalem side believed this rumor of trouble developing for Sennacherib, and will have understood it as a sign of the deliverance from danger for Jerusalem and its peoples. Thus did the enemy leave Jerusalem and its peoples in peace.

Further, in 37:8 we read that Rabshakeh, on returning from his mission, found that Sennacherib had had to leave his old camp in Lachish and move elsewhere, possibly to quell troubles there. So we are told that he moved to Libnah, a town whose location we are not sure of, but maybe somewhere between Lachish and Ashdod.

SENNACHERIB, HEZEKIAH, AND ISAIAH 37:9–38

We now read about a further threat, or at least a renewal of the original threat, of the Assyrians against Jerusalem and it leaders. Thus there is a second phase in the Israelite accounts of the Assyrian siege of Jerusalem. In particular, in Isa 37:9 we read about the Assyrian leader Sennacherib hearing news that Tirhakah of Ethiopia (Cush) had set out to fight against him. We are a little mystified by this statement as in the year 701 BCE Tirhakah was not yet king of Ethiopia, but it may have been in his pre-kingship days that he participated in at least some military action against the Assyrians.

Then in Isa 37:10 we read of the Assyrians appealing to the Israelites in very much the same way they had done earlier (36:18–20). The Rabshakeh suggests that the Jerusalemites should not rely upon the empty promises of their God, which falsely proclaim they will in fact be safe, in particular that they will not be handed over into the power (*the hand*) of the king of Assyria. Thus once again the Jerusalem king is called upon by the Rabshakeh to recall the fate of those other countries who were forced to submit to the Assyrians, *Gozan, Haran, Rezeph* and others, and further to ask where the kings of sundry other nations are now (37:11–13).

---

13. For the prophet Isaiah praying on this occasion, and others, see Thompson, *I Have Heard Your Prayer*, 160–63.

This information about the fates of these kings and their states was put to Hezekiah by letter, which was read to him, and the king's response was to go to the temple in Jerusalem and *spread it before the* LORD (37:14). We are further told that Hezekiah prayed to the LORD, setting out his and his nation's situation of crisis, and ending by asking that the LORD would save them from the power of the king of Assyria (vv. 15-19), *so that all the kingdoms of the earth may know that you alone are the Lord* (v. 20). This prayerful activity was not dissimilar to what we read about kings David (2 Sam 7:18-19) and Solomon (1 Kgs 8:23-53) doing when they and their nations found themselves in similar situations.

Isaiah 37:21 tells us of the response of the LORD to the preceding word of the prophet Isaiah, which had been uttered to the LORD concerning the activities of the King Sennacherib of Assyria. What follows after this is the response of the LORD to the prophet's prayer, this response falling into two sections, the first being in 37:22-29, and it is something of a tirade about Sennacherib, while the second is in 37:30-32, being a word of hope for King Hezekiah concerning the future for the people of Judah and Jerusalem. We consider these in turn.

Isaiah 37:22-29 makes up the deep complaint of the LORD God about the Assyrian Sennacherib, in the first place that he despises the people of Jerusalem (37:22), referring to them as if they are young women, presumably intended to indicate those who were inexperienced in the ways of the world. Yet in fact the real complaint of the LORD is about the fact that Sennacherib has *mocked and reviled* (37:23) none other than the LORD God, here called, once again, *the Holy One of Israel*.[14] Further, this mockery has been given effect through the Assyrian's arrogant entrance into the Judean lands and the taking of some of the finest goods from the land, such as *cedars* and *cypresses* (37:24), and its supplies of *water* (37:25). While, in fact, certain aspects of this entry into, and activity within, the land of Judah by the Assyrian might have been part of the LORD's purposes and will for those peoples within them, even so there has taken place terrible crushing and destructive activities on the part of the Assyrian (37:26-27). Yet the LORD God knows this Assyrian, all about his activities—not least his *raging* against the LORD (37:28). Thus, and also because of his *arrogance*, the divine judgement is upon him, and the LORD will *turn you back on the way by which you came* (37:29). R. E. Clements says, "Sennacherib's returning home without success is seen as a mark of poetic justice in that, for all his arrogant boasting, the king of Assyria was entirely under the hand of Yahweh, the God of Israel."[15]

---

14. On this title, see above on Isa 1:4.
15. Clements, *Isaiah 1-39*, 286.

Thus we come to Isa 37:30–32, and here we have words addressed to Judah's King Hezekiah, these being words of hope about the future for the king, the people, and the land of Judah and Jerusalem. This short piece begins by speaking of a *sign*, the type of sign that we find being spoken about in Isa 7:11. This particular sign concerns a period of three years, in which time there will be the provision of foodstuffs growing in the ground. The special aspect of the sign about this is that there will be the evidence of what can be planted in the ground, that will grow, and then can be harvested and eaten or drunk (37:30). In the following verse the talk is of a remnant, another concept that is spoken about earlier in the Isaiah book, as for example in Isa 10:20–23, signifying that though there may only be a small group left, or only a small offering made, therein is a basis and a beginning of growth into what will become so much greater. We have already come across such talk in Isa 11:16, and here in the passage under consideration the matter is spelled out in 37:32 with its, *for from Jerusalem a remnant shall go out, and from Mount Zion a band of survivors. The zeal of the* LORD *of hosts will do this* (37:32).

The final piecing together in this story tells us of the word of the LORD concerning the Assyrian king in Isa 37:33–35, where we are informed that far from conquering Jerusalem the Assyrian will neither *shoot an arrow* into it, nor come with *shield*, nor even *cast up a siege ramp against it* (37:33). Indeed, Sennacherib will not get even as far as that, for he will by then be on his way home—taking the route back that he had used when he had first come (37:34)—and this due to the fact that the LORD himself *will defend this city to save it, for my own sake and for the sake of my servant David* (37:35).

How could this be, and what brought about it happening? We are given the down-to-earth practical and earthly details of the crisis for the Assyrian that caused what looked like their seriously hurried departure from Jerusalem as recorded in Isa 37:36–38. We are told in v. 36 that it was *the angel of the* LORD causing a huge death toll in the Assyrian camp that brought about the departure back home for the remaining remnant of the Assyrians. Presumably we are to understand that the talk of *the angel of the* LORD is to represent the direct action of God in the world; this is portrayed as being the LORD's chosen way of delivering his people, the kind of happening that has already been spoken about in Isa 29:6 and 31:8. Thus Sennacherib made his departure from Jerusalem, going to live in Nineveh (37:37), but was soon to meet his end with something that reads like a "palace coup," and thus his son Esar-haddon succeeded him as ruler of Assyria (37:38).

Meanwhile, Christian readers of this story will perhaps be asking how they are understand what actually took place in this deliverance of the people and city of Jerusalem, that is, in particular what we read about in Isa

37:36, speaking of the angel of the LORD striking down 185,000 in the camp of the Assyrians, and when morning dawned, they were all dead bodies. Some commentators on the book of Isaiah quietly move on at this stage, and do not stop to discuss what it might have been that actually happened, and by what means it was that Jerusalem was spared, because in its seriously weakened state the Assyrian army perhaps had little else it could have done but return to its homeland. Others take one of two possible happenings, explanations, or at least discuss these possibilities. The first of these two possible explanations is that this event was a direct act of deliverance of the LORD God, who surely can do all such things. Two works of scholarship that set forth this approach are the commentaries of E. J. Young,[16] and Alec Motyer.[17] For some Christians this will seem to be the most likely, even obvious, explanation for the deliverance of Jerusalem. A certain variation on this approach is that of Walter Brueggemann, who says "Sennacherib will not succeed because Yahweh will protect the city and deliver it,"[18] and leaves the matter there.

The second way of explaining this happening is by what we might call a liberal, critical approach, which will perhaps be adopted by those who feel that their explanation needs to be more anchored into the real historical world. In other words, a specific "physical" worldly event took place—such as what is spoken of in Isa 37:36, the deliverance of Jerusalem being understood as having been effected by something like an invasion of field-mice who had maybe gnawed through the Assyrian soldiers' bow-strings and shield-thongs, or other possible important items of soldiers' equipment.[19] Perhaps we each of us as we read this part of Isaiah have either to make our decisions on these matters, or else possibly go on thinking about and considering such issues.

HEZEKIAH'S SICKNESS AND RECOVERY 38:1–22

We are able to read about this sickness and the associated recovery of King Hezekiah of Judah both here in the book of Isaiah, and also in 2 Kgs 20:1–22, but there are some changes between them, both by way of omissions and also additions. Once again we accept that the Kings version is the earlier one, and that therefore the changes are particularly to be noted

---

16. Young, *The Book of Isaiah*, 505.
17. Motyer, *The Prophecy of Isaiah*, 284.
18. Brueggemann, *Isaiah 1–39*, 299.
19. Brevard S. Childs in his volume, *Isaiah*, 276–78, has a helpful discussion of what are clearly problems for some readers at this point in the book of Isaiah.

in the Isaianic version. Overall, the Isaiah account is a good deal longer than that of Kings, in all probability indicating the greater importance and significance attached to the event, and the person to whom it was happening, on the part of the Isaianic book's author(s) over that of the author(s) of Kings.[20] Verse 1 tells us of what was understood at the time to be the serious state of health of King Hezekiah of Judah, and that the prophet Isaiah counselled him to set his affairs in order because he, the prophet, did not expect the king to recover. This was in fact something of a very serious time for the people and cities of Judah, for Hezekiah was undoubtedly one of the more successful of their kings, one who had made good and positive contributions to the lives of his people and their country, both in terms of their peace to live in the land and also their worship of and (personal and corporate) obedience to the LORD. Verse 2 with its talk of the king turning his face to the wall is hardly about seeking to ignore the prophetical word, but rather represents the reaction of the man who is too seriously ill to go to the temple, who has been beset with an illness, in fact, a life-threatening illness, and who therefore must make his prayers where he is, in his bed.

Verse 3 speaks of how the words of the king's prayer come before the LORD. Hezekiah does not seem to feel that he should approach the LORD with any confession of sins, and nor does he protest to God about his afflictions. Rather he calls on the LORD to remember all the good things that he, the king, has done in his life. Is this perhaps really about the fact that the writer wishes to make the point that Hezekiah is a good and pious king, who has done good things as regards his national responsibilities?

With vv. 4-8 we have the divine response to the prayer of Hezekiah, and it is singularly positive, for it affirms that the LORD will add no less than fifteen years to Hezekiah's life, and further, will deliver Jerusalem from the Assyrians, and then moreover even defend it. We may note that in the Isaiah version of 38:6 there are some words omitted from the 2 Kings version, namely, "for my sake and for my servant David's sake" (2 Kgs 20:6). This makes the Isaiah account of deliverance more general, in particular that it is not just for Hezekiah's sake, but rather for the whole city and all its populace.[21] Then additionally, Hezekiah will be given a sign that the LORD will do this, this being through a variation in the indicated reading of a sundial, a happening that we are not able to explain. Presumably we have to accept

---

20. There is a considerable volume of scholarly literature on this subject, but hardly as yet any consensus on the subject of which of the accounts in the book of Isaiah and the books of Kings should take precedence. Useful summaries of this ongoing debate may be found in Seitz, *Isaiah 1-39*, 66-71, and Williamson, *The Book Called Isaiah*, 189-211.

21. See Williamson, *The Book Called Isaiah*, 206-7.

that we are here dealing with an expression from long ago of a miraculous happening effected by the Lord. It is surely intended to indicate that the Lord did indeed hear the king's prayer, and that he made a full response—a much more generous response than the one praying was perhaps expecting.

In vv. 9–20 we have what is called a *writing* of the king, Hezekiah. This composition is not found in the books of Kings version of these events, and we are somewhat surprised to find it having the title *writing*. It seems to be rather a psalm of thanksgiving, in which the king rejoices over his deliverance, for which he gives thanks to the Lord. Though it is not stated here, one cannot but be aware that alongside the apparently enforced departure of the Assyrian king from Jerusalem, it will be not too long hence that this king, Sennacherib (see Isa 37:37), comes to the end both of his kingship and also of his earthly life. This is here in striking contrast to the king of Judah and Jerusalem, giving thanks to the Lord for his deliverance from illness. For a not dissimilar psalm of thanksgiving for deliverance from death, see Jonah 2:1–10. All this is to say that what is being set forth here is about a dramatic change of circumstances, both for the people of Judah and Jerusalem, at what certainly looked like a particular time of crisis for them, and also for the Assyrians, who had looked as if they were in the ascendency.

As far as Hezekiah was particularly, and personally, concerned, he had thought he was having to face an earthly death, and thus he spoke of his having to *depart* in *the noontime of my days* (v. 10), what NEB translates as "in the prime of life." *Sheol* is the place to which in Old Testament thought it is believed that people go when they die. For the coming of better hopes of life after death, see above on Isa 25:6–9 and 26:19. In the meantime (v. 11) the Old Testament's hopes of life after death are limited, and thus Hezekiah's psalm speaks of future life in which he will not see God (as in life he might have done in worship on earth—see for example Ps 42:5). The apparent frailty of earthly life is spoken of in v. 12 in a series of images. Further, there seems to be little hope for the royal psalmist in Sheol even by crying out to the Lord (v. 13).

This psalmic composition certainly brings home to us what limited hopes of a life beyond earthly death there are in so much of the Old Testament; here in this chapter what we read about in *I moan like a dove*, or in *looking upward* (v. 14), it is hard to see any help being found that will bring benefit or satisfaction to the psalmist. Further, there is rather here portrayed a real sense of hopelessness on the part of the author regarding the future, as indeed we read in v. 15, which speaks of the sick king's lack of sleep, and to a real sense for him of *the bitterness of my soul*.

Verse 16 has some difficult text to understand and to translate, but it and the following verse (v. 17) do perhaps indicate a certain transition on the part of the psalmist to some sense of hope, so that he is apparently able to speak of something within him enabling him to live in at least a certain element of hope for the future. These thoughts are put into the prayer of King Hezekiah, who is portrayed as coming to an acceptance of the fact that his previous suffering was mysteriously *for my welfare that I had great bitterness . . . for* God apparently did not hold the psalmist's sins against him, *for you have cast all my sins behind your back.*

With vv. 18–19 we have expressed a comparison of life in Sheol (v. 18) and life on earth (v. 19). Those in Sheol cannot praise the LORD, whereas those on earth can thank the LORD, as the psalmist is now doing, and it is the responsibility of fathers to make known to their children this great faithfulness of the LORD. Thus it is that while we are living on earth we should indeed sing in accompaniment to our stringed instruments our praise of the LORD *all the days of our lives, at the house of the LORD* (v. 20).

What could have brought about this great change for the king? In v. 21 we read about the application of a quantity of figs to Hezekiah's boil, and it could indeed have been that his healing was due to those items which were at that time believed to have such healing properties. As far as v. 22 is concerned it is widely felt that this should have been inserted—or was perhaps originally inserted?—before v. 7 in this chapter, as it was in fact rendered in the NEB translation.

It does have to be said that there is a definitely limited amount of material in the Old Testament about life after death, and that what we do have tends to be of a comparatively late date. This would seem to be a conviction of a divine provision that it took many centuries of the experience of life in the world for some in Israel to become convicted of. Clearly the writer of the composition we have in Isa 39 shares the belief that there can be no surety of there being a good future for individual people after their death, however worthily they have lived or however God-centered their lives may have been. Thus in v. 18 we have words here such as, *For Sheol cannot thank you, death cannot praise you.* Further, it would seem to be that the only reality giving assurance to the suffering and maybe near-to-death King Hezekiah is that he begins to feel better, and this is simply because it becomes clear that his human life will be prolonged. Yet as this chapter makes clear, that could really have been due to the application of the cake of figs, believed to have healing properties, such as we read about in v. 21.[22]

---

22. For more about the Old Testament and the future life, see Johnson, *Shades of Sheol*; Thompson, *The Old Testament and Christian Spirituality*, 136–50. Further, see above pp. 137–38 about what there is in the Isaiah book about life after death.

HEZEKIAH, AND MERODACH-BALADAN'S DELEGATION 39:1–8

Here, we are introduced to a new kingly personality, Merodach-baladan, who was ruler of Babylon twice, and was further at times enabled to fulfill various of his responsibilities through being allied to Tiglath-pileser III of Assyria. However, in 705–4 BCE Merodach-baladan was able to become involved in a plot to set in motion a rebellion against the Assyrian rule, and this seems to be the likely setting for what we read about in Isa 39:1–8, and in the very similar account in 2 Kgs 20:12–19. It is probable that the visit of the Babylonian envoys to Jerusalem to make gifts to, and to meet with, Hezekiah, was to secure his approval and help in their ambition to secure the Assyrian defeat in Babylon. The accounts that we have of these matters maybe point us to the year 703 BCE for their occurrence.

Thus we read in Isa 39:1 of the visit of envoys of Merodach-baladan to Jerusalem with a gift for, and letters to, Hezekiah, and presumably the purpose of these was to secure the support, and perhaps also the assistance of the Jerusalem king to help Merodach-baladan in his various Babylonian struggles with the then-present Assyrian rule. Verse 2 speaks of the apparent full welcome made on the part of Hezekiah in Jerusalem, including the showing of his treasures of *silver, gold, spices, oils*, and—perhaps of even greater significance for this visit of these foreigners—*his whole armory, all that was found in his storehouses*.

Thus we come to hear of the questioning of King Hezekiah by the prophet Isaiah as to what the king had actually shown to these envoys, and what they wanted to know, and of Hezekiah's open declaration to the prophet of what he had explained to them, and shown them, everything that was in his places of storage (vv. 3–4). Thus comes the prophetical word that the days are now surely coming when all these treasured things in Jerusalem would be carried away to Babylon, and further, so much else in terms of goods and persons. Nothing, he says will be left, and even some of the king's own sons will be taken away and become servants in the palace of the king of Babylon (vv. 5–7).

What are we to make of the response of Hezekiah to this prophetical word? The words of the king saying all this will be good, because it means *There will be peace and security in my days*, may sound singularly irresponsible on the part of the nation's leader, and perhaps may seem also to make a somewhat strange ending to a whole collection of prophetical words and to so much else in these first thirty-nine chapters of the book of Isaiah.

"Hezekiah's reaction to this disconcerting prophecy will seem laconic to a fault" says Joseph Blenkinsopp.[23]

And yet there was truly a sense in which, however, taking the long view, and seeing historical events on a larger scale, *could* be said to be good, or at least to have good aspects. Because the life in what was then a far-away and exceedingly foreign place and culture, would open up for these people of God matters concerning wider experiences and issues of life, to introduce them to peoples of other nations, other religions, and other cultures, and above all to the living out of the faith in a whole series of wider and varied settings. Further, there would surely be valuable experience for them in having to be residents in a foreign land, dwelling in a faraway setting; to be subject people, maybe indeed even having to become the more a servant people than they had known for many years, even centuries. There could surely be here remarkable opportunities about the learning of a variety of new aspects concerning being the people of the LORD in a much wider world than they had experienced in the past. As indeed, it did reveal itself to be. Further we, some of the latter-day readers of their work, are thus enabled for our part truly to see and understand that there was yet much more to be contributed to, and incorporated into, the growing collection of documents associated in one way or another with the ministry of the prophet Isaiah of Jerusalem in the eighth century BCE.

---

23. Blenkinsopp, *Isaiah 1–39*, 489.

Table of Dates

Shown here are the main events and also the names of some of the kings of Israel and Judah. Dates of kings shown for their accessions.

Date BCE	Judah	Israel	Assyria
783–742	Uzziah		
750		Menahem	
750–735	Jotham (co-regency)		
744–727			Tiglath-pileser III
742	Death of Uzziah		
737–732		Pekah	
735–715	Ahaz		
734	The Syro-Ephraimite War		
732–722		Hoshea (last king of Israel)	
726–722			Shalmaneser V
722		Siege and capture of Samaria	

Date BCE	Judah	Israel	Assyria
722–705			Sargon II
715–687	Hezekiah		
705–704			Merodach-baladan II
704–681			Sennacherib
701	Besieged by Assyria		Campaign in Judah
689			Assyrians capture Babylon
687–642	Manasseh		
680			Esarhaddon becomes ruler
668–627			Ashurbanipal
640–609	Josiah		
605			End of Assyrian rule
598–587	Zedekiah		
587	Fall of Jerusalem		
539			End of Babylonian/Chaldean rule

Select Bibliography

COMMENTARIES ON ISAIAH 1-39

Blenkinsopp, J. *Isaiah 1-39*. Anchor Bible. New York: Doubleday, 2000.
Brueggemann, W. *Isaiah 1-39*. Westminster Bible Companion. Louisville: John Knox, 1998.
Childs, B. S. *Isaiah*. Old Testament Library. Louisville: John Knox, 2001.
Clements, R. E. *Isaiah 1-39*. New Century Bible Commentary. Grand Rapids: Eerdmans, 1980.
Coggins, R. "Isaiah." In *Oxford Bible Commentary*, edited by J. Barton and J. Muddiman, 433-86. Oxford, Oxford University Press, 2001.
Duhm, B. *Das Buch Jesaia*. Göttingen: Vandenhoeck & Ruprecht, 1922.
Kaiser, O. *Isaiah 1-12*. 2nd ed. Old Testament Library. London: SCM, 1983.
Mauchline, J. *Isaiah 1-39*. Torch Bible Commentary. London: SCM, 1962.
Motyer, A. *The Prophecy of Isaiah*. Leicester: IVP, 1993.
Oswalt, J. N. *The Book of Isaiah, Chapters 1-39*. New International Commentary on the Old Testament. Grand Rapids: Eerdmans, 1986.
Roberts, J. J. M. *First Isaiah*. Hermeneia. Minneapolis: Fortress, 2015.
Sawyer, J. F. A. *Isaiah, Vol. I, chapters 1-32*. Edinburgh: St Andrew, 1984.
———. *Isaiah, Vol. II, chapters 33-66*. Edinburgh: St Andrew, 1986.
Seitz, C. R. *Isaiah 1-39*. Interpretation. Louisville: John Knox, 1993.
Smith, G. A. *The Book of Isaiah*. Expositor's Bible. London: Hodder, 1897.
Stacey, D. *Isaiah 1-39*. Epworth Commentaries. London: Epworth, 1993.
Wildberger, H. *Isaiah 1-12*. Continental. Minneapolis: Fortress, 1991.
———. *Isaiah 13-27*. Continental. Minneapolis: Fortress, 1997.
———. *Isaiah 28-39*. Continental. Minneapolis: Fortress, 2002.
Williamson, H. G. M. *Isaiah 1-5*. ICC. London: T. & T. Clark, 2006.
———. *Isaiah 6-12*. ICC. London: T. & T. Clark, 2018.

———. *Isaiah 13–27*. ICC. London: T. & T. Clark, forthcoming.
Young, E. J. *The Book of Isaiah, Vol. 1*. Eerdmans: Grand Rapids, 1965.

ARTICLES AND BOOKS

Abernethy, A. T., M. G. Brett, T. Bulkeley, T. Meadowcroft, eds. *Isaiah and Imperial Context: The Book of Isaiah in Times of Empire*, Eugene, OR, Wipf and Stock, 2013.

Albright, W. F. "The Chronology of the Divided Monarch of Israel." *Bulletin of the American Schools of Oriental Research* (1945) 16–22.

Berges, U. F., *Isaiah: The Prophet and His Book*. Sheffield: Phoenix, 2012.

Blenkinsopp, J. *The Beauty of Holiness: Re-Reading Isaiah in the Light of the Psalms*. London: T. & T. Clark, 2019.

Brueggemann, W. *The Land*. London, SPCK, 1977.

Clements, R. E. *Abraham and David: Genesis XV and Its Meaning for Israelite Tradition*. London: SCM, 1967.

———. "Isaiah 1.1–31: Israel Summoned to Repentance—The Introduction to the Isaiah Book." In *Jerusalem and the Nations: Studies in the Book of Isaiah*, 213–28. Sheffield: Phoenix, 2011.

———. *Isaiah and the Deliverance of Jerusalem: A Study of the Interpretation of Prophecy in the Old Testament*. Journal for the Study of the Old Testament, Supplement Series 13. Sheffield: Sheffield Academic Press, 1980.

———. "Isaiah: A Book without an Ending?" In *Jerusalem and the Nations: Studies in the Book of Isaiah*, 35–52. Sheffield: Phoenix, 2011.

———. "Written Prophecy: The Case of the Isaiah Memoir." In *Jerusalem and the Nations: Studies in the Book of Isaiah*, 53–65. Sheffield: Phoenix, 2011.

———. "The Unity of the Book of Isaiah." In *Old Testament Prophecy: From Oracles to Canon*, 93–104. Louisville: Westminster John Knox, 1996.

Collins, J. J. "The Sign of Immanuel." In *Prophecy and the Prophets in Ancient Israel*, edited by J. Day, 225–44. London: Bloomsbury, 2012.

Day, J. *Psalms*. Old Testament Guides. Sheffield: JSOT, 1990.

Firth, D. G., and H. G. M. Williamson, eds. *Interpreting Isaiah: Issues and Approaches*. Nottingham: Apollos, 2009.

Goldingay, J. "Isaiah 56–66: An Isaianic and a Postcolonial Reading." In *Isaiah and Imperial Context: The Book of Isaiah in Times of Empire*, edited by A. T. Abernethy and M. G. Brett et al., 151–66. Eugene, OR: Pickwick, 2013.

———. "The Theology of Isaiah." In *Interpreting Isaiah: Issues and Approaches*, edited by D. G. Firth and H. G. M. Williamson, 168–90. Nottingham: Apollos, 2009.

Habel, N.C. *The Land Is Mine: Six Biblical Land Ideologies*. Overtures to Biblical Theology. Minneapolis: Fortress, 1988.

Hayes, J. H., J. M. Miller, eds. *Israelite and Judaean History*. London, SCM, 1977.

Irvine, S. A. *Isaiah, Ahaz, and the Syro-Ephraimitic Crisis*. SBL Dissertation Series 123. Atlanta: Scholars, 1990.

Johnson, P. S. *Shades of Sheol: Death and Afterlife in the Old Testament*. Nottingham: Apollos, 2002.

Lundblom, J. R. *The Hebrew Prophets: An Introduction*. Minneapolis: Fortress, 2010.

Macintosh, A. A. *Isaiah XXI: A Palimpsest*. Cambridge, Cambridge University Press, 2008.

Miscall, P. D. *Isaiah 34–35: A Nightmare/A Dream*. Sheffield: Sheffield Academic, 1999.
Oswalt, J. N. *The Holy One of Israel: Studies in the Book of Isaiah*. Eugene, OR: Cascade, 2014.
Otto, R. *The Idea of the Holy*. Translated by J. W. Harvey. Oxford: Oxford University Press, 1939.
Reimer, D. J. "Isaiah and Politics." In *Interpreting Isaiah: Issues and Approaches*, edited by D. G. Firth and H. G. M. Williamson, 84–103. Nottingham: Apollos, 2009.
Rowland, C. *The Open Heaven: A Study of Apocalyptic in Judaism and Early Christianity*. London: SPCK, 1985.
Seitz, C. R. *Reading and Preaching the Book of Isaiah*. Philadelphia: Fortress, 1988.
———. *Zion's Final Destiny: The Development of the Book of Isaiah*. Minneapolis: Fortress, 1991.
Smart, J. D. *History and Theology in Second Isaiah: A Commentary on Isaiah 35, 40–66*. London: Epworth, 1967.
Stacey, W. D. *Prophetic Drama in the Old Testament*. London: Epworth, 1990.
Stromberg, J. *An Introduction to the Study of Isaiah*. London: T. & T. Clark, 2011.
Thomas, D. Winton, ed. *Documents from Old Testament Times*. London: Harper & Row, 1961.
Thompson, M. E. W. *Greatly to Be Praised: The Old Testament and Worship*. Eugene, OR: Pickwick, 2016.
———. *I Have Heard Your Prayer: The Old Testament and Prayer*. Peterborough: Epworth, 1996.
———. *Isaiah 40–66*. Epworth Commentaries. Peterborough: Epworth, 2001.
———. "Isaiah's Sign of Immanuel." *Expository Times* 95.3 (1983) 67–71.
———. *The Old Testament and Christian Spirituality*. Eugene, OR: Pickwick, 2019.
———. *Situation and Theology: Old Testament Interpretations of the Syro-Ephraimite War*. Sheffield: Almond, 1982.
———. "Vision, Reality and Worship: Isaiah 33." *Expository Times* 113.10 (2002) 327–33.
———. *Where Is the God of Justice? The Old Testament and Suffering*. Eugene, OR: Pickwick, 2011.
Williamson, H. G. M. *The Book Called Isaiah: Deutero-Isaiah's Role in Composition and Redaction*. Oxford: Clarendon, 1994.
———. "The Theory of a Josianic Edition of the First Part of the Book of Isaiah: A Critical Examination." In *Studies in Isaiah: History, Theology, and Reception*, edited by T. Wasserman, G. Andersson, and D. Willgren, 3–21. London: Bloomsbury, 2017.
Wilson, L. "Wisdom in Isaiah." In *Interpreting Isaiah: Issues and Approaches*, edited by D. G. Firth and H. G. M. Williamson, 145–67. Nottingham: Apollos, 2009.

www.ingramcontent.com/pod-product-compliance
Lightning Source LLC
Chambersburg PA
CBHW030113170426
43198CB00009B/611